Faith,
Power, and
Politics

———————

Faith, Power, and Politics

*Political Ministry in
Mainline Churches*

AUDREY R. CHAPMAN

THE PILGRIM PRESS
New York

Scripture quotations are from the New Revised Standard Version Bible,
copyright 1989, Division of Christian Education of the National Council
of the Churches of Christ in the United States of America, and are used
by permission. Quotations have been modified to eliminate pronouns in
references to the Deity.

"Hope Without Risk" (p. 129) is quoted from Dom Helder Camara, *Hoping
Against All Hope* (Maryknoll, N.Y.: Orbis Books, 1984), and is used with
permission of the publisher.

Cover design by Jim Gerhard

Library of Congress Cataloging-in-Publication Data
　　Chapman, Audrey R.
　　Faith, power, and politics : political ministry in mainline
　　churches / Audrey R. Chapman.
　　　　p. cm.
　　Includes bibliographical references.
　　ISBN 0-8298-0904-X (acid-free paper)
　　　1. Christianity and politics–Protestant churches. 2. Liberalism
　　(Religion)–United States. I. Title.
　　BR526.C43 1991
　　261.7–dc20　　　　　　　　　　　　　　　　　　91-11841
　　　　　　　　　　　　　　　　　　　　　　　　　　　　CIP

This book is printed on acid-free paper.

Printed in the United States of America.

10　9　8　7　6　5　4　3　2　1

The Pilgrim Press, 475 Riverside Drive, New York, NY 10115

To my husband,
Karim

Contents

Contents

Acknowledgments

This book is the result of a personal journey on which others supported me. During my tenure at the United Church Board for World Ministries Dan Romero encouraged me to continue the project and enabled me to have time to complete the writing. My reflections about the role and problems of mainline churches benefited greatly from my frequent conversation with Bonganjalo Goba. I would like particularly to acknowledge the assistance of Larry Rasmussen who spent many hours reading over and commenting on successive drafts of various chapters. His suggestions for revisions significantly improved the manuscript. Beverly Harrison also offered helpful criticism on several chapters. My husband Karim Ahmed kindly accepted long periods of preoccupation and contributed to the editing of several of the chapters. I would also like to thank Hwa Jin Lee for patiently typing and retyping endless drafts.

Introduction

Ten years ago, after a long period of residence overseas, I returned to the United States with a sense of a calling to a new vocation within the church. As a political scientist involved in applied social science research related to development issues, most recently as an advisor in the Central Bureau of Statistics in Kenya, I had become disillusioned with conventional development models. I was also interested in working within an environment based on a commitment to the religious values that motivated me. Moreover, my experience in Kenya and the other African countries in which I had lived had changed my conception of the church and its potential role in promoting peace, justice, and human rights. I was in many ways a product of reverse mission, converted to a different and more vital Christianity by the Christian leaders and faith communities with whom I had interacted.

Within months of my return I was elected to the position of the World Issues Secretary of the United Church Board for World Ministries, responsible for coordinating the peace, justice, human rights, and corporate social responsibility ministries of the international agency of the United Church of Christ. In this role I was able to participate in many significant denominational and ecumenical projects and programs during the next ten years that confirmed some of my hopes about the potential of the church. Perhaps most notably I was able to work with Christian leaders in a number of countries, such as South Africa, Korea, the Philippines, and El Salvador, where their commitment to a God of peace, justice, love, and compassion had led them into ministries of risk, suffering, and martyrdom. Through my denominational staff position and as chair of the National Council of Churches Human Rights Committee and of the Interfaith Center on Corporate Responsibility's South African Working Group, as well as through serving on the executive committees of several other ecumenical organizations, I was actively involved in advocacy partnerships between churches in Two-Thirds World countries and the mainline American denominations as described in chapter 4. My office was also part of the staff team that established and serviced justice and peace networks within the United Church of Christ to educate and mobilize church members on critical foreign policy issues. During my tenure on the national staff, the United Church of Christ affirmed its identity as a just peace church. Subsequently, I directed a six-year study and drafting process within the denomination that led to the adoption of the pronouncement on "Christian Faith: Economic Life and Justice" by the General Synod. As cochair of an interagency committee, I played a central role in another denominational priority, the use of economic pressure activities, divestment, and public policy advocacy in an effort to bring about political change in South Africa.

Yet from my first weeks on national staff I had questions about the ways in which mainline churches conducted their justice, peace, and human rights ministries. Having come to the church from a secular background, I had assumed that I would now work from an explicit faith framework. Instead, I soon discovered that theology and scripture had little relevance for the day-to-day operation of my denomination. Although mainline churches had committees and projects related to theological formulation, theology often seemed more of an "alongside" event rather than the source of inspiration for institutional shaping or for programs. Frustrated, I discovered that there often was little difference between the projects and style of church agencies and those of secular institutions doing comparable work. Moreover, as I urged a more distinctively religious approach to advocacy, I found little support. Colleagues, almost all of whom were ordained ministers, were resistant to an approach that would set them apart from the secular public interest groups with which they were affiliated, even in their internal communications and publications on peace and justice issues directed to the church constituency. My concerns and desire to develop a more explicit biblical and theological foundation eventually led to seminary study and ordination, which confirmed my views but did not make them any more convincing within national church circles.

In addition, I was alternatively amazed and appalled by the unstrategic way in which the church conducted justice and peace ministries. As someone who had worked in a variety of professional environments — academic, foundational, and governmental — I took for granted an approach based on the development of clear objectives, identification of the means to achieve these goals, and evaluation of projects, which seemed to be almost completely absent within the church. Because little goal setting or planning was attempted, decisions about projects and programs appeared to be based primarily on the identity of the recipient or partner agency, with little if any effort to undertake an evaluation of potential or actual accomplishments. A shopping-list approach, in which new concerns were taken up without assessing whether there was staff time available or serious constituency interest, led to ongoing issue proliferation and a lack of focus or priority identification. Rarely were there serious efforts to map out a long-term strategy or plan of action that might result in specific tangible results. I could never understand whether the resultant character of peace and justice ministries that opted for witness at the expense of effectiveness was intentional or simply reflected an inability or disinclination to make hard choices and to formulate appropriate strategies.

I also came to be profoundly disturbed by the disparity between the churches' glib adoption of a variety of resolutions and pronouncements and its inability or reluctance to act on them. Again, I seemed to take church policies far more seriously than many of my colleagues, assuming that they were voted for with the express intention of acting on them. My strenuous efforts to promote implementation of several policies relating to church investments generated controversy but at least temporarily resulted in divestment of proscribed stocks by several national agencies. I was less effective on other issues. Despite the years of study, drafting, debate, and evaluation that preceded the General Synod decision, for example, there was little willingness to deal with the pronouncement "Christian Faith: Economic Life and Justice." Despite or because of the considerable work done in advance of adoption, the church seemed to lose interest once this policy was voted, as was the case with so many other documents that I was involved with over the years.

As time went on I came to believe that the failure of mainline churches to incarnate systematically their visions of peace, justice, and compassion within their own corporate lives was a serious failing. Gradually it became far more important to me to attempt to convert the church than to change the world. Church priorities and the decentralized and fragmented polity of my denomination, however, severely hampered any kind of effective outreach from national agencies to engage members of local congregations in faith-based peace and justice programs. And my views advocating a redirection of church peace and justice ministries toward more intentional and systematic internal transformation were often dismissed as sectarian.

This book is an outgrowth of both my commitment to and disappointment with the mainline churches. As I write this introduction I am contemplating my final weeks as a staff member of the United Church of Christ. I have accepted a position directing the human rights program of the American Association for the Advancement of Science. It is my hope that this study may be more successful in stimulating some kind of meaningful reevaluation and revision of mainline political ministries than I was able to achieve during my ten-year tenure within the church.

As I attempted to clarify my disagreements with the prevailing mainline approach, I came to understand that they involved fundamental conceptions of what it means to be a church. Based on the biblical model, this study conceptualizes the church as a community called into a partnership with and for a God of peace, justice, and compassion. It argues that responding to God's summons to participate in redeeming all who remain in bondage and restoring a creation ravaged by sin to the *shalom* state in which peace, justice, and righteousness prevail is central to the churches' vocation. Although mainline churches often articulate theologies with similar views, particularly in the various peace and justice pastorals written during the 1980s, there seems to be a fundamental contradiction between these writings and their actual character and priorities. Most mainline congregations approximate voluntary organizations more than communities of commitment and transformation. Reflecting a consumerist approach to religion, mainline Christians seem to assume that local congregations exist primarily to serve the spiritual and social needs of their individual members, which is quite different from being dedicated to God's purposes.

This study presents a view of faith that underscores its social character, ethical dimensions, and incarnational and transformative qualities. In contrast to the secular tendency to separate faith and politics, it argues that the commitment of the faith community to emulate and embody God's peace, justice, righteousness, and compassion in the world means that faith by its very nature has a political dimension. Politics in this study is defined as the realm in which people come together to decide how to organize collectively their common life. As such, politics has relevance both to the life of the church and to the world. It involves central questions of meaning and purpose, the restoration of communal bonds, and the formulation of collective priorities within the church as well as in the world.

Building on this understanding of faith and politics, the study develops a model it terms *political ministry* and evaluates its potential application to mainline churches. The three components of political ministry are clarification of the community's identity and vocation; development of communal structures, lifestyles, and goals consistent with the character and intentions of the God who is worshiped; and activity by the community to convert and transform the world in the direction of the kingdom. In these three interactive and overlapping stages the faith community would first formulate a shared understanding about the nature of God and God's relationship to the creation, making a radical commitment to place God and God's purposes at the center of the community's life. As in the biblical communities, worship in the form of gratitude and praise and efforts to express fundamental beliefs of today's believers would then have an incarnational dimension. It would lead to active and ongoing efforts to shape and reshape their lives together in accordance with their understanding of the nature and intentions of God. As indicated in the third component, the community would move from a focus on faithfulness in its own fellowship to action directed toward the structural transformation of society. In doing so it would be ever mindful that the faith community, to be true to its calling, must use strategies and modes of involvement consistent with the presence of the kingdom.

The tridimensional model of political ministry developed here differs from the positions both of those who claim the priority of the churches' worldly mission and those who argue that the task of church is to be the church rather than to transform the world. My problem with the "mission first" perspective is that it either assumes the existence of a strong sense of identity and vocation or underestimates the need for such a clarification of beliefs within the churches. My experience with mainline denominations, however, underscores that such a communal articulation of the very being of the church as a faith community cannot be taken for granted. In the absence of such understandings about identity and vocation, mission tends to lack theological grounding and strong membership support and involvement. Moreover, the mission priority orientation usually depreciates the significance of intentional community formation and reformation. Yet a community that espouses norms and policies that it does not itself embody loses one of its most effective means of conversion and transformation, the modeling of God's peace, justice, and compassion to the world.

Writers who argue the contrary position, the "church first" approach, compensate for these deficiencies but frequently do so at the expense of neglecting transformational ministry. Their prescriptions for developing a more cohesive and committed faith community often leads to an inward focus, sometimes to a kind of sectarian withdrawal from the world. These inclinations, however, contradict the basic message of the Gospels: Jesus' mission was to proclaim the good news of the coming of God's reign to the world, not to a select few, and he did so through signs and acts that sought to bring release to the captives, recovery of sight to the blind, and freedom to those who were oppressed. The ministry of Jesus went beyond eliciting individual and community conversion to taking on the principalities and powers. Far from confining his efforts to establishing an alternative community to serve as the model of the redeemed creation, Jesus, as portrayed in the Synoptic Gospels, actively and nonviolently confronted and sought to transform relationships of inequality and domination, albeit through an unconventional nonviolent revolution from below. Affirmation of a partnership with and for God, the human community, and the creation therefore invites engagement rather than withdrawal, particularly service to and advocacy on behalf of the poor and oppressed. Partnership entails responding to God's summons to share in God's efforts to restore a creation long ravaged by sin and injustice to *shalom*, a state in which righteousness, peace, and justice prevail.

Peace and justice ministries emanate not from the triumphalist expectation that the kingdom is at hand, nor from discounting the magnitude of sin and brokenness, but from the relatedness of a

God of compassion with the faith community. Partnership with God means identifying with, serving, and sharing the burdens of all those who suffer. To take seriously the narratives about the loving, caring, empowering Savior of the Gospels who destabilizes conventional expectations, even those about the very nature of divinity, underscores the radically interdependent character of God and creation. Intimate covenantal bonds mean that when one part of the creation suffers, all suffer. In a world of Good Fridays, God's identification with the creation continually brings pain and punishment, sometimes to the point of death. Therefore, the most profound moments of faith revelation between God and God's people come through a willingness to take on and share the brokenness, injustice, poverty, and conflict in God's world. Beyond this, the very nature of the human condition leads to the mandate for transformation, with the realization that, like the kingdom, the very possibilities for change are always "now and not yet."

The scope and orientation of the study is broad, perhaps too much so. It attempts both the delineation of a model as to how the churches should engage in political ministry, as well as an analysis and critique of contemporary mainline peace and justice ministries. The perspective is eclectic, combining elements of Reformed, liberation, and feminist theologies with the thought of some pacifist writers in a synthesis that does not fully subscribe to any of these positions. Judging from reactions to some of my unpublished pieces, the emphasis on the quality of life, faithfulness, and consistency of the churches may be criticized by some mainline Christians as a sectarian withdrawal from the world. These groups are also likely to be uncomfortable with the repositioning of the churches as alternative communities outside the establishment, able to offer an alternative vision but unable to impose it on the rest of society. Yet for those writers who argue that the true role and destiny of the church is to be the church, this study will have too great a concern with political and social transformation.

As a social scientist I realize the limited possibility of effecting the major transformation of the mainline churches that I have in mind, but as a deeply believing Christian I have faith that with God all things are possible. Although I am leaving my position with the United Church of Christ with a deep sense of frustration bordering on despair, I still can identify many causes for hope. I find

two possibilities particularly compelling. Just as I did, I believe that
people who are able to interact and form partnerships with many
Two-Thirds World churches can experience a new understanding of
and commitment to the faith. I also place great hope in biblical study
methodologies that enable the Word of God to speak to contemporary situations. In this moment of *kairos*, of grace and opportunity,
God still beckons, calling the mainline churches and other faith communities into a partnership to serve, suffer with, and participate in
the healing of a broken and unjust world.

Chapter One

Issues and Perspectives

W hen historians, particularly those interested in religion, review the 1980s they may well note the expanding political involvement of churches in many parts of the world. In the United States major Protestant denominations with traditions of social and political concerns increased their activism, moved into direct forms of corporate political ministries, assumed a more critical and prophetic style of political witness, and sought more systematically to educate and mobilize members on a variety of issues. Likewise, the National Conference of Catholic Bishops chose to engage more publicly and visibly in the political process through a variety of means, including drafting major pastoral letters on peace and economic justice, seeking to influence the positions of Catholic office holders, and encouraging the election and appointment of candidates opposed to abortion. Emerging from a state of political apathy and isolation, conservative and fundamentalist white Protestants briefly became a political force within the Republican Party, helping to elect Ronald Reagan and shape his political agenda. After Pat Robertson's failed bid for the Republican presidential nomination, however, they pulled back from such an active role in national politics.

Political involvement by churches and individual leaders in Two-Thirds World* countries was even more pronounced during the decade. Injustice and oppression propelled Christian political activism in countries in Central America, Southern Africa, East Asia, and Latin America. In political systems where repression had stifled and crushed other forms of dissent, churches frequently became the conscience of the nation and last bastion of opposition. Their political ministries took a variety of forms. In many of the countries, including the Philippines, Chile, El Salvador, and Korea, church agencies documented human rights abuses and activated networks linked to churches in other parts of the world in an effort to protect victims. In others, such as South Africa and El Salvador, church initiatives were central in protesting policies of oppressive regimes, ministering to their victims, and fostering democratic alternatives. Despite admonitions from the Vatican nuncio against political involvements, a conservative Catholic prelate called Filipinos into the streets in a great exercise of "people power" to topple Ferdinand Marcos. One of the few viable institutions surviving South African colonialism, the churches in Namibia played a vital role in resettling returning refugees and facilitating the constitutional transition to independence in their country. Churches challenging the status quo often suffered severe penalties, among them assassinations, detention of clergy and lay leaders, disappearances of members, unwarranted accusations of radical/communist ties, seizure of church property, and constraints on operations.

At the close of the decade, churches in several Eastern European countries played major roles in the upheavals that toppled communist regimes and substituted more pluralistic and democratic political systems. During the forty-five years of communist domination, churches in many of these countries participated actively in underground opposition networks and particularly in two cases — the Catholic church in Poland and Protestant churches in the German Democratic Republic — maintained free space for discussion

---

*The term Two-Thirds World is used in this study to refer to the countries of Asia, Africa, and Latin America. Such a designation is more appropriate than the more common term of Third World in that two-thirds of the global population reside in these countries.

of critical issues. Whereas the church in Poland, the symbol of the nation during the period of communist hegemony, retained considerable independence and influence, churches possibly made an even more decisive contribution to political change in East Germany. The number of clergy in the first postcommunist government headed by Prime Minister Lothar de Maiziere attests to this role. Maiziere's cabinet included four Protestant pastors, among them the Defense and Disarmament Minister and the Foreign Minister, and fourteen of the four hundred members of the parliament were pastors. A Catholic priest banned by the state from serving the church for eleven years became one of the top leaders of the Civic Forum, Czechoslovakia's major reform movement, and the head of the major Protestant church was appointed vice prime minister. In Romania, efforts by the government to arrest a dissident local church pastor set in motion the process that ultimately brought down the government.

Ironically, with the occasional exception of articles on East Germany and South Africa, media coverage of these events has rarely dealt with the role of the church. Individual Christians have been acclaimed or castigated, but little has been said about institutional churches' involvement. The limited debate on religion and politics during the 1980s were more likely to deal with the positions of church groups on abortion and other sensitive issues and the appropriateness of clergy holding political office than with the broader issue of the implications of the churches' participation in political ministry. Although religion has been rediscovered by several academic disciplines, published writings have tended to focus on the rise of the religious Right and the decline in membership and influence of the mainline Protestant denominations.

This book seeks to stimulate discussion of the political role of the institutional church and its theological and ecclesial implications. It seeks to move debate away from side issues to the central questions of the relationship between faith, politics, power, and transformation. Far from relating only to questions of strategy, efficacy, or issue orientation, participation by churches in the political sphere involves understandings about the nature of faith, the conception of the divine, the character and vocation of the faith community, and the manner by which the people of God should live out their faith in the world. These issues will be explored primarily from the perspective of their implications for churches and their members rather than the impact of religion on public life. Accordingly, the book is concerned not so much with politics as political ministry, a quite different subject. The use of the term *political ministry* underscores the intrinsic relationship between the political witness of the church and other dimensions of its life as a faith community. As such, political ministry must rest upon and embody the fundamental beliefs of each faith community and be consistent with other dimensions of its institutions and lifestyle.

As conceptualized here, political ministry differs considerably from conventional understandings of politics. Politics usually is defined as the art or science of government or of influencing governmental policy. Alternatively, it is equated with competition between groups or individuals for power or leadership. There is also an older and more comprehensive notion of politics as the total complex of relationships between persons in society. This latter usage comes closer to its meaning in this study. Here "politics" is defined as the realm in which people come together to decide how to organize collectively their common life. Thus politics involves central questions of meaning and purpose, the restoration or reinforcement of communal bonds, and the formulation of societal priorities — all matters relevant to the religious community. Christian political involvement has a special purpose. It is one dimension, albeit a fundamental component, of a faithful response based on love, shared responsibility, and commitment to a God whose love, compassion, and justice for and within the creation have no limits. Through its political ministry the faith community identifies with and participates in the creative, redemptive purpose that is seeking the restoration of the whole creation within the universal order of *shalom* (Hanson 1986, 467).

In contrast to the secular tendency to separate faith and politics, this study reasserts the biblical claims that God is the ultimate source of meaning, authority, and inspiration for all spheres of life, including the political. And counter to the narrow conception of the role of religion in contemporary secular cultures, it emphasizes that a faith that is social, ethical, and incarnational — three central attributes of biblical Christianity — has by its very nature a political dimension. Building on Paul Hanson's analysis of the growth of community in scripture (1986), the perspective here relates the faith community's political witness to its fundamental constitution as "the people called." In the faith dialogue recounted in biblical texts, as

Hanson demonstrates, human response to divine initiative appeared in two essential modes: worship and prayer expressing gratitude and praise, and efforts by the community to shape its life and reshape the world in accordance with its understanding of the nature and intentions of the God to whom it owed its existence. The commitment to express and emulate God's righteousness, peace, justice, and compassion underscored the biblical experiments in community as well as the initiatives of the faith community to bring the *shalom* order to a broken world. It therefore follows that "the people called" have always had a political ministry in the more comprehensive and important sense of the word, understanding politics as "action directed toward structurally transforming society in the direction of the reign of God" (Sobrino 1988, 80).

Political ministry is both broader and narrower than political participation as it is conventionally understood. More specifically, political ministry as conceptualized here has three dimensions: clarification of the faith community's identity and vocation; development of communal structures, lifestyles, and goals consistent with the character and intentions of the God who is worshiped; and activity by the community to convert and transform the world in the direction of the kingdom. Of these three components, only the latter comes close to what is typically equated with political involvement. Yet even this aspect of political ministry places special demands on the church, specifically to act in accordance with faith mandates rather than its own inclinations, that go beyond most self or group interests. Thus, political ministry fundamentally limits political participation. Always required to shape a political witness consistent with its fundamental beliefs, understanding of its faith vocation, and the character of its corporate life, the church is more constrained than other political actors.

CONTEMPORARY PERSPECTIVES ON THE POLITICAL ROLE OF CHURCHES

Neoconservative Critiques of Mainline Churches

In February 1989 the Biblical Witness Fellowship, a caucus within the United Church of Christ with links to the neoconservative

Institute for Religion and Democracy, sent a special issue of its newsletter to all churches within the denomination, in which it questioned the appropriateness of the church's engaging in public policy advocacy. The newsletter attacked nineteen grants made in 1986 by national agencies of the United Church of Christ, primarily by the United Church Board for World Ministries, on the grounds that the recipients were involved in political activity, critical of United States foreign policy, sympathetic to liberation theology, and/or deficient in their opposition to communism. Criticizing the position that the United Church of Christ had taken on a wide range of political, social, and economic issues, the Biblical Witness Fellowship labeled many of the denomination-supported advocacy groups with the epitaphs "partisan," "liberal," and "leftist." Their major criterion in determining whether an organization fell into one or more of these categories appears to be the degree to which it disagreed with the policies of the Reagan administration. More fundamentally, the Biblical Witness Fellowship expressed the view that the church should not support with mission funds any group involved in political ministries, whether liberal or conservative. To underscore this belief, it described respected ecumenical organizations in which the United Church Board for World Ministries and other agencies of the United Church of Christ participated as political action groups (Biblical Witness Fellowship, February 1989).

The Biblical Witness Fellowship claimed to be raising issues about financial accountability as a means to evaluate the definition and focus of mission of the national agencies of the United Church of Christ. Although acknowledging that the grants questioned represented a relatively small percentage of the total budget of the church (they actually totaled only $229,390 of a national church budget of over $30 million, and only four grants were for more than $10,000), the newsletter maintained that the church should not spend even one cent that does not bring glory to Christ Jesus and bear witness to Christ's will and way. Instead of investing funds and staff time in political ministries, the Biblical Witness Fellowship asserted, the moneys of the church should "promote the bringing of men and women into a living relationship with Jesus as their Lord and Savior" (February 1989). Interpreting the ministry and teachings of Jesus of Nazareth very narrowly, the newsletter assumed that church involvement in political, social, and economic issues was incompatible and inconsistent with such a living relationship.

Counterpart groups related to the Institute for Religion and Democracy in the United Methodist, Episcopal, Presbyterian, and Evangelical Lutheran churches have raised similar issues regarding the mission orientation of their own denominations. To the extent that there has been anything in recent years resembling a debate on the political role of the church, the initiative has come from the Institute for Religion and Democracy and these neoconservative caucuses. Although the issues they have identified are important, the contentious and ideological thrust of the attacks and the defensive nature of the responses have made true dialogue difficult.

Formed in April 1981 by a group of neoconservative political thinkers and activists, the Institute for Religion and Democracy, according to its prospectus, seeks "to illuminate the relationship between Christian faith and democratic governance... and to oppose policies and programs in the churches which ignore that relationship" (quoted in Reichley 1985, 336). In contrast to the global perspective and the peace and justice orientation shaping the political ministries of mainline Protestant denominations, neoconservative thinkers affiliated with the Institute for Religion and Democracy have been characterized by an intense anticommunist position and unconditional approval of a strong American military and political presence in the world. The statement of principles setting forth the organization's operating assumptions asserts that Christians must be unapologetically anticommunist (quoted in Reichley 1985, 337). The Institute's anticommunist stance, coupled with its strident commitment to democratic political institutions and limited government, shape a role for the church as the legitimator of the American democratic order, capitalism, and United States foreign policy. Because many of the major Protestant denominations do not provide unqualified support for American institutions and policies, these neoconservatives argue that the churches are eroding the normative bases of the United States' power in the world (Wogaman 1988, 72–84). The Institute for Religion and Democracy goes so far as to characterize some persons holding positions of authority in the churches who do not share their understanding of democracy and America's role in the world as "apologists for oppression" (quoted in Reichley 1985, 337).

Many neoconservative thinkers affirm a political role for religious bodies, as well as for individual Christians, but dispute the priorities and concerns of the ecumenical church movement. Richard John Neuhaus, for example, states that "Christian truth, if it is true is public truth. It is accessible to public reason. It impinges on public space. At some critical points of morality and ethics it speaks to public policy" (1984, 19). He is apprehensive about the emergence of what he terms the "naked public square," by which he means the exclusion of religion and religiously grounded values from the conduct of public business. His book on this subject savagely attacks the two major forms of contemporary religious involvement in the American political system, which he identifies as politicized fundamentalism and mainline or liberal churches. In evaluating the role of the new religious Right, Neuhaus expresses alarm over the substance of its claims and the absolutist and intolerant style of participation (1984, 16–18). He then criticizes mainline churches on other grounds: their liberal political positions (1984, 226–47), their close identification with and support for New Deal policies (1984, 235), their failure to articulate their positions on a Christian basis invoking distinctive Christian claims (1984, 223–24), and their posture critical of American society (1984, 224). Neuhaus later modified his position, becoming more sympathetic to the political resurgence of fundamentalist Christianity, but he never moderated his attacks against the liberal church (1987).

Underlying this critique of the liberal or ecumenical church is Neuhaus's view, like that of many other neoconservatives, that religion serves a vital culture-forming role. He claims that the mainline, liberal, or ecumenical Protestant denominations, using these terms interchangeably, once served such a formative role within the American political system but no longer do so. With a reading of church history that many would dispute, Neuhaus writes that these churches abandoned their culture-forming task when key leaders identified the New Deal experiment as the working out of God's purposes in history, thus assuming an ancillary and supportive posture toward American culture. At the same time, however, Neuhaus argues that the leaders of contemporary mainline churches, far from being conformed to the American political system, are now so critical that they cannot contribute to its moral legitimation (1981). Thus Neuhaus alternatively characterizes the major Protestant churches as being too establishment-oriented and too antiestablishment-oriented, too accommodating and insufficiently accommodated to the American political system, and too well identified with and too critical of American culture and the role of the United States in the world.

A Mainline Position

Like many of the other mainline Protestant churches, the United Church of Christ has been shaped by an ethical, activist, community-oriented approach to religion very different from the Biblical Witness Fellowship's assumption that Christian faith and theology relate only to the private and personal relationship of the individual with God. Coming out of a Reformed tradition, indeed tracing its roots back to the Pilgrims landing at Plymouth and Puritan Congregational efforts to establish a religious commonwealth in North America, the United Church of Christ has consistently affirmed the appropriateness of the church's engaging in political ministries. In contrast to the Biblical Witness Fellowship, which apparently wants the national church to spurn involvement in justice and peace advocacy, the United Church of Christ testifies in its Statement of Faith to a God who "judges persons and nations by God's righteous will declared through the prophets and apostles," a God who promises "courage in the struggle for justice and peace" (General Synod of the United Church of Christ 1959, 113). Along with adopting the Statement of Faith, the Second General Synod of the United Church of Christ also voted a "Call to Christian Action in Society," which states that "God holds political life under [God's] providence and judgment." It confesses that "God as revealed in Jesus Christ is the ruler of all human affairs — nations, social orders, institutions." Identifying political life as "an area in which [people] and nations make some of the most fateful decisions of our time," the Call envisions "a church with bonds of Christian fellowship so strong that it dares to discuss and act upon civic and political issues" (General Synod of the United Church of Christ 1959, 171, 174–75). It goes on to set forth a detailed agenda on social, economic, and political issues, asking the church to pray and work for the end of racial segregation and discrimination, support for the United Nations, full implementation of the Universal Declaration of Human Rights, reduction of all national armaments, and the use of wealth, personal resources, and trade polities in a worldwide attack on human misery (General Synod of the United Church of Christ 1959, 171, 174). Subsequent General Synods have approved additional pronouncements and resolutions articulating the United Church of Christ social teaching and developing the denomination's public policy agenda.

The United Church of Christ and the Biblical Witness Fellowship reflect but two of many contemporary perspectives on these issues. Two others with particular relevance for this study have come from Two-Thirds World churches and from the Anabaptist stream of the Christian heritage. Frank Chikane's autobiography, described below, offers a kind of narrative confession of the faith evolution of a thoughtful and compassionate black South African Christian, raised in an apolitical pietist tradition, whose experience of injustice and oppression brought him to a liberation theology orientation. As one who has spent nine years in various countries in Africa and another nine relating to churches and ecumenical institutions in Two-Thirds World countries, I am sympathetic to these concerns about the universal nature of the Christian fellowship and its demands on American Christians. John Howard Yoder, a Mennonite theologian, like Chikane, raises the fundamental question of whether churches can be both faithful and accommodated to prevailing structures of culture and power. As mainstream churches reconsider their role in American society, I believe Yoder's ethic of the prophetic minority has much to offer.

A Gospel Message from South Africa

Frank Chikane, like many other church leaders prominent in the antiapartheid movement, once was a fugitive from the South African police. In an autobiography written during this period, Chikane, later to become General Secretary of the South African Council of Churches, recounts his experience as a black Christian in a country where whites in his own denomination refuse to worship with blacks. He reflects on what it means for the church to be faithful to the gospel message of intrinsic human worth in a society where institutionalized racism and oppression prevail (1988). Recounting his religious upbringing, Chikane describes his struggles within the Apostolic Faith Mission Church over its narrow conception of spirituality that excluded the social dimension of faith. His role in ministering to those in the midst of the struggle soon resulted in detention by the police. In one case he was tortured by a church elder, whom he recognized, from the white branch of his denomination. Charged by the police with making political statements and with allowing his church to be used for political purposes, apparently because of his youth work, Chikane was also suspended by the council of the Apostolic Faith Mission Church from his ministry because the council members believed that such activities were inappropriate for a minister.

During the next five years Chikane served as the director of the Institute of Contextual Theology, a position that enabled him to work through critical issues on the role of the churches in society. He met monthly with a group of ministers, many of whom had been detained in circumstances similar to Chikane's. The group eventually reached a consensus that the dominant tradition in Christian theology was not compatible with the demands of the gospel because it viewed reality and understood faith from the point of view of the powerful. Surveying the role of the church since Constantine — the church that served the apartheid system in South Africa, the empires of Europe, the czars in Russia, the Third Reich in Germany — they assessed that in the main the church had taken sides with the dominant classes in society, the very people principally responsible for pain, suffering, misery, and sometimes death of the weak, poor, and powerless (1988, 44–45).

This analysis led Chikane's group to formulate an alternative theology, a theology of taking sides modeled on the Confessing Church in Nazi Germany and other theologies emerging from Latin America, Asia, and Africa. Conscious that they were called to minister to all in the world, both oppressors and oppressed, white and black, they decided that solidarity with the victims of injustice means taking sides with the ideal of the kingdom of justice, righteousness, and peace proclaimed by Jesus. Applied to the South African situation, this required the church to take the side of blacks against the white heresy of racism, which the English-speaking churches in South Africa came only gradually to understand, and the Dutch Reformed Church not at all. Chikane drew inspiration for such a ministry of liberation from the portrayal of Jesus in the Gospels, albeit with an interpretation very different from traditional Christianity's efforts to spiritualize Jesus and to associate him with the kings and lords of society (1988, 46).

What does this theology mean specifically for churches in the United States and elsewhere in the First World? In April 1986, after returning from a trip to several European countries, Chikane wrote a letter to the churches in Europe in which he spelled out some of the implications. The letter reflects the pain of someone who takes seriously the universal nature of the Christian fellowship, only to discover that most members of the churches in the North do not feel connected with the plight of Christians in other parts of the world. This insensitivity to and uncaringness about exploitation and oppression led Chikane to conclude that "primary sin" has eluded churches in these countries, with the result that churches have become obsessed with what he terms "secondary sin." For Chikane primary sin refers to structures of injustice that enable one group or class to exploit and impoverish another. In contrast, secondary sin is the type of personal sin — adultery, theft, falsehood, and drunkenness — that the church has traditionally addressed. Because of this preoccupation with secondary sin, the church representatives with whom Chikane met to discuss the situation in South Africa were largely oblivious to the role of corporations in their own countries in supporting apartheid by continuing to invest in South Africa. They also failed to understand the implications of churches' drawing profits from investments in corporations that operated in South Africa (1988, 75–78).

Like many other Two-Thirds World Christians, Chikane believes that the churches of Europe and North America are in need of radical repentance and conversion. To identify the elements of a faithful response to the gospel in the contemporary world, he cites the 1971 statement of the Roman Catholic Synod of Bishops that "action on behalf of justice and participation in the transformation of the world fully appear to us as a constitutive dimension of the preaching of the gospel, or, in other words, of the Church's mission for the redemption of the human race and its liberation from every oppressive situation" (Third Synod of Bishops, *Justice in the World*, cited in Chikane 1988, 80). According to Chikane, this "transformation of the world," the "liberation from every oppressive initiative," entails the establishment of new structures and systems to encourage a just redistribution of wealth, power, and knowledge to narrow the gap between the rich and poor, the North and the South. To begin such a transformation, First World churches would need to deal more seriously with "primary sin" by studying the causes of underdevelopment, injustice, and inequality; evaluating sociopolitical, economic, and church structures to identify injustices; and perhaps most important, developing a meaningful form of solidarity with those who suffer (Chikane 1988, 80–84).

An Alternative Approach

The Anabaptist/Mennonite tradition, as updated and modified by John Howard Yoder, provides yet another perspective on the relationship between faith and politics relevant to this study. Emerging from the radical wing of the Protestant Reformation, Anabaptists modeled their tradition on the early Christian movement. Like the early Christians, they understood themselves as a distinct minority group based on a voluntary membership set apart from the corrupt established churches of their time. Highly disciplined, concerned with faithful obedience to New Testament ideals, theirs was an ethic of pacifism and nonresistance that precluded their serving in the army or in public office and often resulted in their persecution. Ernst Troeltsch's influential characterization (1931) portrayed Anabaptists as representative of the sect, a form of religious organization whose uncompromising worldview led to withdrawal from society. Troeltsch compared the sects with the church type which seeks to be inclusive in both geography and membership, to control or dominate the social order and culture, and to enact its saving ministry primarily through sacramental participation. Some contemporary Mennonites, heirs to this heritage, have disputed Troeltsch, arguing that the community orientation of the Anabaptists constituted an alternative approach to social change (Yoder 1984, 160–65). Others recognize that much of Mennonite experience fits the sectarian model but maintain that in the twentieth century formerly withdrawn Mennonites have been catapulted into the mainstream, developing a style of political activity that transcends the classic church/sect options (Burkholder 1988).

Yoder's writings, a rearticulation of the Mennonite ethic in a more contemporary form, offer a challenge to mainline models of Christian political ministry. Like those of other Mennonites, his social ethics are based on adherence to New Testament standards, affirmation of nonviolence, and a commitment to costly discipleship. Yoder's innovation is to link this orientation to a reinterpretation of the Jesus community as the "original revolution," the creation of a distinct community with an alternate set of values and a coherent way of incarnating them (1972). Yoder argues that the Jesus ethic entails a new vision of what it means to be human, based on forgiveness of offenders, responding to violence with nonviolence, sharing of goods, new patterns of relationships between men and women, parent and child, slave and master, and a new attitude toward the state (1972, 28–29). Radical commitment to Christian community for Yoder means emulation of the model of the Jesus community as a vehicle of social change.

Like Chikane, but from a different perspective, Yoder questions whether any church that is part of or accommodated to the prevailing power structure can provide an authentic political witness. His models and criteria for political involvement contrast the radical commitment to the New Testament ethic and behavioral norms possible for a minority community with the diluted interpretation characteristic of churches with nonvoluntary or inclusive membership bases. Yoder identifies Constantine's fourth-century recognition of Christianity as a critical dividing line explaining much of the distance between biblical and contemporary Christianity. From this perspective it can be seen that most Christian thought relating to power and society is rendered captive to their systems, even when writers intend a critique. In place of this false universalism, he advocates the minority consciousness and stance of what has been variously labeled as sect, peace church, or radical reformation.

Yoder's more sectarian understanding of the church characterizes the true church as an alternative community whose minority status enables it to choose its own agenda and hold fast to a morality based on principle. He describes it as having a modeling mission. "The church is called to be now what the world is called to be ultimately" (1984, 92). Another dimension of its role is the cultivation of an alternative consciousness based on the Jesus ethic. Although a minority community can appeal to the conscience of society at large and thus bring about significant change, Yoder believes, as a minority the true church trusts in the power of weakness (1984, 91–101).

CONFLICTS AND TENSIONS
IN THE AMERICAN HERITAGE

American religious history and traditions have given rise to two opposed dynamics: an ethical, social, and activist interpretation of the role of churches growing out of Puritanism and the Reformed tradition, and a privatistic and more narrowly spiritual understanding of faith fostered by pietism and a variety of the eighteenth- and nineteenth-century renewal movements, which discouraged churches' political involvement. Although both these perspectives have had numerous theological exponents, their influence in many ways has been on a more popular than formal theological level. This dual heritage helps to explain why there are such varied interpretations as to whether religion serves as a legitimation, a critique of, or an escape from American culture and society (Fowler 1989). The answer depends to a considerable extent on a group's basic conception of faith. I believe that the tensions between a public and private understanding of the church underlie many of the conflicts between liberals and conservatives, as documented by Robert Wuthnow (1988, 1989) and others, as well as the divisions between Christians who focus on the local congregation and those whose concept of the church is more global. Moreover, the pluralism and lack of theological coherence characteristic of American churches result in the coexistence of both of these dispositions within mainline denominations, sometimes within the same congregation. Generally, the national church tends toward a public orientation, and the local church inclines toward a private or local perspective.

The Reformed Heritage

Several historians stress the formative role of the Calvinist or Reformed heritage in American religious and cultural history. Sidney Ahlstrom's influential work, *A Religious History of the American People* (1975), for example, accords a central place to Puritan Protestantism in American religious history. A recent book by Mark Noll similarly maintains that the theology and values of the Puritans constitute the enduring foundations for American political life (1988, 19). Robert Handy's study, *A Christian America*, juxtaposes the mainline denominations' respect for the separation of church and state with their resistance to the separation of religion and morals from public well-being (1984).

The Reformed Calvinist conviction of God's radical sovereignty over all spheres of life — family, church, culture, society, economy, and politics — gives rise to a worldview in which faith is intrinsically linked to all human activities, institutions, and sectors. A corollary of this belief in God's sovereignty is that there is no dimension of the world's life that God is not seeking to redeem. Within the Reformed tradition, history is seen as the present encounter with God in Christ, a Christ who is the transformer and converter of all spheres of life. John Calvin's call for the gospel's present permeation of all life was reflected in his close association of church and state and his insistence that the state can play a positive role in the promotion of human welfare. In Calvinist thinking the Hebrew covenant between God and the chosen people, established to embody righteousness within the human community, provides a model of the relationships between members of society expressed in a covenant of mutual responsibility and commitment.

One way to conceptualize the differences between the Calvinist perspective that influenced American culture and the Lutheran dualism that was a major alternative is to use H. Richard Niebuhr's paradigms of Christ and culture. Niebuhr characterizes Martin Luther as an example of a type he labels "Christ and culture in paradox." He explains that in this type the duality and inescapable authority of both Christ and culture are recognized, but the opposition between them is also accepted. In Luther, life in Christ and life in culture — in the kingdom of God and in the kingdom of the world — are closely related and yet always in tension. Like the "Christ-against-culture" believers, Luther refused to accommodate the claims of Christ to those of secular society. However, unlike adherents to this latter type, Luther also emphasized obedience to the institutions of society as well as obedience to the Christ who sits in judgment of that society. This means that individuals are understood to be subject to two moralities and to be citizens of two worlds that are forever in conflict (Niebuhr 1951, 44–45). In evaluating the consequences Niebuhr observes that "more than any great Christian leader before him, Luther affirmed the life in culture as the sphere in which Christ could and ought to be followed; and more than any other he discerned that the rules to be followed in the cultural life were independent of Christian or church law" (1951, 174). The dynamic dualism of Luther led to a cultural conservatism and, in later generations, to a static and undynamic dualistic parallelism that separated spiritual and temporal life (1951, 179), sometimes to the point of rendering Lutherans impotent before or accommodating them to political tyranny.

In contrast to Luther, Niebuhr discusses John Calvin as a primary example of another typology in which Christ is seen to be the converter of culture. In the conversionist model the antithesis between Christ and all human institutions and customs leads neither to Christian separation from the world nor to endurance in expectation of a transhistorical salvation, but instead to Christian transformation. For the conversionist, the creative activity of God and of Christ-in-God makes it possible for sinful and fallen humanity still to live under the rule of Christ, by the creative power and ordering of the divine Word. Among conversionists humanity's good nature has become corrupted — that is, "perverted good," not evil or a "badness of being." As a consequence the problem of culture is the problem of conversion, not of its replacement by a new creation. Conversionists also view history as the presence of God in time, with the divine possibility of renewal (Niebuhr 1951, 45, 190–96). According to Niebuhr,

> The conversionist, with his view of history as the present encounter with God in Christ, does not live so much in expectation of a final ending of the world of creation and culture as in awareness of the power of the Lord to transform all things by lifting them up to himself. His image is spatial and not temporal; and the movement of life he finds to be issuing from Jesus Christ is an upward movement, the rising of men's souls and deeds and thoughts in a mighty surge of adoration and glory of the One who draws them to himself. This is what human culture can be — a transformed human life in and to the glory of God. For man it is impossible, but all things are possible to God (1951, 195–96).

This conversionist perspective leads to an activism, a constant and ongoing effort to change the world to be more consistent with God's intentions, in and through all spheres of society, including the political. But just as Lutheranism tended to transmute Luther's dialectical dualism into a static dualism, Calvinism can sometimes degenerate into an activism for its own sake, and conversionism can flirt with accommodation to culture.

For Mark Noll, who is an evangelical, this Reformed heritage has been a mixed blessing. Failing to make clear whether he is characterizing individual or institutional behavior, Noll describes Christian political action in America as an extension of the revival, with its prevailing characteristics — immediatism, ultraism, and perfectionism — creating a peculiarly American style of political evangelism. Noll relates this political evangelism, or evangelistic politics, to the tendency of American Christians to assume that the public sphere of government exists as a forum in which to promote the virtues defined by an individual's religion (1988, 24–25). Noll also laments the general absence in America of theological reflection on political questions, asserting that Christian political action typically occurs at the level of personal morality rather than theology. Critical of the "Reformed" assumptions that have dominated American political life, Noll suggests that a "Lutheran" contribution, more sensitive to the complexities involved in moving from private moral vision to corporate public policy, would enrich and correct these dispositions (1988, 183). Although he believes that Reformed political action has sometimes confused partisan political imperatives with faith, Noll also acknowledges that the Reformed foundation has done too much good to be cast aside lightly (1988, 183–84).

The contemporary religiopolitical landscape reflects the continuing Reformed legacy. The theological understanding, policies, and activist modes of involvement of major Protestant churches affiliated with the National Council of Churches differ very little, whether or not they emanate from a Reformed heritage. The Lutheran churches and the Methodist, for example, mirror the activism of the United Church of Christ and Presbyterian churches. Most of these denominations have an office for church and society or a functional equivalent charged with overseeing issues of social responsibility. Many have presences in Washington to monitor and influence legislation, one of which dates from the Prohibition era and many others from the post-World War II period (Reichley 1985, 244–45).

The evolution of the Lutheran Church in America, one of the constituent denominations of the recently formed Evangelical Lutheran Church in America, is instructive in this regard. As recounted in a book by Christa Klein with Christian von Dehsen (1989), the Lutheran Church in America moved over two centuries from a focus on individual conversion and personal morality to a broader conception of social responsibility and activism. Key to this process, the Lutheran General Synod, established in 1820 to accomplish projects that district synods could not manage by themselves, also provided a forum to deliberate and formulate Lutheran positions on theological, political, and ethical issues. During much of its early history the Synod focused on missionary work, theological education, ministerial aid, and the publication of worship and catechetical materials. It strongly affirmed a renewal emphasis based on a profound concern for people's recognition of God's saving grace. A preoccupation with the temperance issue between 1866 and 1917, however, drew the Synod into corporate public advocacy, links with a political lobby, and establishment of relationships with the churches that founded the Federal Council of Churches in 1908 (Klein and von Dehsen 1989, 2–16).

In the twentieth century the various Lutheran bodies, coalescing through mergers and development of more complex bureaucratic structures, devoted increasing attention to finding their corporate voice. In doing so and responding to such traumatic events as war and depression, the Lutherans moved away from the earlier denominational focus on conversion and personal morality. In 1918 the newly formed United Lutheran Church created a standing committee for the study of social issues. Meeting during the week in which the armistice ending the war was signed, the delegates adopted a statement critical of "national aggrandizement" and "unbridled commercialism" and urged that weak and small nations "be given free, full and unhampered opportunity to development of their own national life" (Klein and von Dehsen 1989, 20). Two years later, after the passage of the Eighteenth Amendment prohibiting the manufacture, sale, or transportation of alcoholic beverages, the church convention established a second national agency alongside its Inner Mission Board, a Committee on Moral and Social Welfare, to provide a thorough study of moral, social, and industrial problems. By 1930 the Committee on Social Welfare had worked out positions on two issues, marriage and war, the latter of which affirmed the agenda for peace favored by liberal Protestants. During the next thirty years there was an increased engagement of Lutherans in the American mainstream, stimulating denominational leaders and Lutheran teachers in church-related schools to develop theological principles for social analysis. Unsurprisingly then, the Lutheran Church in America, during its twenty-five year life from 1962 to 1987, when it merged with other Lutheran bodies, issued nineteen social statements on subjects as diverse as economic justice, human rights, peace and politics, social criteria for investments, ecology, Vietnam, aging, church and state, and sex and marriage (Klein and von Dehsen 1989, 179–290).

The Pietist Tradition

A strand of religious personalism or pietism, with many of the same dispositions as a Lutheran "two kingdoms" dualism, interfaces with the Calvinist or Reformed legacy in the American cultural and religious heritage. Bruce Birch and Larry Rasmussen attribute this disposition within American Christianity — to spiritualize the material and to subjectivize and privatize faith — to the confluence of three factors: the rise of religious movements that claimed that religion had to do with inner life, the impact of secularization, and the ethos of capitalist individualism. Pietism, a major religious movement emphasizing personal experience and feeling, arose during the seventeenth century as a reaction to the Lutheran and Calvinist emphasis on faith as assent to right belief or correct doctrine. Pietism's focus on developing a living relationship with a personal God leads to a preoccupation with personal sin, grace and forgiveness, and personal testimony. Although pietism encourages acts of charity as an expression of Christian faith, it advocates social transformation through changing hearts and minds, rather than through reforming institutions (1978, 48–49).

Secularization as a societal phenomenon and as a point of view reinforced the tendency of pietism to draw boundaries between religion and political life. In the course of industrialization, urbanization, and bureaucratization in the West, social phenomena and areas of knowledge once dealt with in the context of ethical theology and moral philosophy came to be regarded as independent entities. Social structures, such as political institutions, the economy, and class systems, formerly under the "sacred canopy," were vested with separate and independent identities, meanings, and rules — all unrelated to religion. By the end of the eighteenth century the natural sciences were separated from ethics in an effort to identify the "laws of nature" governing various dimensions of the universe. Religion was relegated to its own separate or semiseparate sphere, thus encouraging the assumption that religion was an individual and personal matter. As Birch and Rasmussen explain,

> As this dividing proceeded, the common cover of a single "sacred canopy" over the whole of society was rent. . . . Rather, religion became a more individual matter, as did so many things in secularization's thrust toward division and pluralism. Religion did not inform economic, political, and social life as enterprises in themselves, or even as parts of a larger whole. It informed, when chosen at all, *individual* searches and needs (1978, 50–51).

Capitalist individualism constitutes the third factor that Birch and Rasmussen identify as encouraging the privatization of religion. Classical capitalism, as exemplified in Adam Smith's *The Wealth of Nations* written in 1776, posited that individuals, each driven by his or her own self-interest, not the community, were the fundamental social reality. Furthermore, Smith contended that the individual, acting on the basis of self-interest, tended to promote the aggregate interests of the society. In Smith's work, market economics reconciled the seemingly competing and conflicting self-interests of members of the society through the metaphorical "invisible hand" (1937, bk. 4, ch. 2). Although self-interest had long been recognized as a critical motivational factor, hitherto it had been considered to be a sin. To acknowledge self-interest openly — even more, to call for economic engagement on the basis of self-interest — involved a fundamental transformation in attitude. It assumed that socially beneficial results can be obtained without an institution's acting for the good of the whole or making an explicit commitment to the common good. In reflecting on the impact of capitalist individualism on American life, Birch and Rasmussen comment that it encouraged an ethos based on the unrestrained pursuit of individual happiness or self-fulfillment that came to pervade the conception of religion and the approach to public life (1978, 52).

An Uneasy Coalescence

This dual legacy, a Reformed dynamic calling the church into public life and politics to pursue God's intentions for humanity and a pietistic inclination toward a privatized religion disengaged from social and political responsibility, leads to confusion, conflicts, and major inconsistencies. In the debate between the Biblical Witness Fellowship and the national agencies of the United Church of Christ, for example, a caucus nominally affirming the Reformed legacy of the United Church of Christ is espousing a conception of faith as first and foremost a personal relationship between the individual and God, contradicting fundamental tenets of Reformed belief. Although the Biblical Witness Fellowship would presumably deny the influence of secularization in shaping its basic understanding of faith, its clear-cut separation between religion and politics reflects such a truncated approach. The Fellowship's attack on the United Church of Christ's political involvement may, however, cloak political goals and motivation in a pietistic theology.

The politicization of the conservative Protestants who have made up the core of the religious Right provides another example of seeming inconsistencies in the intermixing of a pietistic understanding of religion with a Calvinist political activism. (Evangelicals, it should be noted, have a diversity of perspectives, some holding very different political orientations than the conservative evangelicals and fundamentalists who have participated in the coalitions of the new political Right.) Analysts trace the increasing political involvement of this diverse coalition of evangelicals, the heirs of pietism, and fundamentalists (who espouse a form of evangelicalism that regards the Bible as an infallible source of religious and moral authority) to a perceived threat to their autonomy and moral integrity. They link the politicization of the evangelicals and fundamentalists to a series of Supreme Court decisions, beginning in the 1950s, that outlawed segregation, banned school prayer, and legalized abortion. According to Gary Wills, the desegregation decisions and related public demonstrations became a challenge not only to a way of life but also to a religion that had sanctioned racial separation and inequality. Southern religiosity had tended to be noninstitutional; now Southerners responded to protect their way of life through organized and institutional means, particularly through the establishment of religiously based political organizations (1989, 24). A. James Reichley points to the Supreme Court's 1961 decision prohibiting organized prayer in public schools and the 1973 abortion decision as events that so enraged the evangelical community that they propelled it into politics. Reichley disagrees with social scientists who have described the rise of the religious Right as an example of "status politics" or the struggle of a declining social group to recapture some of its lost influence and prestige. Instead Reichley argues that evangelicals have been motivated by their sense of a declining standard of public morality, particularly as related to the family (1987, 76–91).

In moving into the political arena, however, conservative evangelicals and fundamentalists do not necessarily change their basic perspectives or develop a broad sense of social responsibility. Jerry Falwell, founder of the Moral Majority political movement, one of the casualties of the new Right political retrenchment at the end of the decade, claimed that political liberalism had eroded America's traditional values and therefore contributed to its intellectual and moral decline. He argued that the Moral Majority provided a singular opportunity for spiritual revival and political renewal in the United States. As outlined by Falwell, the political agenda of the Moral Majority reflected many of the beliefs and concerns typical of groups that have understood religion as a private matter, including a focus on personal morality, support for the traditional family, and an opposition to abortion, pornography, drug abuse, and homosexuality (Falwell 1987, 111–23).

But does this amount to a new sense of the public and social dimensions of religious concern? Martin Marty, the well-known historian of religion, makes a useful distinction between theological assumptions that are political and public. According to Marty, the political theology of privatist fundamentalists retains their traditional opposition to the secular-pluralist order. He considers politicized fundamentalists to be chiefly motivated by self-interest, seeking to protect their turf, to extend their mission, and to have their way at the expense of others (Marty 1987, 311–13). Jerry Falwell's decision to disband the Moral Majority and withdraw from politics in 1989, in the wake of criticism from other fundamentalists, difficulties in promoting the Moral Majority's political agenda, and the various scandals concerning television evangelists, suggests a transitory and limited interest in political ministry. Political involvement thus may come about to promote the goals of a pietistic faith without changing its premises about the nature of religion and political life.

As the preceding discussion indicates, the debate over the appropriateness of the church's engaging in political ministries touches on basic issues related to the understanding of faith, the interpretation of scripture, and the formulation of theology. It crosses some of the major divides in American religious life between those who have subscribed to a public orientation and those who have held a private conception of religion and its role in society. The situation is further complicated by inconsistencies and the syncretistic way in which individuals and communities have appropriated and applied dimensions of the various traditions. No political theology, however clearly conceptually defined, biblically based, consistently developed, or compellingly argued, is likely to identify a position acceptable across these theological and historical divisions.

THE CHANGING ROLE
OF MAINLINE CHURCHES

This study focuses primarily, but not exclusively, on Protestant denominations often referred to collectively as "mainline" or "mainstream." It does so because of my interest in and experience within these churches and because of the central role they have played historically within the American society and political system. Identifying the parameters of mainstream Protestantism is fraught with problems. Some use the term to refer to specific denominations that historically played a significant role in American history and political life; others employ the term more broadly to include all the Protestant denominations with ecumenical inclinations that are currently affiliated with the National Council of Churches of Christ (NCCC). Of the denominations characterized as mainstream, three that had deep roots in the colonial period — the Congregational (now United Church of Christ), Episcopal, and Presbyterian churches — occupy a central place. These denominations, along with the Northern Baptists, Methodists, Lutherans, and Disciples of Christ, sometimes described as products of the nineteenth-century religious expansion, came to occupy a special niche in American society. The most inclusive and imprecise equation of mainline with ecumenical would mean that at least all of the Protestant members of the NCCC would qualify, including the predominantly black denominations and, given the fluid contours of the ecumenical movement, perhaps even the post-Vatican II Catholic Church and some of the historic peace churches.

In some ways the term mainline as applied to this group of denominations is more appropriate as a socioeconomic rather than a religious designation. According to Charles Strain, the term mainline originally referred to the well-off and well-placed families who were major beneficiaries of and powers in the social, economic, and political structures of major cities that developed during the late nineteenth century. Similarly, mainline Protestants for the most part arrived early on the American scene, occupied a central place in the development of American culture and history, and thus were advantaged in ascending to positions of power and privilege. Statistical data unsurprisingly show that mainline Protestants tend to be comfortably above average in terms of income, formal education, and professional status (Strain 1989, 131). Nevertheless, the relation between social class and religion in this country has been fluid, and, as H. Richard Niebuhr observed, the churches of the disinherited often become the churches of the middle class (1984). Thus while the Episcopalians, the Congregationalists (United Church of Christ), and the Presbyterians have maintained high-status positions during the past two hundred years, other groups have experienced upward mobility to close the gap. The social and economic gains of Catholics in the period since the Second World War, for example, have eliminated Protestant-Catholic status differences and have placed Catholics at the cultural and religious center. In addition, the current tendency, particularly among younger members of the upper-middle class, to reject religious affiliation has further weakened the relationship between membership in a mainline denomination and establishment status (Roof and McKinney 1987, 107–17).

The Realignment Assessed

As some have noted, it is ironic that the term mainline came into vogue just at the point when these churches could no longer be appropriately so designated. General consensus holds that there is a major shift in the American socioreligious order that has reshaped the religious center and displaced the major Protestant churches from their once-dominant positions. Wade Clark Roof and William McKinney summarize the trends as follows:

- The privileged Protestant mainline has fallen upon hard times and no longer enjoys the influence and power it once had.

- Conservative Protestants are flourishing and are now much more culture affirming than they used to be.

- Roman Catholic leadership has assumed a new position in the center and is articulating a social vision to its constituency and the public at large.

- American Jews seem to have experienced a shift in outlook — more concerned now with group interests and survival and less with assimilation.

- Black religionists are now holding up a more inclusive vision of America and are less prone to a separatist outlook.

- Secular humanism is identified as a growing and hostile force in relation to traditional religion and morality (1987, 4–5).

There is less agreement on the causes and implications of this realignment. A few critics of the mainline churches link their declining membership and financial plight to political activism, claiming that church leaders and pronouncements critical of the established order have alienated local congregations (Neuhaus 1981, 1984). Others consider the situation of the mainline denominations to be primarily the product of demographic and cultural shifts (Bass 1989; Roof and McKinney 1987). Another group argues that these denominations, by becoming conformed to white middle-class American culture, failed to challenge their members to make a real commitment based on faith (Kelley 1986; Roof and McKinney 1987). Others date "disestablishment" as occurring decades earlier and view the process as related to secularization and increasing pluralism (Handy 1984; Noll 1988). Still another explanation treats the problem as an educational failure, describing liberal Protestants as confused and tentative about appropriating the Christian tradition and transmitting the meaning and excitement of Christianity from one generation to another (Bass 1989).

This major realignment of the American religious landscape, with its change in the roles of mainline churches, has produced very different assessments of the implications, depending in part on whether the focus is on the American political system or on the future of the denominations. Richard John Neuhaus's lament about "the naked public square" (1984) reflects his thesis that mainline Protestantism formerly served as a culture-shaping force that provided moral and religious legitimacy for democracy in America. His diatribes against these denominations reflect his anxiety about the future of democracy now that mainline Protestantism has lost its power to bind Americans into a common moral and civic order. Roof and McKinney similarly express concern that the breakdown in the national religious culture during the 1960s altered significantly the normative basis of American religious pluralism. According to Roof and McKinney, the absence of a common religious culture and the decline of the tolerance central to the "religion of civility" has the potential to arouse strong authoritarian impulses (1987, 34–38). In looking to the future, Roof and McKinney project ongoing expansion of the boundaries of American religious pluralism and a continued decline in membership, political influence, and social status of the mainline churches (1987, 233–34).

The Benefits of Disestablishment

The analyses discussed above, however, focus on one dimension of a complex series of political, social, religious, and cultural shifts and by so doing provide for an unduly negative assessment of the prospects of the mainline churches. They ignore as well the potential benefits of disestablishment for religious renewal. In the past generation major Protestant denominations have, with some success, responded to two other major challenges: the emergence of a global Christian community based on new types of relationships between First World and Two-Thirds World churches and the need to provide a faith response to the increasing possibility of nuclear destruction, serious economic injustice, and severe environmental degradation. In the second half of the twentieth century the locus of the world Christian movement has moved from North America and Europe to Africa, Asia, and Latin America. Christians from Two-Thirds World countries now constitute a clear majority in membership, which will increase during the twenty-first century. Moreover, the global church of the third millennium of Christianity is coming to consciousness as a church of the poor, anchored in the suffering, struggles, and needs of those who live amid poverty, economic injustice, and, often, political oppression. As Christianity has become explicitly, rather than implicitly, a world or international religion, it has entailed greater theological and cultural diversity, new perspectives and theological emphases, different understandings of social, economic, and political forces, and a recasting of relationships among the churches. Through membership in the global Christian community, churches of North America and Europe that have in the past sent missionaries to developing countries have been transformed from preeminent shapers and financiers of mission into equal partners with the now fully independent churches they helped establish. Many Two-Thirds World churches operating in situations of risk, injustice, and violence regularly appeal to churches in other parts of the world for assistance, often in the form of political initiatives. Thus the plight of suffering churches in other parts of the world plays a major role in shaping the priorities and political witness of the mainline churches.

In the 1980s the major Protestant denominations and the Catholic Church rediscovered and revitalized their peace and justice ministries and, in the process, cast their political ministries in a more prophetic mode. In belatedly confronting the darkening valley of possible nuclear destruction, American Christians have come face-to-face with the realities of the principalities and powers in much the same way as did Two-Thirds World Christians when dealing with dehumanizing systemic injustice and poverty. Like the United States Catholic Conference, several of the Protestant denominations have written peace pastorals acknowledging that the world is at a moment of fundamental crisis and rejecting the production and use of nuclear weapons. They then followed these peace pastorals with theological statements on economic justice that seek to reinstitute moral and religious concerns within an economic system captive to the tyranny of the market. Both of these initiatives begin to address structural issues, not just policies and programs, and they often attempt to link public policy prescriptions with the qualities of life and the behavior of the church and its members.

The globalization of the Christian community, along with the greater peace and justice orientation of these denominations, provides both a challenge and an opportunity. These developments make new demands on mainline churches inconsistent with the comfortable Christianity that accompanied establishment political status. Both also carry the seeds of a more dynamic and meaningful faith. Disestablishment, to the extent that it has occurred, has begun to empower the mainline churches to assume new roles in relationship to American society and the world. Thus the issue is not whether or how much of their prerogatives, power, and influence these denominations will be able to retain, but whether the new situation will be a catalyst for their revitalization and renewal. Although it is far too soon to predict the outcome of this major historical transition, there are signs of hope and promise.

Political ministries play a significant role in this process. The political witness of the mainline churches has reflected the religious, cultural, and social shifts. In addition, it is through political ministry that mainline denominations have often sought to shape and express a faith attuned to current realities and problems. Initiatives in formulating a new type of political role, therefore, have major implications for the future of these churches.

Chapter Two

Faith, Politics, and Power

A s the discussion in the previous chapter indicates, the debate over the appropriateness of the church engaging in political ministry touches on basic issues related to the understanding of faith, politics, and power. This study emphasizes that a faith which is social, ethical, and incarnational, three central attributes of biblical Christianity, by its very nature has a political dimension. And so the church has always had a political ministry in the comprehensive sense of politics as "action directed toward structurally transforming society in the direction of the reign of God" (Sobrino 1988, 80). Politics when infused with faith can serve as the arena in which the community searches for meaning and purpose in its collective existence, seeks ways in which to identify and promote the common good, and formulates the goals and priorities to pursue together, matters of central concern to the faith community. In engaging in political ministry, however, churches must do so very selectively in a manner reflecting fundamental beliefs, structures and practices, areas of expertise, and membership in a global Christian community. Limitations apply as well to the use of power. As an enabling principle or source of energy, power potentially offers the faith community the means of achieving greater justice and righteousness, but in contemplating the use of power churches can never confront the principalities and powers on their own terms or seek political power over society. The faith community must always strive for a consistency between means and ends, for a use of power reflecting Jesus' sharing, self-giving, and empowering love.

FAITH

Faith arises in the midst of a dialogue of divine initiative and human response. We are called, summoned; and we answer, committing our whole being and everything in our lives. Intensely personal, reaching the innermost depths of being, faith is also quite social in character, involving life in relationship with God, the human community, and all of creation. Spiritual in its origin, faith demands expression and embodiment in every aspect of personal and social existence. Faith exists not in the abstract, but in relating and living in the concrete realities of specific situations. For Christians this realized spirituality, this living the faith, occurs most readily within the context of a community in partnership with the God of peace, justice, and compassion.

Peruvian theologian Gustavo Gutiérrez's *We Drink from Our Own Wells* (1984) captures the sublimity, the profundity, the intimacy, and the radically transforming impact of the faith encounter. Following the biblical tradition, he emphasizes the encounter as something personal, gratuitous, and demanding, reminding us that "to encounter the Lord is first of all to be encountered by the Lord. 'You did not choose me, but I chose you and appointed you that you should go and bear fruit' (John 15:16)" (1984, 38). Gutiérrez links the encounter with the divine, with God in Christ, with discipleship, with the total reorientation of life to our following Jesus. Life according to the Spirit for Gutiérrez is not an experience at only the level of the soul but encompasses the total person. He describes it as entailing an existence "*in accord with life,* love, peace, and justice (the great values of the reign of God) and *against death*" (1984, 71).

Gutiérrez also underscores that faith or spirituality is primarily a community enterprise. Spirituality is a journey, "the passage of a people through the solitude and dangers of the desert, as it carves out its own way in the following of Jesus Christ" (1984, 19). Together, not alone, we can discover the living water that springs up in the wells of the experience of faith and from which we must drink (1984, 37). As Gutiérrez observes, paradigmatic experiences of the encounter with God in scripture were those of a community, not of isolated individuals (1984, 72). Although he has a deep kinship with some of the great medieval mystics, he rejects the individualism and elitism of a "spirituality of evasion" concerned exclusively with the interior life. He even claims that such an individualistic spirituality of separation from the world in a quest for a "state of perfection" impoverishes and distorts the following of Jesus (1984, 15).

Biblical historian Paul Hanson concurs with this emphasis on community, developing the theme that the Judeo-Christian faith entered history as people called by God (1986). In the Hebrew Bible Yahweh delivers a community out of slavery and establishes a covenant, creating a people, not a group of individual believers. The "people of Israel" came into being when a gracious God chose those who had no status, no freedom, and no ability to influence their own destiny to live a life of blessing for themselves and others (Hanson 1986, 469). This experience of deliverance from slavery by a God of liberation, recounted in the Exodus narratives, established the basis of a relationship (Hanson 1986, 3): "I will be your God, and you will be my people." In this faith dialogue, human response to divine initiatives was expressed in two essential modes: worship in the form of gratitude and praise, and efforts by the community to shape its life in accordance with its understanding of the nature and intentions of God (Hanson 1986, 524). Hanson views the era from the early Christian period through the end of the apostolic age as continuing the biblical experiments in community. He characterizes Christianity as fundamentally the faith of a pilgrim community called to orient its life toward God and to participate in bringing a divine order to the imperfect structures of this world (1986, 3).

In her book *The Future of Partnership*, theologian Letty Russell writes about the bonding between a God of peace, justice, and compassion and the community of faith. She describes the community as being drawn into a "partnership of service and freedom with and for God, with and for others, and for the future" through which people become part of God's love affair with the world (1979, 23). This partnership, like all relationships entered into by Christians, is lived within the tension of the "already and not yet" of God's kingdom. According to Russell,

> We are *already partners* even before we know one another, because God has reached out to us in Jesus Christ and has reconciled us, making us partners of one another and God. But we are also always in the process of *becoming partners*. And this is very difficult. It involves partnerships where commitments are broken, and persons betrayed, as well as the few relationships where there are signs that partnership might be a possibility. And at the same time we live in the hope that we *will become* partners, when the providential signs of *koinonia* in this life are realized fully in God's promised future (1979, 54–55).

Russell emphasizes that this partnership between the community and God, just like the partnership among members of the faith community, is always living, growing, and changing and therefore requires ongoing commitment, recommitment, and shared struggle toward this goal (1979, 140). Community provides the context and possibility for such a partnership.

Applying Russell's threefold typology of partnership, "the community called" lives constantly within the tension of the already and the not yet. God's initiative, whether or not answered, already initiates the basis of partnership. God's call establishes the possibility of a bond with the community, sets it apart from the world, and dedicates its existence, its very being, to serving God's purposes. In the process of responding and thus affirming its relationship with the God of justice, righteousness, and compassion, the faith community begins actualizing the potential of partnership. Such a beginning, however, does not mean that the faith community achieves full partnership. Struggling, striving, longing for that partnership, human communities will experience many failures, many instances of unfilled commitments, many partial relationships, no matter what their intentions and efforts. Yet in the midst of that brokenness there will also be the hope, the possibility of partnership and perhaps glimpses of God's peace, justice, righteousness, and compassion. Living toward a fuller partnership in God's promised future constitutes the vocation of the faith community.

From Faith to Community

The discovery and affirmation of its "partnership of service and freedom with and for God, with and for others and for the future"
(Russell 1979, 23) provides the faith community with a distinctive
agenda. It invites engagement rather than withdrawal, commitment
to the creation rather than dreams of otherworldly escape. Hanson
writes about the development of a sense of vocation "as a summons to
participate in God's purposes redeeming all who remain in bondage,
and of restoring a creation long ravaged by sin to a state in which
righteousness and peace prevail" (1986, 517). Realization of belonging to God releases a free flow of vitality for life that issues forth
in patient and generous advocacy on behalf of the poor and the oppressed and in loving care of God's creation. The assurance of the
faithful that their lives are secure in the providence of a gracious
God empowers members of the community to dedicate themselves
to the pursuit of God's *shalom*. Experiencing God's *shalom* in its own
life, "the community of faith becomes a nucleus of blessing from
which reconciliation and healing radiates outward into the rest of
the world" (Hanson 1986, 517).

Scripture records the journey of biblical communities as they
sought to understand the intentions of the God who called them
and bound them together and to respond within that context. As
such, the Hebrew Bible was very much a community enterprise of
interpreting, remembering, recording, rewriting, and editing over
the centuries. Through this process later biblical communities dia-
logued with and relived the experiences of their spiritual ancestors.
Many of the recent analyses of the four Gospels also interpret them
as the products of a profound community experience that shaped
distinctive interpretations of Jesus' ministry. These studies identify
each of the Gospels as written within the context of communities of
faith with particular characteristics, needs, and perspectives, whose
interaction with the Spirit was so intense that they sometimes inter-
mix "the time of Jesus" and the "now of the community" (Kee 1983,
141–44). One example is Michael Crosby's *House of Disciples*, which
explores the Gospel of Matthew in the context of its socioeconomic
milieu of the house-church communities of early Christianity (1988).
Howard Kee's *Community of the New Age: Studies in Mark's Gospel*
(1983) and Raymond Brown's *The Community of the Beloved Disciple*

(1979), which reconstructs the Johannine community in the first century, provide others. Robert Banks's book *Paul's Idea of Community: The Early House Churches in Their Historical Setting* offers a counterpart for the Pauline epistles.

Contrary to the preoccupation with individual salvation often characteristic of contemporary Western Christianity, the gospel always had a community and social dimension, and it is from this corporate base that the church developed. As recounted in scripture, Jesus of Nazareth, almost immediately after initiating his public ministry, began calling a group of followers. Once formed, this community, sometimes described as the Jesus movement, played a central role in his ministry. Relationships within the community provided a glimpse of a new kind of social order based on compassion, sharing, forgiveness, equality, peace, and love that embodied the ethic of a kingdom that was both present and not yet fully incarnated into history. Within the community around Jesus, the primitive rural Palestinian and Syrian Christian communities such as portrayed in the Markan Gospel and then in the urban environment of Pauline Christianity, the acceptance of the gospel brought people into a new relationship with God and led the converts into a new personal relationship with one another.

Paul, so often selectively interpreted through Reformation lenses, actually spent most of his ministry nurturing communities, not converting individuals. He invested his time in such efforts because he believed that the gospel bound women and men to one another as well as to God. For Paul, one cannot be a follower of Jesus apart from living within a community whose shared life reflects the gospel faith (Banks 1980, 33). Thus in his letters Paul considers at length the requirements for a faithful life within a community. He writes of the need for mutual affection, love, sympathy, and humility in order that members "look not to [their] own interests, but to the interests of others" (Phil. 2:4). Paul also urges that members do good to one another and "bear one another's burdens, and in this way . . . fulfill the law of Christ" (Gal. 6:2). He warns that the failure to adhere to a Christian lifestyle and standards of behavior invalidates worship and the celebration of the Lord's supper (1 Cor. 11:17–32). According to Paul, the Christian community constitutes a unity so that "if one member suffers, all suffer together with it; if one member is honored, all rejoice together with it" (1 Cor. 12:26). Paul sums up the understanding of Christian responsibility as "faith working through love" (Gal. 5:6), a love that originates with God and is expressed within and through the Christian community.

Paul, for whom Jesus' resurrection and abiding presence within the community of faith were central, imaged the communal character of this new entity as the body of Christ. In the well-known passage in 1 Corinthians 12 he envisioned the body of Christ as having many members, each different and yet essential, each part with distinctive gifts but all having an intrinsic value. In employing this metaphor Paul underscored the symbiotic interconnectedness and mutuality of the Christian community. It is an image of organic relationship, interdependence, and growth akin to the systems of all living things.

> For just as the body is one and has many members, and all the members of the body, though many, are one body, so it is with Christ. For in the one Spirit we were all baptized into one body — Jews or Greeks, slaves or free — and all were made to drink of one Spirit. . . .

> But God has so arranged the body, giving the greater honor to the inferior member, that there may be no dissension within the body, but the members may have the same care for one another. If one member suffers, all suffer together with it; if one member is honored, all rejoice together with it (1 Cor. 12:12–13, 24–26).

Biblical understandings of covenant embody this conception of relatedness as the calling and vocation of humanity. Scripture expresses God's calling the community of faith relationally: "They shall be my people, and I will be their God" (Ezek. 11:20). Biblical covenants, of which there were several different types, created the framework of a relationship between humanity and the divine, a humanity living in community and the God who brings the community into being, nurtures and sustains it, and through the covenant defines the norms for community life. Many of the Old Testament covenants explicitly linked faithfulness to God with human responsibility to neighbor, placing special emphasis on the needs of the poor and disadvantaged. The vision of a household of freedom and justice in the Old Testament, for instance, had many provisions for the rights of those who had no standing in the community. The poor (Exod. 23:6; Deut. 15:7–11), the stranger (Exod. 23:9), the servant (Deut. 24:14), the sojourner (Deut. 10:19), the widow and the orphan (Deut.

24:19–22) were placed under the protection of the covenant. The instruction is clear: "Remember that you were a slave in Egypt and the LORD your God redeemed you from there; therefore I command you to do this" (Deut. 24:18). To protect the interests of the poor, the Pentateuch prescribed that the fiftieth or Jubilee year be celebrated as "God's year of release," in which agricultural land sold to those other than family members would be returned, debts accumulated would be canceled, and slaves freed (Lev. 25:8–55). Maintenance of the covenant was made contingent on fulfillment of these duties; injustice and unrighteousness were often equated with perversions of worship.

God's covenant with Israel was fulfilled and extended in the new covenant in Jesus Christ. The covenant anticipated by Jeremiah that would be written into the hearts of the faith community became a reality in Jesus, shattering the traditional boundaries of community and universalizing covenantal responsibility. Although Jesus did not often use formal covenantal language, his behavior and his teaching expressed the realities of mutual responsibility and interconnectedness with those unable to demand justice and reciprocity. Covenantal themes of dual responsibility to God and neighbor became reinterpreted through the ministry, crucifixion, and resurrection of Jesus into a new synthesis. Love of God and love of neighbor became reciprocal dimensions of an integrated relationship. As recounted in the Gospels, Jesus called into the community those who had been excluded from full membership: sinners, the poor, women, those suffering disability, the oppressed. Universalizing covenantal responsibility, Jesus transformed the stranger and the outsider into the neighbor (Luke 10:29–37), and the enemy whom it was once permissible to hate became redefined as someone to pray for and love (Matt. 5:43). His covenant of love, inclusiveness, and sharing has been commemorated in the celebration of the eucharist by Christians through the generations. "He said to them, 'This is my blood of the covenant, which is poured out for many'" (Mark 14:24). In Jesus Christ the covenant with the people of Israel is made open to all. It breaks through all human boundaries — national, class, racial, gender. "There is no longer Jew or Greek, there is no longer slave or free, there is no longer male and female; for all of you are one in Christ Jesus" (Gal. 3:28).

From Faith to a Way of Life

In conceptualizing the relation of faith to politics and power, its incarnational requirements have great import. Far from being abstract or disembodied as a kind of state of mind or orientation, the Christian faith requires expression in concrete acts, behavioral norms, and social and religious institutions. Bruce Birch and Larry Rasmussen, in their book *Bible and Ethics in the Christian Life*, stress that morality and ethics in scripture serve as an expression of "faithfulness toward God as the way of life of a people" (1989, 20). Thus morality arises as a dimension of community. To be a people of God, for both the ancient Israelites and the early Christians, involved the ethical embodiment of faith. The earliest Christian communities were even known as the "People of the Way." According to Birch and Rasmussen this entailed a particular pattern of living, the instruction and training required for such discipleship, and the continuous recalling of the formative stories, above all the "Jesus story" itself (1989, 21). Therefore, the faith community proceeds from moral identity and deliberation to become an agent of action. As Birch and Rasmussen state,

> In both Jewish and Christian traditions, faith's truth is finally a "performative" one. We know it when we see it, or experience it. It is real when it is embodied, and only then. The test of any moral truth is in the social form it takes, and the difference it makes in society. Moral truth and a way of life always go hand in hand (1989, 137).

Birch and Rasmussen's characterization of the social embodiment of faith is reminiscent of the passage in the letter of James reminding us that "faith by itself, if it has no works, is dead" (James 2:14–17).

Although community is essential for faith development and expression, scripture attests and sociological literature documents the difficulty in maintaining meaningful community life. The realities of behavior among biblical peoples often fell far short of the mandate to be a community called. Particularly after the confederacy grew into a monarchy with a hierarchical class structure, the people of Israel apparently violated their covenantal commitments to one another more often than they fulfilled them. When the early Christian community expanded into settled urban regions and became a multicultural, multiethnic church, it faced a daunting task in cultivating and retaining its sense of common community. Little wonder that the Gospels and letters devote so much effort to community formation. Conflicts between intimate community and institutionalized church became an issue very early in Christianity, as did the related tensions between counterculture commitments and desires for social acceptance. Biblical texts manifest a kind of dialectic between conformity for the sake of the evangelistic effectiveness (Pauline letters, pastoral letters) and the efforts to reclaim the countercultural commitments of early Christianity, particularly that of caring for and changing the status of the poor (Gospel of Luke, Letter of James) (Dudley and Hilgert 1987, 42–59). By the second and third centuries, however, the institutionalization of structures and the growing power of leadership began to dominate the dynamics of community formation and relationships. The Constantinian legalization of Christianity, soon followed by Christianity's elevation as the official religion of the Roman Empire, further eroded the community infrastructure of the faith.

A Crisis of Community

The contemporary crisis of community within the churches most particularly reflects the rise of individualism at the expense of community. Modern individualism, the product of Reformation theologies preoccupied with issues of sin and justification, enlightenment philosophies, secularization, and capitalist market forces, goes beyond the biblical recognition of the transcendent worth and sacredness of human beings to claim the priority of the individual, usually at the expense of community. Intended to displace the Catholic hierarchy with the priesthood of all believers, the Reformation emphasis on the theological priority of the individual believer devolved into the atomistic individualism of such thinkers as Thomas Hobbes, who depicted the individual as having an ontological priority and society as little more than an instrumental collectivity serving the self-interest of the individuals within it. For Hobbes and many other Enlightenment thinkers, community was neither natural nor perhaps even feasible. Hobbesian individualism — alienated, selfish, and competitive, in the mythological state of nature — led to a war of all-against-all that made necessary the establishment of a governmental monopolizing force to impose order on the societal collectivity. Adam Smith's capitalist individualism, portraying the individual somewhat more benignly as dominated by rational self-interest, hypothesized that an "invisible hand," the operation of the market, miraculously reconciled competing interests to produce the best of all possible outcomes. And American utilitarianism, dedicated to the greatest good for the greatest number, further eulogized a life devoted to one's own material interest and pleasure, virtually ignoring the pursuit of the common good.

Modernity has brought into being systems that serve the needs of individuals, not communities, with destructive consequences for religious and social ecology. Secularization transferred functions that were once the prerogative of the churches, that reinforced their sense of purpose and community to other entities. Powerful nation-states relating directly to citizens, rather than through inter-mediary bodies, assumed social welfare functions previously provided by the church and other voluntary organizations. New technologies in transportation, communications, and manufacturing integrated once-autonomous communities into national or even international markets and, in the process, changed the relationships of the persons within them. Within capitalist economies the organization of work, place of residence, social status, and patterns of social relationships were increasingly shaped by economic criteria. Money became the new universal, displacing religion, social morality, and community as the central focus of life. And most of the same trends then oc-curred within socialist systems, with economic production placed at the center of life.

This matrix of extreme individualism and secular modernity has altered the role and the character of the church. In this environ-ment the church becomes primarily a private institution catering to the preferences and needs of its members and serving a more ther-apeutic than community-building function. In his critique of these developments, Jürgen Moltmann characterizes the modern church as having moved from *cultus publicus* to *cultus privatus*. According to Moltmann, the church as *cultus privatus* serves three roles in moder-nity: first, it is the cult of subjectivity where matters are dealt with on individual, existential levels; second, it is a membership where lonely individuals come for community but which exists as a collection of individuals, not as a meaningful community; and third, it is an institu-tion that maintains itself, like other institutions in the modern world, through bureaucracy and management (1967, 311–24). Commenting on these developments, Rebecca Chopp observes that when the church is both ahistorical and individualistic it cannot be realized as constitutive for Christian life. Christians may attend church to nurture their Christianity, but weekly services are more likely to bring together individuals each seeking to express, develop, and share their Christian growth and development than to be a gathered community (1989, 79).

Signs of Hope

Between individualism and bureaucracy, are there still possibilities for true community? A central theme of this study is the critical need and possibility of resurrecting and revitalizing this dimension of the churches so that they may once again become a community called. Although difficult, requiring little short of a conversion experience, the recovery of the church as a worshiping, incarnating, and transforming community is critical to its reformation and renewal. The model of political ministries developed in this study is intrinsically related to this task of returning the church to its character as a community called by God to worship God and serve God's purposes in the world.

There are signs of hope in the number of church renewal movements currently seeking to strengthen community bonds, much as the medieval religious orders, Reformation sects, and American denominations did in earlier periods. The formation of base communities has enabled the Catholic Church in several Latin American countries and in parts of the Philippines to foster vital centers for their members' biblical study, action, and reflection. The movement known as women-church enables women who are marginalized within official church structures, theologies, and liturgies to construct new types of faith communities for women and men, affirming women within or apart from parent denominations. The growth of conservative Protestantism in Latin America and the United States is often related to its ability to provide communities of support and meaning. Many statements of mainline churches during the past decade, particularly the economic pastoral letters and pronouncements, stress the importance of community. The letter of the National Conference of Catholic Bishops, for example, affirms the dignity of the human person realized in community with others as the fundamental criterion in evaluating all institutions and endeavors (National Conference of Catholic Bishops 1986, 15).

Yet we are still far away from this vision of the church as a community of faith communities. Expanded and reinterpreted to apply both to congregations and the relations among them, Paul's metaphor of the church as the body of Christ offers a glimpse into a church that is very different from a series of institutions or a collection of voluntary associations catering to individual needs. As a community of faith communities the church would respect, indeed nurture, the diversity, integrity, and autonomy of its member communities. Reciprocally, the member communities would be linked organically, not hierarchically, one to another through shared faith commitments and undertakings. Inclusive and open, the communities would seek to support, assist, and encourage their members, other communities, and those outside the community. Like parts of a body joining to perform certain tasks, the communities would group and regroup into ever-more inclusive partnerships of communities. They would seek to orient their lives toward God and to participate in bringing the divine order to the imperfect structures of this world.

The dynamic of living within and struggling toward partnership suggests a need both for the intense bonds of small primary communities and for more comprehensive contexts, particularly the more inclusive church, in which these communities receive nurture and support. The image of the church as a community of faith communities balances the possibilities inherent in an intimate community in which members have ongoing face-to-face relationships, with the benefits of the support systems, kinds of mission projects and initiatives, and possibilities for action that come with larger-scale organization. Envisaged is a series of partnerships reaching outward toward ever-more inclusive forms of partnership within the global Christian community. Such partnerships would enable members of the primary communities to experience the direct personal fellowship, shared intense commitment, and mutual support characteristic of sect-type communities without giving up the broader network of relationships, skills, and mission activities possible within church-type structures. As a community of faith communities in which the various communities are in a dynamic and organic partnership with one another and undergirded by strong shared faith commitments, the institutional church would be more than a loose voluntary association based on legal contractual agreements among its parts. It would once again be an *ekklesia*.

Does this image of the church have contemporary relevance or is it merely a hopelessly unrealistic vision? Can the church or churches become a community of faith communities? Susan Thistlethwaite observes that Paul used the metaphor of the church as the body of Christ to stimulate the imagination of the Corinthians so that they might be inspired to create among themselves the kind of cooperation, integration, and affiliation that would make them truly one (1983, 23). Paul did not describe a then-contemporary reality but provided an inspiration and a goal. The early Christian communities had to strive to achieve Paul's vision of the church, and at least some seem to have had considerable success in reaching the norms he prescribed. Like Paul's, my efforts to push beyond the realities of the contemporary church are intended to open the future, this time for a restored and revitalized church. By envisioning the church as an integrated, mutually related and supportive partnership of ever-more inclusive faith communities, I hope to revive the manifold possibilities of the community called.

POLITICS

The secular or liberal model of society that has shaped much of contemporary American thinking posits that the religious, political, cultural, and economic constitute autonomous or quasi-autonomous spheres. As noted in the first chapter, secularization redefined religion, narrowing its scope, privatizing its focus, and spiritualizing its content. In doing so, it erected conceptual barriers between faith and politics to the detriment of both. Assumptions about the separation of faith and politics have not prevented religious involvement in the political process. The activist character of American religion, linked by some analysts to the Reformed tradition or Puritan legacy, has propelled faith into social and political life. These categories, however, have often made it difficult to analyze, justify, or appreciate the political role of churches or other religious groups. This model has also tended to privatize and impoverish political life by removing it from an ethical and community foundation. By positing that the individual is the primary social reality and that the community is at best instrumental and fragile, Anglo-American liberalism casts politics as the realm in which individuals, interest groups, or competing parties contend for power. By denying the social nature or even the full humanity of members of society, it strips from politics its ability to serve as the arena in which the community searches for meaning and purpose in its collective existence, seeks ways in which to identify and promote the common good, and formulates the goals and priorities to pursue together.

Faith and Politics

A faith that is social, ethical, and incarnational, however, cannot abide by such an arbitrary delimitation of life into independent compartments. Like the God it worships, the faith of the community called, by its very nature, informs all dimensions of life. An understanding of faith affirming God as the Creator, Redeemer, and Sustainer of all that is, present in and concerned with all areas of society and creation, cannot countenance the liberal delineation of politics and religion as unrelated to each other. Such a separation of faith and politics, moreover, contradicts the biblical perspective that time and again affirms God as the ultimate source of meaning, authority, and inspiration over all spheres of life. Scripture conceptualizes divine intention, creation, human responsibility, and commitment — inclusively, wholistically, and synoptically — in ways that are disturbing and disruptive to secularized compartmentalization. As H. Richard Niebuhr points out, the very nature of radical monotheism, of faith toward the one beyond the many, is inconsistent with the postsecular conventional separation of human activity into domains such as the religious, the political, the scientific, the cultural, the economic, and the aesthetic. Niebuhr underscores that the modern perception of Moses, the prophets, even Jesus of Nazareth, as great religious leaders reflects contemporary categories and that each of them actually had a much broader societal role (1943, 39–40).

In contrast to modern societies, biblical communities lacked sharp demarcations between religion, government, and culture. Faith dominated, shaped, and defined all dimensions of life. Ancient Israel was a theocracy in which faith was the normative center of the political system. In the initial centuries of the Israelite confederacy

Yahweh was both God and Israel's only king (Lind 1980, 32). The institution of the Davidic kingdom made Israel more like the other nations, but Israel's kings were intended to rule in accordance with fundamental religious precepts, thus fostering the basis of a righteous society. This meant that major issues regarding the society and its future usually had both religious and political expression and that conflicts were also played out in both spheres.

The Roman Empire in which Christianity evolved also had complex interlocking social, political, economic, and religious structures. In the Roman imperium the public worship of an emperor as a god was central to the civic religion binding together an empire of many languages, cultures, and belief systems. As elsewhere in the ancient world, religion was an instrument to legitimate the existing social and political systems. Virtually every aspect of public life incorporated the dual representation of the emperor as both a political and a religious figure. Moreover, because the Romans made use of traditional authority patterns for governing subject peoples, the Temple and the religious establishment of the Sadducees, chief priests, and scribes served a political as well as religious role in first-century Palestine. The Temple was not only the center of a religious ideology of purity and holiness that governed all religious, political, and social relationships within the Jewish community; it was also the national treasury, the seat of government, and the high court (Jeremias 1969; Borg 1987).

Jesus was born into a society marked by the clash of two interlocking social, political, economic, and religious systems, the Jewish and the Roman. Already looming during Jesus' lifetime, the conflict was to culminate thirty-five years after his death in a series of wars that devastated and dispersed the Jewish community. For the Jews, Roman conquest and the resulting loss of political independence and the severance of the political dimension from the integrated life of the community, precipitated a major crisis about their religion and identity. Key issues dividing early first-century Jews into religiopolitical factions or subgroups tended to revolve around relationships with Rome, payment of taxes, and the legitimacy of the collaborating Jewish elite. Messianic longings for the restoration of the political expression of the community, this time under a king who would truly be just and faithful, shaped much of Jewish life during the first century. As a religious and spiritual leader concerned with

the quest for faithfulness and righteousness, Jesus could not have ignored the burning social, ethical, and political issues of his time. Put
another way, in virtue of the incarnation and the historical nature
of his ministry, Jesus was a part of the society of Israel with all its
political tensions and conflicts (Ellacuría 1984, 94–95).

Political Implications of the Gospel

Like the Israelite prophets before him, Jesus of Nazareth preached
an ethic of complete commitment transcending contemporary distinctions between faith and politics. The Gospel of Mark records that
after John was arrested, Jesus came into Galilee preaching, "The
time is fulfilled, and the kingdom of God has come near; repent,
and believe in the good news" (Mark 1:14). Warning that people of
faith cannot divide their lives into compartments, expressing their
religious conviction in some but ignoring their beliefs in others, he
dedicated his life to the call for the complete repentance, conversion,
and societal transformation entailed by the imminent arrival of God's
kingdom. Far from being concerned with only a narrow spiritual dimension, Jesus demonstrated an acute sensitivity to and compassion
for human need, suffering, and oppression. In the Gospel of Luke
Jesus inaugurated his public ministry in Nazareth by announcing,

> The Spirit of the Lord is upon me
>   because God has anointed me
>   to bring good news to the poor.
> God has sent me to proclaim release to the captives
>   and recovery of sight to the blind,
>   to let the oppressed go free,
> to proclaim the year of the Lord's favor
>   — Luke 4:18–19.

Jesus identified his ministry with the good news to the poor,
anticipated in Isaiah (61:1–2), and incarnated the radical hope of
a new age. Like the Hebrew prophets who took their stand with
the poor, Jesus embodied the covenantal promise to the poor that
they were not forgotten. In the Beatitudes he anticipated an inversion of the contemporary order, proclaiming that those who were
poor, those who hungered, those who were weak, and those who
were persecuted, were blessed or favored by God (Luke 6:20–22).

Near the close of his public ministry, in the parable of the great judgment, Jesus warned that the criterion by which individuals and nations would be judged was their ability and willingness to meet concrete human needs (Matt. 25:31–46). The people with whom Jesus associated and with whom he had a fellowship defying societal norms and purity laws, were socially marginalized and even outcasts. He indicted the ruling elites of power, wealth, and religion for their exclusion of and domination over the marginal and powerless.

For Jesus, as for the prophets, God's covenantal responsibility extended to the realm of politics and power. He warned those with power and privilege that they served as stewards of their people at the behest of a God who would one day judge how they had used their gifts, because "from everyone to whom much has been given, much will be required" (Luke 12:48). He showed contempt toward King Herod, calling him a "fox" (Luke 13:32), roughly the equivalent of skunk or rodent (Borg 1987, 163). He criticized the kind of power exercised by "those whom [the Gentiles] recognize as their rulers" and enjoined his disciples to emulate a very different standard of behavior (Mark 10:42–45). He condemned the governing order of the Temple economy and the Roman imperium because they did not conform to God's norms of righteousness, justice, and compassion, and he did so in a public and confrontational manner. In his final week of ministry Jesus entered the seat of the dual Roman-Jewish power, Jerusalem, in a planned political demonstration, enacting a passage from Zechariah that spoke of a king of peace riding on the foal of an ass (Borg 1987, 174). He then challenged the established authorities in a prophetic and symbolic act in the Temple, overturning the tables of the money changers. And in his teachings in the Temple he questioned and undermined the legitimacy of the established order. Far from positing the comfortable coexistence of religious and secular authority, his maxim, to "give to the emperor the things that are the emperor's, and to God the things that are God's" (Luke 20:25), assumes the overriding claims of God's realm over Caesar. At his trial he refused to cooperate with Pilate and Herod, implying nonrecognition of their authority over him. As a nonconformist, as a controversial figure, he excited both strong support and opposition. Jesus' challenge to the existing religious, social, and political order contributed to his death on a cross as a political revolutionary. His trial and death were political events.

New methodologies for studying scripture that enable the text to speak to contemporary culture and social situations have helped to recover the political meaning and implications of Jesus' life and teachings. Like many Latin American liberation theologians, Leonardo Boff's Christology interprets Jesus as a liberator whose message about the kingdom had a political connotation (1984). Richard Cassidy's study of Luke's Gospel concludes that although Jesus consistently rejected the use of violence against persons and was not a Zealot, his ministry still posed a threat to Roman rule (1978, 77). John Howard Yoder, identifying Jesus with the Jubilee vision of restoration and transformation, portrays the kingdom of God anticipated by Jesus as "a visible, socio-political, economic restructuring of relations among the people of God" (1972, 39). For Yoder, the cross and the crown were two political choices confronting Jesus, and he considers that within the framework of radical political action, the cross serves "not as a ritually prescribed instrument of propitiation but as the political alternative to both insurrection and quietism" (1972, 43). Although acknowledging that Jesus neither claimed to be nor behaved as a revolutionary or political leader, Ignacio Ellacuría underscores that Jesus' religious and political message generated a dynamism of sociopolitical change for his time and for all history. Ellacuría traces the most fundamental political consequences of Jesus' message to four themes: his relativization of Roman totalitarianism by his asserting the overriding claims of God, the call to the poor to make up God's kingdom, the universalization of the proclamation of the kingdom beyond the frontiers of Jewish nationalism, and the renewal of Israel's prophetic and moral consciousness (1984, 94–98). Summarizing the findings of much recent biblical scholarship, Marcus Borg characterizes Jesus' initiatives to foster the renewal and transformation of Israel as political in character. Borg writes:

> We are not accustomed to thinking of Jesus as a political figure. In a narrow sense, he was not. He neither held nor sought political office, was neither a military leader nor a political reformer with a detailed political-economic platform. But he was political in the more comprehensive and important sense of the word: politics as the shaping of a community living in history (1987, 125).

And so the community called and the church have always had a political ministry "in the more comprehensive and important sense

of the word: politics as the shaping of a community living in history."
Jon Sobrino has defined Christian political involvement as "action
directed toward structurally transforming society in the direction
of the reign of God" (1988, 80). A faith that is social, ethical, and
incarnational by its very nature has a political component. Political
activity, far from being inappropriate or irrelevant, is an intrinsic expression of the faith commitment of the community called. Political
activity is one dimension, one fundamental component, of a faithful
response based on love, shared responsibility, and commitment to a
God whose love, compassion, and justice for and within the creation
have no limits. Through its political ministry the faith community
identifies with and participates in the creative, redemptive purpose
that is seeking to restore the whole creation within a universal order
of *shalom* (Hanson 1986, 467).

More specifically, political ministry as conceptualized here has
three dimensions: clarification of the community's identity and vocation; development of communal structures, lifestyles, and goals
consistent with the character and intentions of the God who is worshiped; and activity by the community to convert and transform the
world in the direction of the kingdom. The clarification of vocation
involves members of the community coming to a realization that
they are "a people called" by the grace of a loving and compassionate God. As such the process involves the community's formulating
a shared understanding about the nature of God and God's relationship to the creation, making a radical commitment to place God and
God's purposes at the center of the community's life, and articulating the fundamental beliefs and goals of the community. Ongoing
adaptation and remodeling of communal structures, lifestyles, and
priorities are a contemporary expression of the incarnational nature
of Christianity. For "people of the way" Christianity's truths first and
most fundamentally require embodiment so that the community can
model its ethic and vision of the world. Through action directed toward the structural transformation of society, the faith community
seeks to bring about a greater correspondence between the world
and the kingdom, ever mindful that the kingdom is now and not
yet, both a standard against which to evaluate all systems, structures,
and policies, and a goal never to be fully achieved in human history. In confronting the realities of a broken, divided, unjust, and
violent creation, the faith community, to be true to its calling, uti-

lizes strategies and modes of action consistent with the presence of
the kingdom.

Although logically independent, each of these dimensions is
interrelated with the others. A community's faith journey necessarily involves continuous and overlapping cycles of prayer, worship,
study, self-examination, confession, conversion, and action in the
world, each interacting with and building on the other. Liberation
theology's emphasis on the interconnectedness between reflection
and action, or what is termed the praxis of the life of the believing community as the basis for formulating theology, captures this
dynamic. It also reflects the traditional Christian perspective that to
know God in Jesus Christ one must first become a disciple. Even
worship and ethics have an intrinsic relationship that is sometimes
obscured or forgotten. John Howard Yoder speaks of the unity of
worship and morality, describing worship as "the communal cultivation of an alternative construction of society and history" (1984,
43). The dual movement toward internal embodiment and external
transformation is more than an act of consistency. The modeling
mission of the faith community constitutes one of the most effective
means to convert the world.

The Church's Mandate

In its political ministry the church expresses its fundamental commitment to place God at the center of all of life and to counter
the secular tendency to push faith to the periphery. Through its political role the church contributes to the reconstitution of a public
sphere permeated by a sense of unity, reconciliation, and wholeness. Justice and peace advocacy reflects the church's efforts to
model its own life and mission on the initiative of a God who
is ceaselessly active, seeking to incarnate divine righteousness, justice, compassion, and peace in a broken world in order to make
it anew. In its participation in politics the church contributes a
unique gift, a vision of the society better able to order its life
on the basis of a common good. In contrast to the secular tendency to focus on the utility of immediate political advantage,
the faith community's partnership with God provides a fundamentally different perspective transcending private interests and
reaching across geographic boundaries. Stewardship of God's cre-

ation means responsibility to and for all living things, particularly the poor and powerless.

The need for the moral agency of the church to participate in politics is particularly great in contemporary societies. In political systems that threaten to become little more than arenas for the interplay between various organized private interests, the church remains one of the few institutions with a capacity for vision and a commitment to the common good. Within competitive political processes where access to resources — money, organization, influence, media, voting blocs — often matters more than the merit or rightness of positions in determining outcomes, the church can be the voice of principle urging that the morally correct and just action be taken. In contemporary political systems in which coalitions of wealth and power reinforce the power of the affluent, the church has a mandate to empower and speak for the poor and those disadvantaged by current power arrangements. Community commitment to the common good and to the societal covenant of mutual responsibility, while always important, is even more essential to sustain modern, complex societies, reinvigorate institutions with meaning and purpose, and resolve many of the most fundamental social, economic, political, and environmental problems. As the virtual paralysis within the American political process grimly attests, there is no invisible hand benignly or justly reconciling clashing private interests into fair and wise public policies. A government of the people, by the people, and on the people's behalf requires a community's strong commitment to and defense of the common good.

Governments in modern political systems daily make fundamental decisions that determine peace or violence, justice or injustice, public good or private gain. Just as no individual or group can avoid the effects of this collective determination of the future, the faith community often can pursue enactment of the fundamental Christian norms of peace, justice, and righteousness only through public policy channels. Moreover, the awesome power for good or evil conferred by modern technology confers means that many public policy debates address significant issues with long-term consequences. The title of Jonathan Schell's book *The Fate of the Earth* refers to the contemporary nuclear predicament. As Schell has starkly stated, "The question now before the human species, therefore, is whether life or death will prevail on the earth. This is not metaphysical language but a literal description of the present state of affairs" (1982, 113, 115). A faith community instructed, "I have set before you life and death, blessings and curses. Choose life so that you and your descendants may live" (Deut. 30:19), cannot be silent when the very future of the creation is at stake, when public policy decisions will shape the very prospect as to whether there will be future generations.

The nuclear predicament is not the only fundamental issue affecting the collective future to which the church can speak as one of the few communities that transcend particular interests and contribute on behalf of the common good. Human activity and technology also imperil global ecosystems. As the twentieth century draws to a close, major changes are taking place in the atmosphere, the biosphere, and the hydrosphere that threaten the viability of God's good creation. Modern industrial societies, succumbing to an ethic of technological domination over nature, have pursued unlimited and unrelenting growth at the expense of the environment. A century of exploiting the earth's resources, polluting its rivers and air, and haphazardly disposing of toxic substances has plundered God's good creation. Pollution now endangers whole regions of the world. The global greenhouse effect may bring fundamental climatic changes, and ozone depletion in the upper atmosphere threatens the life-supporting capacity of the earth. Confronted with these dangers to the creation, the faith community is called to rediscover that faithfulness and respect for the Creator entail reverence for the whole of creation, because "the earth is the LORD's and all that is in it" (Ps. 24:1).

Another crisis of contemporary society demanding a faith perspective is the contradiction between society's ability to eliminate poverty and the economic conditions that subject a majority of the human community to live without adequate income, food, clothing, shelter, or medical care. In a world that has already developed the technology needed to lift the burden of poverty from all people, the distribution of economic resources and the operation of a global market literally maintain a system by which the rich grow richer and the poor become further impoverished. Despite increases in production, despite the unprecedented wealth and affluence of the industrialized market economies, the world continues to be divided between the one-third who are affluent and the two-thirds who are poor. And appallingly, massive starvation, malnutrition, and hunger persist in the midst of a considerable global food surplus. In the face of this moral outrage, Christians, to be faithful, cannot forget the Savior who in the parable of the great judgment thus separated the righteous from the unrighteous:

> I was hungry and you gave me no food, I was thirsty and you gave me nothing to drink, I was a stranger and you did not welcome me, naked and you did not give me clothing, sick and in prison and you did not visit me.... Truly I tell to you, just as you did not do it to one of the least of these, you did not do it to me (Matt. 25:42–43, 45).

Beyond and in addition to these issues, the period in which we live is one of major structural change affecting most of the world's people. The global economy, communications networks, and new technologies have knit countries together without kindling the awareness that the human family has a common origin and shares a common destiny. Once primarily an abstract theological concept, the oneness of all people has become an economic, environmental, and existential reality without engendering a commensurate sense of ethical and social responsibility. Interdependence arising from the globalization of issues and problems has made national boundaries more and more irrelevant. Yet such globalization has not generated the evolution of international institutions with broad bases of participation, able to plan common strategies and undertake projects and programs on behalf of the wider human community. Just as the Great Depression beginning in 1929 could not be resolved without major changes in capitalist domestic economies, among them a new form of social commitment to the poor, the world seems to have reached a watershed requiring new commitments, policies, and structures. Churches are perhaps the only international institutions able to advocate and work for a new international order based on greater equity and justice for and toward the overwhelming majority of the members of the human community who are poor.

Conditions for Political Ministry

Nevertheless, in engaging in political ministry churches must do so in a manner consistent with fundamental commitments. John Howard Yoder characterizes the Christian witness to the state as substantially different from traditional self-interest lobbying. Beyond the church's serving as a model for society, Yoder proposes that the Christian community has the obligation to attempt to rectify major injustices within the society. He sets three conditions for this political ministry. The witness must (1) be representative of the church's clearest convictions, (2) be consistent with the church's own behavior, and (3) relate to subjects on which the church has a relevant contribution to make (1964, 20–22). I would add three other norms: that political ministries (4) reflect membership in a global Christian community dedicated to serving the needs of the poor, unfortunate, and oppressed, (5) deal with fundamental structural matters that shape the social, political, and economic order and determine the integrity of creation, and (6) seek to go beyond representation of needs to empower those who suffer most from violence, poverty, and injustice.

Just as faith as conceived in this study leads to participation in the political realm, it also severely restricts the nature of that involvement. The Latin American Bishops' 1979 statement at Puebla, which differentiates between politics "in the broad sense" and "party politics," captures something of this distinction between political ministry and partisan political activity. The bishops enjoin the church to be active in seeking a political order that will respect human dignity, establish justice, and ensure harmony and peace, but to refrain from organizing political parties and seeking political office (Eagleson and Scharper, eds., sect. 5.1–5.3, par. 501–34). I would go further and impose additional conditions. As a constituent dimension of the church's vocation as a people called, political ministry must be fully consistent with the fundamental beliefs of the faith community and express its sense of identity and vocation. The social and covenantal dimensions of life in the faith community require that the conceptualization and exercise of political ministry come through a shared and broadly participatory process. Christians, as adherents of an incarnational faith, need to apply to the world the norms they already embrace and live by. If the church is to help the kingdom vision to break into an unjust and sinful world, it has to employ means that reflect these goals, including and particularly an approach to power based on the ministry of Jesus of Nazareth. Thus the conception of political ministries in this study, because of its stringent limits on political engagement, shapes a political witness of a very special character.

POWER

Christians have often had difficulty in dealing with questions of power. The Argentine ethicist José Míguez Bonino describes Christian attitudes as oscillating between the poles of absolute rejection and total submission, between the cult of powerlessness and the claim to absolute power (1983, 95–96). But the faith community cannot simply turn its back and pretend that it can avoid dealing with power. Faith seeking embodiment encounters resistance in the world, sometimes referred to biblically as the principalities and powers. As a restricting boundary, power is the limit of faith's possibility. As an enabling principle or source of energy, power offers the prospect of faith's realization (Bonino 1983, 94).

A God of Power

The faith community from the time of its inception has been dealing with issues of power. Scripture portrays Yahweh as a God of power deeply and universally active in the world (Newman 1987, 75). In the Creation narratives in Genesis divine power brings the heavens and earth into being out of the original chaos and establishes order and harmony. Throughout the Bible God's active presence becomes known to God's people through powerful acts of liberation, protection, vengeance, or punishment (Bonino 1983, 96). Bonino identifies God's power as God's justice in action — in defense of the weak, judgment of the unjust, protection of the powerless, and strengthening of those who are given a mission (1983, 96). The Magnificat of Mary in the Gospel of Luke celebrates this God of power.

> God has shown strength with God's arm,
>   God has scattered the proud in the thoughts of their hearts.
> God has brought down the powerful from their thrones,
>   and lifted up the lowly;
> God has filled the hungry with good things,
>   and sent the rich away empty.
> God has helped God's servant Israel,
>   in remembrance of God's mercy.
>   — Luke 1:51–54

Although scripture portrays Yahweh as a God whose power is overwhelming, singular, and unmatched, it also recognizes that Yahweh chooses to exercise that power in ways that are distinctively different from those of the figures of power of Middle Eastern history and mythology with which Israel was familiar or, for that matter, Israel's own kings. Unlike that of the imperial hierarchies that seek control and dominion over the lives of others, God's power is expressed most typically in acts of love, compassion, and justice that liberate, empower, inspire, and transform from within. In contrast to that of secular rulers who seek self-aggrandizement, God's power is self-giving, self-emptying, self-limiting, leading not to glory but to death on a cross. And faith does not bring subservience to the power of God, but instead the gift of sharing in it. As Carter Heyward writes, God is "creative power, which effects justice — right relationship — in history." Heyward describes the power of Jesus as also the power of all persons with faith in this power, "a shared power-moving, given, received, passed on, celebrated, held in common as ours, not mine alone or his alone or hers alone" (1984, 119).

Although the New Testament is clear that the ministry, crucifixion, and resurrection of Jesus of Nazareth provide the paradigmatic revelation of the nature of God, over the centuries Christian thinkers and the church have frequently used images and metaphors of the divine more appropriate to hierarchical secular power systems than to the relational, compassionate deity of the Gospels. The self-limiting and self-giving of a Savior who enjoined his followers to abjure the manner in which those who ruled over the Gentiles exercised power as domination (Mark 10:42–46) was ignored and transmuted into metaphors of God and parallel structures for the church that resembled the very imperial power that Jesus railed against. Ignoring that "Christ Jesus, who though he was in the form of God, did not regard equality with God as something to be exploited, but emptied himself, taking the form of a slave" (Phil. 2:5–7), the church has imaged God and sometimes itself as king, ruler, lord, master, and governor. Preferred, sometimes official, theologies have described God as absolute, complete, immutable, and transcendent rather than relational, caring, loving, and empowering. Thus they violated the spirit and the meaning of the Jesus story. It is almost as if the relational God of the Gospels who destabilizes conventional expectations and worldly standards has been no more acceptable to the Christians than to the Jewish religious authorities and Roman governors of first-century Palestine.

The Royal Metaphor

Like the disciples who resisted Jesus' definition of his ministry and his anticipation of his death, the church historically has often seemed unaccepting of the Messiah who came in the form of a spirit-filled preacher and reformer, and not as a conqueror or king, whose chosen instrument of power was the cross, not the crown. Just as the disciples longed for a Davidic king, the church has sought a God of unlimited power, able to inspire awe and reverence, whose "godness" is evinced through absolute control and domination over the world. And although the disciples eventually came to understand and accept Jesus' definition of his messiahship through the resurrection and the pentecostal vesting of the Spirit in the Jesus community, the institutional church has rarely had profound experiences able to destabilize its images of deity and restore the Galilean vision of a God of love and relationship. As many scholars have noted, the dominant model of God's relationship with the world employed by the church through the centuries has been the royal metaphor in which God is imaged as an absolute monarch, male in gender, ruling over his kingdom. The monarchical model initially developed in Jewish thought, with God portrayed as Lord and King of the universe, was taken over in medieval Christian thought, which emphasized divine omnipotence, and in Reformation theology, especially in Calvin's insistence on God's sovereignty (McFague 1987, 53).

By casting the exercise of God's power in imperial form, the monarchical model has contributed to the deformation of Christian theology and church structures. Commenting on the dangers implicit in this metaphor, Sallie McFague points out that it results in a pattern of "asymmetrical dualism" in which God and the world are only distantly related and all power, whether understood as domination or benevolence, is on God's side. Because God and the world are assumed to be separate and distinct from each other, God can exercise power or rule the world only externally, either directly through divine intervention or indirectly through controlling the wills of God's subjects. The absolute power assigned to the deity in this model comes at the cost of vesting any meaningful power in humanity:

the all-powerful God and the passive human subjects totally dependent on God's will are two sides of the same theological model. By assigning all power to God the model implies an absence of humanity's capacity to make a fundamental contribution or control its own destiny. Therefore, according to McFague, the monarchical model encourages either a propensity toward domination of the world or a passivity to it, both of which inhibit human growth and ownership of responsibility (McFague 1987, 63–69).

Moreover, this dualistic and hierarchical way of thinking has encouraged and legitimated human structures of oppression and domination through the ages, both in the church and in the wider society of which it has been a part. The prevalence of the monarchical model has undoubtedly contributed to the church's imaging its own structures and its role in the world in terms that approximate Caesar's rather than the paradigm of Godship incarnated by Jesus of Nazareth. The hierarchical and dualistic qualities of the deity in the monarchical models have given rise to corresponding hierarchical church institutions characterized by the complete dominance of clergy over laity and the centralization of power. Like the all-powerful God imaged to rule from a transcendent position over the world, the church in many historical periods has claimed near absolute power over its members. This monarchical model of church polity historically undergirding Roman Catholicism, Orthodox Christianity, and classical Reformation Magisterial Protestantism envisages a unidirectional exercise of power that excludes choice of membership, freedom of theological and biblical interpretation, and meaningful forms of participation. And by imaging the deity as king, as monarch, as the source of absolute and unshared power, the church has encouraged male representations of deity and legitimated female exclusion from full participation in clerical roles and church leadership positions.

Alternative Images

In contradistinction to the monarchical model, Jesus' ministry, crucifixion, and resurrection provide a fundamentally different conception of power and relationship for theology and church institutions. As Sallie McFague argues, it is essential for Christians to look to the paradigmatic story of Jesus for formulating metaphors appropriate in describing the relationship between God and the world, and between human beings and the world. In contrast to traditional theological claims that God the King becomes a servant only for the brief duration of Jesus' ministry and sacrifice on the cross, but then returns to full power and glory, McFague understands the cross not as a passing phase but as permanently and genuinely revelatory of God's way with the world. The mode of the cross, the sign of God's radical identification with creation, reveals God's destabilizing, inclusive, nonhierarchical vision for the world. According to McFague, Jesus does not "do something on our behalf" but instead manifests in his life and death that unqualified love working to befriend the outcast, the oppressed, the needy is the ultimate reality (1987, 55).

Because McFague finds in the Jesus story a destabilizing, inclusive, nonhierarchical vision of fulfillment for all of creation, she correspondingly emphasizes the need for radically egalitarian, non-dualistic images of God's way of being in the world. Abjuring both of the traditional metaphors, God as king and God as the suffering servant, McFague explores alternative metaphors based on the paradigm of the cross as revelatory of God's way with the world. In addition to rejecting the royal metaphor, McFague does not believe that the traditional servant metaphor adequately conveys the interdependence of all life, including the life of God with the world, or reciprocity, including human responsibility to work with God for the care and fulfillment of all that lives. Four alternative models developed in her metaphorical theology are the world as God's Body, God as Mother, God as Lover, God as Friend. For her these images provide associations of caring, mutuality, attraction, nurturing, supporting, empathy, responsibility, self-sacrifice, forgiveness, and creativity, as well as underscore the self-sacrificial and self-giving nature of God's way of being in and with the world (1987, 55–57). Without discussing or evaluating the content of these models, it is essential to affirm the effort to image and understand God's relationship with the world in ways consistent with the fundamental themes of Jesus' life and death, particularly his teachings on power.

Power in the Church

As an institution the church has an internal power structure that shapes its character and, in turn, affects its relationship with and role

in society. The distribution of power within the church raises at least
five major issues. The first is the extent to which the organization
and power structure foster or discourage the development of community. Second, do the organization and power structure facilitate
inclusiveness and openness to the gifts of members, to meaningful forms of participation, and to the recruitment and election of
a representative leadership drawn from the membership? That few
churches historically did so and that the Catholic, Orthodox, and
many Protestant churches still relegate women, usually more than
half of their members, to second-class status, has been one of the
sins and scandals of Christianity. Third, to what extent and in which
ways do the maintenance functions of the church shape and interface
with the conception and execution of its mission? Recent studies have
been particularly critical of the Roman Catholic hierarchy on this
point, but the question can be asked of virtually all church structures.
Fourth, considering the church as the institutional embodiment of
an incarnational faith, does its structure and exercise of power reflect Jesus' unique teachings on power? Unfortunately, this has been
one of the most neglected dimensions of church history. Fifth, how
does the power structure within the church affect the manner in
which the church deals with the issue of power outside the church,
particularly in the political realm? How does the church recognize,
encounter, and confront oppression and other distortions of power
in the world?

The dilemmas of institutionalization have faced the church
from the first century onward. To exist within the world, to retain
some stability from generation to generation, the church requires
ministerial offices, ritual, liturgy, and theology. The very concept
of *ekklesia* implies not only community but something more structured, accessible, and future-oriented. In its origins *ekklesia* reflects
both the intimate covenant of the Jewish heritage and the more
structured process of the Greek community councils (Dudley and
Hilgert 1987, 34). Some Christian thinkers perceive institutionalism, a system in which institutional elements become primary, as a
deformation of the true nature of the church which has affected
the church at certain periods of its history (Dulles 1974, 35). Others
go so far as to argue that institutionalism has been and is pervasive. One variant is the claim that contemporary churches, at least
those categorized as mainline, are just bureaucracies shaped by the

same "logic" of functional specialization, personnel relations, and institutional maintenance as are secular bureaucracies (Berger 1967, 140–45). Churches historically have often allowed institutional maintenance concerns to dominate over mission, with support for the institutions becoming an end in itself to such a degree that it distorts all dimensions of church life.

Two groups of Christian thinkers have been particularly sensitive to the implications of power relations within the church — Two-Thirds World theologians and feminists, appropriately two groups at the margins of the institutional church. Two-Thirds World Christians characteristically attempt to hold church structures accountable to the fundamental beliefs of Christianity, something that many First World Christians fail to do. Feminist theology has examined the extent to which the religious sanctification of patriarchy by dominant traditions within Christianity has perverted interpretations of the redemptive paradigms, diminished and distorted the full humanity of women, and contributed to the establishment of hierarchies of domination and control within the church and the society.

One example of such a pervasive critique is Leonardo Boff's *Church: Charism and Power* (1988). Its description of the Catholic Church as having an authoritarian and centralized structure that contradicts the gospel and violates the human rights of its members brought about his silencing by the Vatican for a year. In Boff's analysis the church, like every institution, has faced the risk of imposing itself on the community it is meant to serve. He identifies Constantine's recognition of the church in the fourth century as the critical point at which the institutional prerogatives and power of the church began to intrude. Over the years the church began to understand itself as the epiphany of the promises it safeguards. Corruption by power eventually led the church to substitute the institution for God and Jesus and to serve as an instrument of domination (1988, 48).

Others, also critical of the Catholic Church, describe it as oscillating between the logic of mission and the logic of maintenance operative in every organization. Gregory Baum, a Canadian Catholic theologian, like Boff, writes that the Catholic Church suffers from what sociologists term "professional deformation," the tendency for an excessive concern for maintenance to become dysfunctional and undermine the institution's well-being. But in an analysis that has implications for all church institutions, Baum believes that special moments of distancing and fidelity enable the Catholic Church to break through the logic of maintenance and recover its sense of mission. Baum interprets recent contradictions between Catholic social teaching and institutional behavior as the result of the as-yet unresolved contradictions between the logic of mission and the logic of maintenance. According to Baum, defensive, narrow, and sometimes paranoid institutional concerns incline church leaders to act against principles that in fact belong to the church's official teaching (1987, 234–45).

The more well-dispersed power systems within mainline Protestant churches have attracted less attention, but they too are a major factor in shaping these institutions and their role in society. In contrast to Catholicism's efforts to concentrate power at the center, the complex structures of contemporary Protestantism with their specialized agencies, layers of authority often unclearly related to one another, and elaborate processes often seem to provide the ecclesiological equivalent of the United States Constitution's checks and balances. The decentralized nature of the polities in most of these denominations, based on considerable or complete congregational autonomy and the segmental organization of national bureaucracies, make coordination, focus, and accountability difficult. Although the presbyterian, congregational, and other conciliar systems are less hierarchical than Roman Catholicism, they also inhibit the development of a shared sense of community among their fragmented parts.

Power and Evil

Issues of power are interwoven with the mission of the church to join in God's struggle for justice and righteousness. Scripture imparts a realistic sense of the strength of evil and sin, particularly its social and institutional embodiment in the "principalities and powers." Many biblical narratives recount the struggle between God's will for justice, righteousness, compassion, and peace, and the concrete historical conditions of human sinfulness, societal evil, and structural oppression. From the first chapter of Genesis onward, human beings, vested with the responsibility of caring for God's household of creation in accordance with God's intentions, more often than not fall short of the mark. The Bible chronicles account after account of human proclivities to disobedience, unfaithfulness, disloyalty, and apathy, and the tendencies of such behavior to distort, disrupt, and undermine relationships with God, neighbors, and all of creation. Scripture also underscores the extent to which personal sinfulness pervades and warps institutions and systems. As Albert Nolan has pointed out, sin in the Bible refers to something more than individual acts of wrongdoing. Sin is simultaneously personal and social, personal in the sense that only individuals can commit sin, societal because sins become embodied in social structures, laws, and customs (1988, 42–43).

In the world the church confronts what is described in scripture as the "principalities and powers." In a well-known passage in Ephesians, for example, the faithful are told to be strong in the Lord and to put on the whole armor of God so as to be able to contend against the principalities, "against the rulers, against the authorities, against the cosmic powers of this present darkness" (Eph. 6:12). In a study of the language of power in the New Testament, Walter Wink argues that the principalities and powers are not disembodied supernatural spirits or forces. Rather, "they are the spirituality of institutions, the 'within' of corporate structures and systems, the inner essence of the organizations of power" as well as the political systems, appointed officials, laws — "in short, all the tangible manifestations which power takes" (Wink 1984, 5).

When the principalities and powers become idolatrous and sinful, when they set themselves counter to God's intentions, when the powers of death thwart God's will for all members of the human community to have life, the task of the faith community is to unmask this evil and to seek to recall this aberration of power from God's created purpose (Wink 1984, 5). To do so is to deal with structures and systems that distort, deprive, and dehumanize, and with the underlying norms and ethos that animate and legitimate these perversions. In the midst of pervasive oppression it is necessary and possible to speak God's truth to address the source of human oppression, domination, inequality, and injustice. This necessitates countervailing power — power to discern God's intentions, power to join together in a community of faith to participate in God's struggle for righteousness and justice, and power to overcome evil and begin to incarnate God's *shalom* in history.

Power and Love

In dealing with the issue of power, particularly in the political realm, the faith community has a fundamental dilemma. Its mission to go beyond witness to transformation, that is, to seek to restore the righteousness, peace, justice, and wholeness of creation, requires effectiveness in the use of power. But in contemplating the use of power it can never confront the principalities and powers on their own terms. Putting on the armor of God never countenances the use of force, manipulation, deception, or destruction. The faith community must strive for a consistency between means and ends, for a use of power reflecting God's sharing, self-giving, and empowering love. God's people are therefore enjoined to respond to enmity with love, to violence with nonviolence, and to division and suffering with healing; to convert, not to displace, destroy, or overturn the principalities and powers.

These fundamental dilemmas in the nature and use of power come into sharp focus in Jesus of Nazareth's ministry and teachings. In dealing with the issue of power, Jesus is reported in Mark to have told his disciples:

> You know that among the Gentiles those whom they recognize as their rulers lord it over them, and their great ones are tyrants over them. But it is not so among you; but whoever wishes to become great among you must be your servant, and whoever wishes to be first among you must be slave of all. For the Son of Man came not to be served but to serve (Mark 10:42–45).

What does this passage mean? To begin with, it is a radical critique of the political power based on oppression and domination characteristic of the political empires surrounding Palestine. The most obvious model of a political system in which the rulers exercised authority for their own benefit over members of society is the Roman imperium. In many passages in the Synoptic Gospels, some mentioned in this chapter, Jesus is reported to have indicted Roman political rule and the related Temple economy of the Sadducee collaborators. In doing so, Jesus reflected the agonies of a subject people suffering under the political, economic, and cultural yoke of a tyrannical and efficient foreign empire, a community whose dreams of regaining independence inspired periodic outbursts of religiopolitical messianism. For Jesus, particularly in this pericope, however, the issue is not political independence but the achievement of power arrangements consistent with human dignity, liberation, and equality. He implies that these goals require a fundamental transformation of human relationships and the reordering of prevailing political systems.

The passage contrasts self-interested authority with self-giving and self-sacrificing service. In the presence of the kingdom, society's hierarchies of privilege are shattered. The one who aspires to be first does so not through seeking power for self-advancement or privilege, but through self-emptying. In the kingdom's new order everything is inverted, and the slave of all, the very bottom of the conventional social ladder, displaces the great men of the Roman imperium. Here, as elsewhere in the Gospels, the disciples are given Jesus' life as their model.

Jesus' ministry and the alternative community he founded offer a new model of social relationships consistent with life in the presence of the kingdom. John Howard Yoder describes the new social order incarnated by this community based on the principle of servanthood as one in which human beings lived together on the basis of love, offenders were accorded forgiveness, and violence responded to by suffering love (1972). Elisabeth Schüssler Fiorenza reconstructs the praxis of the discipleship of equals in the Jesus movement in which women shared leadership and missionary work as full members of the community (1983). Marcus Borg cites compassion as the defining ethos of the Jesus movement, negating the social boundaries of the Jewish social world and offering a much more inclusive understanding of community (1987, 129–37). Rosemary Ruether portrays Jesus as manifesting the "kenosis of patriarchy," the announcement of the new humanity through a lifestyle that calls for a renunciation, a dissolution, of the status relationships by which societies define privilege and deprivation (1983, 137).

A Reinterpretation of Power

For twenty centuries the church has mostly ignored or forgotten this radical critique of power and Jesus' model of social relations. Among contemporary Christian thinkers feminists come the closest to recapturing Jesus' reinterpretation of power as reciprocal, shared, and leveling all hierarchies of privilege. Some, Monika Hellwig among them, understand the Resurrection as a challenge to recognize the power of God in a new way, as the inversion of ordinary concepts of power (1983, 106). Their reconstructions of the nature of the early Christian community, most notably Elisabeth Schüssler Fiorenza's *In Memory of Her* (1983), recapture its inclusive vision. They document also the perversion of the community of equals through the progressive elimination of women from church leadership in the post-Pauline period as the church accommodated to the Roman social structure. Feminist contributions illuminating power issues appear in devastating critiques of patriarchy as defining and deforming the theology and structure of church and society. Mary Daly's *The Church and the Second Sex* (1975) was a landmark work. Other feminist writers have raised questions about the nature of power, rejecting power as domination and recasting it as a shared and relational process (Hartsock, 1983).

Does the passage from Mark then imply that the Christian community and the church should abstain from the exercise of power? If the life and ministry of Jesus of Nazareth is taken as the norm, this would be the wrong conclusion. Although Jesus clearly refrained from exercising direct political authority, he did not abstain from cultivating and employing power. For example, Jesus sought to strengthen a form of power social scientists define as "authority," claiming time and again to have authority from God as his source or grant of legitimacy. This divine authority cast him as God's instrument and vested his teachings with a power undercutting the Jewish religious establishment of the priests, scribes, and Pharisees who opposed him. He also cultivated a form of power that contemporary social scientists identify as "attraction." Through his parables, his teachings, the example of the community around him, he sought to provide incentives for voluntary conversion and transformation.

Jesus' teachings and ministry exemplify a very sophisticated understanding of power dynamics. Individual conversion and social transformation are shown to be possible through creative new techniques of active nonviolence. In a provocative book, Walter Wink discusses what he terms Jesus' Third Way, the alternative that Jesus provides to submission or withdrawal on the one hand, and violence on the other, as a response to conflict. Wink claims that when understood correctly, the well-known injunction in the Gospel of Matthew to turn the other cheek is one of the most revolutionary political statements ever uttered (1987, 12).

> You have heard that it was said, "An eye for an eye and a tooth for a tooth." But I say to you, Do not resist an evildoer. But if anyone strikes you on the right cheek, turn the other also; and if anyone wants to sue you and take your coat, give your cloak as well; and if anyone forces you to go one mile, go also the second mile (Matt. 5:38–41).

According to Wink, in the three enigmatic maxims in this passage Jesus is counseling and empowering victims of oppression and injustice. By turning the other cheek the victim would require the attacker to use the back of the hand, the normal way of admonishing inferiors. By so doing the victim would rob the oppressor of the power to humiliate. In the second part of the passage, referring to a lawsuit for indebtedness, Jesus admonishes the victim to strip off not only the outer garment held as collateral, but also the inner garment, leaving him or her naked. Wink understands this as an act of clowning or lampooning that deflates the creditor, possibly also unmasking the system that results in a victim's perpetual indebtedness. And Wink understands the third teaching, on responding to the forced labor of carrying a Roman soldier's pack for one mile by offering to do so for a second mile, as a way for the victim to overturn a situation of servile impressment, to take the initiative and perhaps rebalance the power relationship (1987, 12–21). He concludes, "This message, far from being a counsel of perfection unattainable in this life, is a practical, strategic measure for empowering the oppressed" (1987, 19).

Wink interprets Jesus' Third Way as including the following elements:

Seize the moral initiative
Find a creative alternative to violence
Assert your own humanity and dignity as a person
Meet force with ridicule or humor
Break the cycle of humiliation
Refuse to submit or to accept the inferior position
Expose the injustice of the system
Take control of the power dynamic
Shame the oppressor into repentance
Stand your ground

Make the Powers make decisions for which they are not prepared
Recognize your own power
Be willing to suffer rather than retaliate
Force the oppressor to see you in a new light
Deprive the oppressor of a situation where a show of force is effective
Be willing to undergo the penalty of breaking unjust laws
Die to fear of the old order and its rules (1987, 23)

Comparing the Third Way with Saul Alinsky's principles for nonviolent community action, Wink characterizes Jesus' teaching as a kind of "moral jujitsu" (1987, 30–31). In contrast to Alinsky, however, Wink emphasizes that the active nonviolence entailed in Jesus' Third Way holds open the possibility that both sides will win. It opposes the enemy in such a way that it holds open the possibility of the enemy's transformation and responds to ill treatment with a love that can be found only in and through God (1987, 32–33).

These characterizations of the Jesus movement, as well as the Gospel passages delineating Jesus' encounters with women, the poor, sinners, the sick, and others on the margin of society, offer a model that is contemporarily known as empowerment. Time and again scripture records scenes in which Jesus, rather than effecting conversions and healings unilaterally on the basis of his power, elicited new strength, understanding, and self-transformation from those to whom he ministered. Typically, he credited these seemingly miraculous changes to the faith or inner power of his subjects, not to himself, telling them "Go in peace, your faith has made you well," not "I have healed you" nor even "God has healed you." Jesus thus emphasized participation, sharing in the healing process. By doing so, he redefined the very nature and impact of power.

One contemporary interpretation of political power that captures much of the meaning of the passage in Mark is John Swomley's *The Politics of Liberation*. Swomley distinguishes between the politics that is concerned with achieving or maintaining political power and that makes concessions to special interest groups at the expense of the people, with a politics concerned with sharing power with others rather than exerting power over others. He terms the latter a politics of liberation. Swomley recognizes that anyone who acts to liberate human beings anywhere in the world, by that very fact functions politically. He cites Moses, Jesus, Gandhi, and Martin Luther King Jr. as examples (1984, 10). For him, however, the means by which the individual or movement exercises power is the determining factor. According to Swomley,

> A politics of liberation, however, is concerned with empowering people rather than controlling them, with meeting their needs rather than exploiting them. It must necessarily be concerned with transforming the social structures that oppress people. It must also oppose the whole ideology of domination that makes the structure of oppression acceptable to many of those who suffer most from them (1984, 13).

The faith community, therefore, is called to a politics of liberation, of the pursuit of power not for its own self-interest but to continue Jesus' ministry of service, empowerment, and transformation, and to do so in a manner consistent with these goals.

Chapter Three

Mainline Political Ministries

Political ministry as conceptualized in this study has three fundamental dimensions, clarification of the community/church's identity and vocation; development of corporate structures, lifestyles, and goals consonant with the character and intentions of the God who is worshiped; and efforts by the community to transform the world in the direction of the kingdom.

The "mission first" or "mission only" approach characteristic of the mainline churches, however, focuses predominantly on the third component of political ministry. Sensitive to the brokenness and suffering of the world, imbued with a sense of social responsibility, mainline churches conceptualize their role as rectifiers of social problems. They generally neglect or depreciate the importance of providing opportunities for clarification and education about the community's fundamental beliefs as a basis for formulating and implementing mission. Although these denominations devote considerable resources and staff time to internal operations and the provision of services to their members, their efforts seem directed more toward system maintenance rather than toward community building or corporate faithfulness. In the absence of shared understandings about identity and vocation, mission of all types, and political ministry in particular, tends to be unfocused and diffuse, lacking explicit theological grounding and sustained membership support and involvement. Political witness tends to become a specialized mission activity undertaken primarily by national agencies and sometimes intermediate judicatory bodies on behalf of the denomination, rather than an expression of the community's faith journey.

SOCIAL AND HISTORICAL CONTEXT OF POLITICAL MINISTRY

The Churches and the Constitution

The mainline political ministries in the United States today evolved within a constitutional system defined by the free exercise of religion and the legal separation of church and state. The First Amendment to the Constitution voted in 1791 states that "Congress shall make no law respecting an establishment of religion, or prohibiting the free exercise thereof." In framing the First Amendment its drafters sought to assure that the United States government could not emulate the European practice of establishing and supporting an official religion, which they believed had led to oppression and the denial of basic freedoms. Although most of the men who wrote the Constitution welcomed its influence in public life, they preferred that religion serve as the context for public behavior rather than becoming a direct participant in the political process (Noll 1988, 65–68). The First Amendment institutionalizes the right to religious liberty by disestablishing all churches on an equal basis. In exchange for the right to function independently of governmental authority, churches accepted a legal status as voluntary associations.

The practical results of this arrangement have been somewhat different from those intended by the framers of the Constitution. Rather than erecting a wall between church and state, the First Amendment merely prohibits governmental restraint on religion. It does not, however, impose a reciprocal constraint on churches' participation in the political process. By enabling churches to compete as voluntary associations, the innovation of the constitutional separation facilitated and perhaps even encouraged religious involvement in secular politics. In contrast to established European churches, Protestant denominations in the United States were free to determine their own policies and priorities, express their activist impulses to shape and remake society, choose their own leaders, regulate their internal affairs, and attempt to influence public policy without interference from the state. There were no positive incentives of status or money or negative sanctions to deter churches from embarking on religious campaigns involving major public policy issues, such as abolition of slavery and prohibition. As Robert Bellah comments, "Indeed it might be argued the peculiar nature of U.S. church-state 'separation' meant churches entered the political fray with greater abandon" (Bellah 1980, 69).

In a sense the major Protestant churches could affirm this novel and innovative arrangement of the separation of church and state because they were already assured a formative role in American society. Historian Sydney Ahlstrom describes the American colonies as the "most thoroughly Protestant, Reformed, and Puritan commonwealths in the world" (1975, 1:169). He notes that Puritanism provided the moral and religious background of 75 percent of the people who declared their independence in 1776 (1975, 1:169). After the legal establishments of religion by the former colonies were terminated in the late 1700s and early 1800s, Robert Handy relates, Protestants believed that they could still realize their dream of a Christian America through voluntary action. To do so many of the denominations formed voluntary societies, first at the local or state level and then gathered into national societies, to accomplish specific mission or reform tasks. Well into the twentieth century, even as the country became more religiously and ethnically diverse and the "Protestant era" in American history came to a close, many of the churches retained the evangelical vision of a Christian commonwealth and society (Handy 1984).

Although never achieving the Puritan, and then evangelical, mission to make America into a holy commonwealth, these churches were remarkably successful in putting a religious stamp on American culture and politics, albeit often of religious form rather than substance. Mark Noll's study *One Nation Under God?* (1988), cited in the first chapter, develops the theme that Reformed assumptions about culture and politics have dominated American political life in every period — Puritan, evangelical, and then secular. Both critical and appreciative of this heritage, Noll associates the Reformed legacy with the activist character, revivalist style, crusading zeal, and pursuit of political goals defined on the basis of religious belief. Noll traces the dominant pattern of American political involvement, which he describes as "a straight line from personal belief to social reform, from private experience to political activity" (1988, 24–25), to the Puritan and evangelical assumption that it was necessary to move directly from passion for God to passion for the renovation of society. Noll comments less about another theme, the commitment to the public good which also came into American politics through the Reformed influence.

A National Religious Community

The forms and symbols of religion also entered into American political life through another avenue. Robert Bellah argues that religious liberty and voluntarism had the concomitant effect of churches' relinquishing their monopoly on religious symbols and sharing them with the government. According to Bellah, the Great Awakening of the 1740s, a wave of religious revivalism that swept across the colonies, was gradually given a more political interpretation, conferring providential religious meaning on the role of the American colonies. By providing the basis for a national community with religious inspiration, Bellah believes, the emergence of this "civil millennialism" made the American Revolution possible and created the new nation. It also, however, meant that the imagery of the "chosen people" and "God's new Israel" became embedded in American public theology (Bellah 1980, 10–15). With the passing years, the country itself became a transcendent object of reverence, a source of civic obligations as well as faith and hope. The Puritan sense of divine mission, melded with national ambitions, transformed apocalyptic visions of a virtuous "city on a hill" into an imperialist manifest destiny. Moreover, given the task of upholding the sacred trust and yet avoiding the temptations of idolatry, of reminding citizens of the country's ideals and yet preaching that the God of Israel was a judge of all nations, the churches were deficient. "Patriotism would protect and enliven the churches, yet threaten their integrity" (Ahlstrom

1975, 1:464–65). Despite the legal separation of church and state American churches through much of our history "found themselves as completely identified with nationalism and their country's political and economic system as had ever been known in Christendom" (Mead 1975, 157, quoted in Fowler 1989, 78).

Church Involvement

Church involvement in political activity and major social reform initiatives has been episodic. During the Revolutionary period, public spokespersons for Christianity played a significant role. They promoted the movement for independence from Great Britain and contributed to the pursuit of the war, to such an extent that some historians believe that Christian political action was instrumental in the achievement of independence. This direct involvement, like subsequent unqualified support for American war efforts, came at the cost of sacrificing the integrity of the faith to an undiscriminating patriotism. In contrast, church participation was more indirect, restrained, and qualified during the debate on the drafting of the Constitution. Opposition to Thomas Jefferson's candidacy, much of it deriving from his advocacy for the disestablishment of the Anglican church in Virginia, made the presidential election of 1800 a religious event on a very partisan level. Two of the most significant nineteenth-century Christian reform efforts, the campaign to abolish slavery and the effort to restrict the sale and consumption of alcoholic beverages had important political components. Taking advantage of the guarantee in the First Amendment of the right to petition the national government for a redress of grievances, abolitionists in the 1830s inundated Congress with letters. A single-issue antislavery party was formed to contest the 1840 and 1844 elections, splitting the moderate/progressive vote. From 1840 through the passage of the Civil War amendments banning slavery in 1865, Christian agitation on this issue waxed and waned. After the passage of the constitutional amendments, however, leading abolitionists ceased their advocacy even though racism and systemic oppression of black people continued. The movement to restrict and, later, to ban the sale and possession of alcoholic beverages, which the Methodist Church spearheaded, similarly moved from an evangelistic revival against a social evil into the political arena, including the formation of a Prohibition party in 1872 (Noll 1988).

Although the activist temperament and social orientation that Protestant churches brought to American political life implies the need to change, improve, and reshape society, the mainline denominations have not been inclined to raise fundamental structural issues. Protestant reformism has generally been supportive of the established system and optimistic about the possibilities of rectifying injustices within it, more so than Roman Catholicism's consistent critique of capitalism. The Social Gospel movement during the final two decades of the nineteenth century and the early part of the twentieth century, an exception to this trend, questioned the capitalist system and expressed a strong interest in socialism. Never more than a minority voice within liberal Christianity, the progressive and hopeful spirit of the Social Gospel was largely silenced by the crusading nationalism and carnage of the First World War. Responding to the suffering and difficulties of the Great Depression, the General Council of the Congregational Christian Churches in 1934 voted overwhelmingly to condemn the competitive, profit-seeking economy and pledged to work toward abolishing the market system (General Council of the Congregational Christian Churches 1971, 226–27). The Congregational Christian Churches, however, disclaimed this position eighteen years later. In an essay published in 1935, H. Richard Niebuhr described the church as imperiled by its identification with Western culture, economic systems, and political ideologies and challenged the church to find an identity of its own, independent of the world (Niebuhr, Pauck, and Miller 1935), seemingly to back away from this critique in his later work.

The Contemporary Situation

Whether or not religion formerly provided the basis for a coherent civil religion and political culture, a question that is now being debated, there is general consensus that it does not do so currently. Robert Bellah, a proponent of the concept, now writes about the unraveling of the symbiotic relationship between religion and the political order. Like several other analysts, he understands the traumatic events of the 1960s, the civil rights struggle, the assassinations of John F. Kennedy and Martin Luther King Jr., and the domestic response to the war in Vietnam, to have undermined the salience of the religious heritage that once provided an ethical vision for the nation. In *The Broken Covenant* he laments that "today the American civil religion is an empty and broken shell" (1975, 142). Others concur in his assessment that the old cultural faith has collapsed, a casualty of the violence and organized protests of the 1960s, resurgent privatism and individualism, and cultural and religious fragmentation. Robert Booth Fowler (1989), for example, argues that religion, far from intentionally serving as the underpinning for American liberal culture, now serves as a refuge from its skepticism, rampant individualism, and lack of meaning and values. Wade Clark Roof and William McKinney's study of *American Mainline Religion* (1987) links these developments to the "disestablishment" of the mainline churches, a term they use to refer to the decline in membership, status, and influence of these churches during the past three decades. Richard John Neuhaus's theme of the "naked public square" (1984) makes the claim, considerably overstated, that religious values and symbols have been effectively eliminated from the conduct of public discourse.

The implications of the "disestablishment" of the mainline churches for political ministry will be discussed at length in the next chapter, but it is important here to note the point-counterpoint movement between the greater involvement of mainline churches in major public policy issues and their decreasing status and influence. A. James Reichley and others point to the civil rights movement as a watershed in the churches' participation in the national political process. Although I would dispute Reichley's explanation, I agree that the past thirty years have been especially important for mainline denominations' political ministries. According to Reichley, although the churches were relatively late in identifying as morally unacceptable the legally enforced racial segregation in the South and the racial discrimination throughout the country, once they took official positions on this issue, beginning with the United Church of Christ in 1959, they made civil rights a priority and contributed significantly to the struggle for enactment of the Civil Rights Bill. Reichley, who compares the political role of mainline churches unfavorably with the neoconservative Institute for Religion and Democracy (1985, 331–39), claims that after the civil rights legislation was approved, church leaders, flushed with their success, arbitrarily shifted their churches' energies to economic and foreign policy concerns. Because he downplays the ethical content of these issues and regards the church as having no special expertise, he considers these initiatives inappropriate foci of church attention (1985, 246–50).

In contrast to Reichley, I understand the heightened political involvement of mainline churches during the past three decades as a more gradual and episodic development. Motivated by the increasing scope of state expansion and their own activist and ethical impulses, mainline churches have had a long history of raising issues of peace, foreign policy, and economic justice. During the first half of the twentieth century, for example, the American Baptist Churches, or their predecessor bodies, voted policy positions on a wide range of social and political issues, among them the reduction of armaments, church and state relations, conscientious objection, the applicability of the Golden Rule to social, industrial, and international relations, the international arms race, national health insurance, public corruption, and self-determination in international relations (American Baptist Churches in the U.S.A. 1989). For several decades prior to the emergence of the civil rights movement, many of the denominations and the ecumenical organizations to which they belonged, such as the Federal Council of Churches and its successor, the National Council of Churches, had actively championed racial equality. The Congregational Christian Churches, one of the predecessor bodies of the United Church of Christ, for instance, voted nine separate actions on race relations and social equality between 1931 and 1956 (General Council of the Congregational Christian Churches 1971, 154–60). The turning point in the churches moving from resolutions and pronouncements on the subject to social activism coincided with the march on Washington led by the Reverend Martin Luther King Jr. in 1963. Robert Wuthnow attributes this change, I think correctly, to the inability of white church leaders to stand by while their black counterparts were staging demonstrations, engaging in active civil disobedience, and becoming the targets of increasing racial violence (1988, 145–46). The civil rights movement represented more an acceleration than a watershed, more a translation of social positions into greater social activism, more a change of style toward a corporate and sustained public policy participation than the discovery of a public policy ministry.

Contrary to Reichley's claim, the political role of these denominations has very much reflected their belief that these issues involved ethical questions highly appropriate, indeed necessary, for churches to address. Beginning with the civil rights struggle and then during the war in Vietnam, there have been a series of political issues that were perceived by the churches as critical to the future of the society and to the global order. The very absence of a moral and political consensus invested political decisions about these concerns with an even greater significance. And, in some ways, disestablishment thrusts the mainline churches ever-more into the political process, perhaps the only arena in which basic social and ethical issues can be resolved in a pluralist society. That Reichley and various neoconservative critics of mainline churches deny the ethical implications probably says more about their political views than about the issues themselves. Yet despite the significance of many of these issues for the churches, the mainline denominations have been very slow, almost reluctant, to cast their responses in a moral and religious framework, thus leaving themselves vulnerable to misunderstanding and misrepresentation.

The activism of the mainline churches during the post-Vietnam period, motivated by a sense of urgency about a series of critical issues, has developed in an inhospitable climate. Distrust of American institutions, an outgrowth of the 1960s, was turned inward toward the churches as well as outward toward the political system. Disillusionment with the American system rather than resulting in a reform movement led to increasing privatism and alienation in both the religious and the political spheres. Years of unrest produced a conservative backlash and the "America first" nostalgia of the Reagan years, not a disposition to deal with critical issues and problems. As the gap between the rich and poor widened and poverty and homelessness became more pervasive, the society exhibited a kind of compassion fatigue, accepting the increasing inequality and ignoring New Deal social commitments to key sectors of society. Meaningful political debate became more and more difficult as the political system took on the characteristics of a one-party system in which money was the key arbiter of political outcomes. The balance of power shifted visibly in favor of the large economic interests and the wealthy, with a concomitant weakening of the influence of organizations representing the interests of the poor, labor, immigrants, and women. All of these factors tended to make the mainline churches the advocate/opposition of last resort.

CHURCH CONTEXT
OF POLITICAL MINISTRY*

Recent Findings on Faith

As an expression of faith as a lived reality, political ministry requires five elements often absent among mainline Christians: a dynamic and mature faith, the intention to shape patterns of behavior and institutions to be consistent with faith mandates, a deep sense of connectedness with and responsibility for the welfare of others, a commitment to ongoing political activity to promote peace and justice, and strong community bonds and a coherent structure to facilitate and sustain this process. Recent research profiling faith, loyalty, and congregational life in five mainline Protestant denominations (the Christian Church [Disciples of Christ], Evangelical Lutheran Church in America, Presbyterian Church [U.S.A.], United Church of Christ, and United Methodist Church) and the Southern Baptist Convention, for example, concludes that only a minority of Protestant adults evince an integrated, vibrant, and life-encompassing faith (Benson and Eklin 1990). This study of 11,000 church members in 561 randomly chosen congregations conducted by the Search Institute for the Lilly Endowment reveals that the vast majority of mainline adults tend to lack both a traditional deep personal piety and a strong social commitment. Or, as the two research directors comment, "Loving God wholeheartedly and loving one's neighbor as oneself is a basic biblical mandate, yet two-thirds of adults and almost ninety percent of adolescents in the mainline

---

*In undertaking this social analysis of the ecclesial context, as well as in the succeeding sections of this chapter, I am relying primarily on my own observations and secondarily on published sources. During the nine years prior to writing this study I served as the World Issues Secretary of the United Church Board for World Ministries, the international agency of the United Church of Christ. As a direct participant in denominational and ecumenical initiatives in political ministries, I came to have an increasingly critical perspective, sympathetic to the objectives but questioning the priorities and strategies.

churches give evidence of a faith that is deficient in one or the other or both" (*Effective Christian Education* 1990, 65).

Conceptualizing faith as a way of living, not just an adherence to doctrine or dogma, researchers posited that faith has a life-transforming, dramatic impact on the believer. They identified eight facets of faith grouping them into two overall themes: a strong personal relationship with God, which they refer to as the vertical dimension; and a consistent devotion to others, which they term the horizontal dimension. Only about one-third of the adults interviewed evinced such a mature faith characterized by balance. Slightly more than one-third of respondents provided answers that placed them in the category of having an undeveloped faith, lacking both a strong relationship to God and a social commitment. Another third were considered to be either vertical or horizontal types, in which one of the two themes predominated at the expense of the other. Whereas there were no significant denominational differences among members of the five mainline denominations, women were much more likely than men to have an integrated faith. The disparity was particularly pronounced in the forty to fifty-nine age range (15 percent as compared with 40 percent). Although the sample of ethnic and racial congregations was too small to yield a reliable result, this group also had a higher index of faith maturity than other mainline Christians (Benson and Eklin 1990, 13–16).

According to the research findings, the most problematic areas of faith development were those having to do with spiritual growth (prayer and Bible reading), talking with others about one's faith, involvement in social service (helping other individuals) and participation in the pursuit of social justice. Of those interviewed, less than half reported that they sought out opportunities to grow spiritually and only a third indicated that they devoted time to reading and studying the Bible. Many adults did not experience a sense of well-being, security, or peace in the faith. As a group, mainline members apparently had serious difficulties in witnessing about their faith to others. And most claimed to do little to serve others either through directly helping people who have problems or needs, or through pursuing justice. Only a third of respondents devoted time to assisting others, and there was an even greater disinclination to become active in initiatives to promote social justice (13 percent) or world peace (7 percent) (Benson and Eklin 1990, 11).

Equally discouraging, many of the factors identified as promoting faith maturity and enhancing community ties were weak or absent. Of the areas of congregational life that were examined, the Search Institute/Lilly Endowment study concluded that involvement in effective formal Christian education programs had the strongest tie to growth in faith and to loyalty to the congregation and the denomination (Benson and Eklin 1990, 2). This hopeful finding on the efficacy of exposure to Christian education, however, was coupled with two other discoveries: There is a distinct proclivity for mainline youth and adults to avoid Christian education, because they perceive programs as appropriate primarily for children; and few congregations had effective Christian education programs. Of the adults interviewed, only 28 percent were involved in Christian education, and among youth in grades 10 through 12 the figure was 35 percent (*Effective Christian Education* 1990, 53). Particularly relevant for political ministries, it was discovered that growth in mature faith was associated with education that linked faith to political and social issues and stressed life experiences as the occasion for spiritual insight. Yet only 17 percent of the congregations studied had programs that related biblical knowledge and insight to an understanding of the social, political, and cultural contexts of human life. Less than a third (31 percent) emphasized global awareness and understanding (*Effective Christian Education* 1990, 55).

Characteristics of Mainline Churches

Writings about mainline denominations, this book among them, discuss these entities as if they were coherent organizations with fixed identities and characters. With some exaggeration, it would be more accurate to regard them as coalitions of congregations linked together by tradition, liturgy, doctrine, and weak institutional ties. Mainline churches exist as coherent entities in the meetings of their synods and assemblies, where the denomination in all of its diversity periodically comes together to affirm mutual commitments. In the meanwhile, their national agencies and instrumentalities symbolically represent the unity of the denominations. Much of the time, however, mainline churches are beset by the centrifugal forces, regionalism, and localism that affect virtually all American institutions. This means that it is erroneous to speak about a particular denomination in terms that suggest that the activities or decisions of national bodies automatically frequently characterize other levels of the church or the general membership. Some denominations, among them the various Baptist churches, the United Church of Christ, and the Christian Church (Disciples of Christ), have polities in which the congregations are constitutionally recognized as the basic units and decisions of other bodies have only advisory status. Denominations with other types of polities, however, have also been "congregationalized" over time, the congregations assuming or maintaining basic control over their programs and priorities. These institutional tendencies have been further reinforced by the new "voluntarism" characterizing mainline churches. In today's individualistic culture in which religious affiliation is viewed as a matter of taste and preference rather than of family heritage, many adults select church membership on the basis of the programs and climate of particular congregations, with their denominational identity a relatively insignificant consideration. Reciprocally, many congregations feel a greater inclination to pick and choose which missions and denominational programs to support (Roof and McKinney 1987, 40–71).

Moreover, in the complex structures characterizing mainline denominations, there is considerable specialization and fragmentation of power. To a considerable extent, each level of authority operates independently of the others, which results in a layered, onion-like structure. Functional specialization has led to fragmentation of authority and proliferation of centers of initiative. Relational ties between levels of the system tend to be weak. The effective authority of higher judicatory bodies is generally greater in areas related to provision of services and resources, liaison among local churches, training, placement and support of clergy. In this division of labor, most of the subject matter pertaining to political ministries is vested primarily in national agencies of the denomination that have few direct linkages with congregations.

Added to this already complex configuration, hundreds of special-purpose groups have proliferated since 1960. Such special-interest groups, which now function at all levels of the denominations, often reflect significant ideological/theological cleavages in the membership. Describing denominations as diverse federations of special-purpose groups rather than monolithic, homogenous structures, Robert Wuthnow locates much of the concrete action in which religious people are engaged, including initiatives related to political and social witness, in such specialized groups functioning within or across denominational lines (1988, 125). Wuthnow also believes that the growth of these special-purpose groups has heightened the propensity of religious communities to become fragmented along the lines of the larger society (1988, 130).

Political ministry is among the areas in which the decentralized nature of the denominations is manifested most concretely. To speak about political ministry in a particular denomination is to refer to the sum total of initiatives at various levels of the denomination and within many of its special-purpose groups, each body making its decisions and seeking to implement its own programs. This leads to issue proliferation, sometimes even to contradictory initiatives. At any one time a denomination is likely to be pursuing a wide range of social and political concerns without attempting any serious effort to coordinate them. Regardless of the constitutional situation within the denominations, local churches generally consider the social policy formulations of higher judicatory bodies as optional, a kind of menu from which they can choose their activities and involvement. Moreover, in at least one, and very likely in most of these denominations, the national structures are so distant and invisible that the majority of members cannot even identify the national agencies by name or cite their functions, let alone describe General Synod or Assembly decisions (United Church Board for Homeland Ministries 1988).

As denominations have become less distinctive and many of the traditional doctrinal differences and social and economic sources of religious subcultures that gave rise to their formation have become of less interest and relevance to the lives of their members, they have also been beset by greater pluralism and polarization. One major source of cleavage afflicting all levels of the churches are conflicts between religious liberals and religious conservatives. This is a division that intersects and reinforces the differences in orientation between those conceptualizing the church primarily in terms of its corporate partnership with the creation, and those understanding the church primarily as a voluntary association serving its members. Robert Wuthnow places the origins of the current conflict not so much in the fundamentalist/modernist debate early in the twentieth century, as in congregational splits relating to the contro-

versial social and political issues of the 1960s (1988, 133–53). The
expansion of higher education has also been a contributing factor.
According to Wuthnow, educational levels have become the most reliable predictors of people's values and attitudes, eclipsing ethnic,
income, and regional factors, and even denominational affiliation.
Many of the significant attitudinal divergences in congregations occur between less well-educated laity, who tend to be conservative,
and college-educated laypeople and clergy, who are more likely to
hold liberal views (1988, 159–64). As rising levels of education have
inclined mainline denominations to espouse more liberal positions,
these shifts have generated countermovements, some of which have
encouraged the establishment of special-purpose organizations on
both sides of the issue. This in turn has resulted in greater polarization between the Right and Left and increasing dissension within the
churches regardless of the positions taken (Wuthnow 1988, 164–72).

VOCATION AND IDENTITY

The mainline church has traditionally had a broad and diffuse sense
of social responsibility, without a clear delineation of the boundaries
separating the church and the society. This disposition, a product
of the historical involvement of mainline churches as well as their
theology, underpins political ministry. Foundational documents in the
various denominations assign the church such an inclusive role vis-
à-vis the welfare of society that it becomes the functional equivalent
of the arbiter of everything in general and nothing in particular.
This has deprived mainline denominations of a clear definition of
vocation and has overwhelmed denominational staffs and members.

Policy Statements of Mainline Churches

Among the mainline denominations, the Presbyterians have generally been the most theologically articulate on the subject of political
ministry, many of its General Assemblies voting actions on the rationale for and nature of its corporate social witness. Beginning with the
Reformed belief in God's sovereignty over all spheres of life, going
on to assert the social relevance of the gospel and the Christian faith,
the body of Presbyterian social teaching has a comprehensive concep-

tion of Christians' social and political responsibility. "The Reformed Faith in Relation to Social Concern and Action," prepared by a committee representing both branches of the then-divided Presbyterian Church, for example, underscores the responsibility of Christians "to seek as far as their influence may extend to bring national life and all the institutions of society into conformity with the moral government of God, and into harmony with the spirit of Jesus Christ" (Board of Christian Education n.d., 9). Other statements affirm the intrinsic relationship between faith and politics. A 1983 action, *Reformed Faith and Politics*, develops the biblical and theological bases for a comprehensive political vocation. This vocation rests on a series of declarations, one of which states that "just as nothing human is outside the rule of God, nothing is outside the potential concern of the church" (General Assembly Presbyterian Church [U.S.A.] 1983). As delineated in these documents, the church has a prophetic ministry to engage in the reform of institutions that do not conform to Christian norms of justice. "Obedience to our Lord's commandment to love our neighbor requires that the church work to achieve a more just social order, and that achieving a more just social order requires not only the redemption of individuals but also the changing of patterns and corporate structures of society" (1959 General Assembly, quoted in Board of Christian Education, n.d., 25).

Coming out of a different theological tradition, the United Methodist's Social Principles nevertheless have many similarities. They were adopted by the General Conference in 1972, four years after the uniting of the Methodist Church and the Evangelical United Brethren, and then revised in 1976. The document begins with a reference to the Methodists' long history of concern for social justice and willingness to take forthright positions on controversial issues involving Christian principles. In the first section, on the natural world, it acknowledges that "all creation is the Lord's and we are responsible for the ways in which we use and abuse it" (United Methodist Church 1988, 16). It repents of human devastation of the physical and nonhuman world and recognizes the responsibility of the church toward lifestyle and systemic changes in society that will promote a more ecologically just world. The second section focuses on support for social climates in which human communities are maintained and strengthened for the sake of all persons and their growth. Affirming all people as equally valuable in the

sight of God, the section on the social community makes a commitment to work toward developing societies in which each person's
value is recognized, maintained, and strengthened. Because the Social Principles claim all economic systems to be under the judgment
of God, no less than other facets of the created order, the section
on the economic community deals with such diverse concerns as
property, collective bargaining, work and leisure, consumption, poverty, migrant labor, and gambling. Similarly, the recognition of the
political community as a principal vehicle for the ordering of society leads to subsections on basic freedoms, political responsibility,
freedom of information, education, civil obedience and disobedience, crime and rehabilitation, and military service. The pledge to
seek the meaning of the gospel in all issues that divide people and
threaten the growth of world community is translated into a focus on
such problems as war, injustice, exploitation, privilege, population,
international ecological crisis, proliferation of arsenals of nuclear
weapons, development of transnational business organizations that
operate beyond the effective control of any governmental structure,
and the increase of tyranny in all its forms. And these issues are
then further elaborated in the book of resolutions. At the time the
1988 edition was compiled, there were 181 resolutions dealing with
social issues: 14 on the natural world, 12 related to the nurturing
community, 64 on the social community, 17 on the economic community, 37 on the political community, and 35 related to the world
community — a comprehensive, even daunting, policy base (United
Methodist Church 1988).

An Assessment of Policy Statements

As a foundation for political ministry, these and other denominational documents are problematic in several regards. They assign
the denominations a comprehensive role responsible for virtually
every facet of society, for which they have neither membership commitment nor staff resources. Such a broad and diffuse responsibility
often means a possible lack of a tangible and specific vocation. And
there is little basis within the statements on which to set priorities
or develop a focus. Often written serially, they reflect the American
penchant for discovering issues with an evangelical zeal but retaining
only short-term interest. Each new problem, each new issue clam-

ors for denominational commitment, with the result that few can be pursued effectively.

Many statements are also inadequate on a theological level. With the exception of the Presbyterian statements and the various peace and economic pastorals written in the 1980s, few of the foundational pronouncements and virtually none of the resolutions provide a comprehensive biblical or coherent theological grounding. The links between scriptural commitments to peace and justice and the specific subject matter of the documents often remain implicit rather than explicit. They are frequently alluded to rather than spelled out, obvious to the drafters but not to the people in the pews. This is unfortunate. Several studies have pointed out that the membership's perception and commitment to implementation depend on whether policies reflect the fundamental values of the church, particularly biblically based concepts depicting the church as the servant of a just and compassionate God. James R. Wood's survey of seventy-five members in each of fifty-seven churches in Indianapolis belonging to seven of the mainline denominations, for example, underscores the importance of establishing a link between general values and a specific policy in order to make an effective claim to legitimacy (1981, 84–86). Similarly, Marjorie Royle and Richard Bolin's study of the responses of congregations in the Pacific and Southwest Annual Conference of the United Methodist Church to the sixteen resolutions voted by the 1982 Conference concludes that resolutions are more likely to have an effect if they are biblically based (1983, 11).

Many of the policy statements offer a devastating critique of social directions and governmental policy, but the denominations are bound by a self-imposed theological orientation that precludes their offering an alternative vision of the future as it ought to be. Their commitment to a theologically "realistic" standpoint, which is explicit in Presbyterian documents and implicit in others, is a legacy of Reinhold Niebuhr's continuing influence. The Christian realism approach ostensibly commits the churches to social analysis of the patterns and structures of life that block or enhance healthy social reforms (Board of Christian Education n.d., 24), but, as in the evolution of Niebuhr's theology, it can also imprison them within the existing system. Niebuhr's efforts to weld together an anthropology infused with a profound sense of human limitations and sinfulness, and a quest for justice, particularly in his later work, often verge into an acceptance, even a justification of the status quo. Although denominational social policies are predicated on the need for social change, their realism binds them politically within the confines of existing structures and processes and deprives them theologically of a critical element of transcendence. Thus the denominations' analyses of current inadequacies and proposals for incremental policy changes often differ little from those of secular political actors.

Absent from most of these documents is what might be termed a compelling religious vision, a sense of the now and not yet of God's kingdom that challenges and opposes the injustices of the dominant reality by invoking God's peace and justice. This means that no matter how profound the criticism, the mainline denominations never really engage in prophetic ministry. As Walter Brueggemann notes, "The task of prophetic ministry is to nurture, nourish, and evoke a consciousness and perception alternative to the consciousness and perception of the dominant culture around us" (1978, 13). He suggests that the biblical vision challenges the dominant consciousness and delegitimates the present order while energizing persons and communities through the promise of another time and situation toward which the community of faith may move (Brueggemann 1978, 130). In another context Pope Paul VI's 1971 encyclical *Octogesima adveniens* discusses such a religious vision not as an impossible dream that inhibits action but as a protest against "bureaucratic socialism, technocratic capitalism, and authoritarian democracy" with the function of "stimulating creative imagination to perceive ignored possibilities in the present and as orienting towards a new future" (quoted in Bonino 1983, 92–93). As can be seen in the recounting of the Creation, the Exodus, and the resurrection of Jesus, God's promises of the kingdom express the possibility of God's power acting as the negation of determinations, of breaking through the injustices and limitations of the present toward creating the possibility for a new reality in which signs of the kingdom will be ever more in our midst. Such a sense of radical hope — that all things can and will be made anew, that with and through God all things are possible — is noticeably absent from mainline formulations. Without this eschatological horizon the faith community cannot remain forever unreconciled to society, cannot be a constant disturbance, a source of continual new impulses toward the realization of God's righteousness, freedom, and humanity.

Policy Statements and the Membership

Since political ministries are part of the spiritual journey of a community, it is important to evaluate the extent to which the views expressed in denominational policy statements reflect the beliefs of members. Various surveys conducted by denominational offices and by the Search Institute do not provide conclusive answers, but insofar as it is possible to discern patterns within them, it appears that there is support for denominations' involvement in social issues. The levels of endorsement of particular denominational stands vary by issue. At the same time, however, the surveys reveal a low level of interest and commitment on the part of laity on matters related to political ministries. The general sense of the legitimacy of congregations or denominations engaging in peace and justice ministries seems to be combined with a lack of inclination to participate in such activities. Moreover, there seems to be a difference in the political orientations of members when they speak for themselves and when they define appropriate positions for the church. Mainline adults appear to be more liberal or progressive in reference to denominational social and political positions than when identifying their own orientations. None of these trends, however, characterize all members, and there are significant minority views on virtually every issue.

Denominational surveys tend to report support for church involvement in peace and justice ministries, but it is somewhat ambiguous as to what this really means. A Presbyterian Panel Report based on 1987 survey results of a sample of some 2,500 members, elders, pastors, and special clergy, for example, indicates that, of those questioned, at least two-thirds of the laity and 90 percent of the clergy agree with the statements "Peacemaking is central to the gospel" and "Sometimes Christians must respond in faith, even if this means opposing government positions." When the study begins to delve into specific issues, however, the levels of support decline. On the subject of abortion, just over one-half of the pastors, but seven out of ten members and clergy serving in specialized ministries, identified with the position that the ultimate decision should be the choice of the woman and her physician. When asked about South Africa, only 42 percent of members and seven out of ten clergy reported that they agreed or strongly agreed that "the U.S. govern-

ment should do everything it can to end apartheid in South Africa"
(Presbyterian Panel Report 1988).

A 1989 survey conducted by the Evangelical Lutheran Church
in America on a national sample of about 2,000 members and clergy
reports an even stronger disposition toward a comprehensive social and political witness. Strong majorities of members and an even
higher percentage of clergy affirmed that they wanted the "church
to be an active force in the world, challenging our society to be more
like what God intended it to be." Similar numbers responded that
"congregations exist just as much to affect the world around them
as to nurture members." When asked questions about the relevance
of faith, more than three-fourths of members and over 90 percent
of clergy said that Christian principles are applicable to almost every
social issue and that Christian ethics have many implications for economic policy. Far from having a spiritualized conception of faith,
the majority believed that faith concerns our material lives just as
much as our spiritual lives. Lutherans who participated were also
overwhelmingly optimistic about the possibility to achieve major im-
provements in our society. In looking at the role of the congregation,
a majority of the respondents agreed that it would be appropriate to
promote prayers for peace and justice, teach members to have high
ethical standards, help operate a food pantry for the needy, and encourage members to develop a personal understanding of what faith
has to say about current social and political issues. In considering the
role of the church beyond the congregation, a majority of respondents were willing to join with other organizations in coalitions to
influence public policy. Clergy rated this activity as more important
than did laity (Office for Research, Planning, and Evaluation 1990).

Results of the Search Institute/Lilly Endowment survey reveal
a low interest and lack of participation in social service, justice, and
peace ministries in all five mainline denominations. To summarize
some of the relevant survey findings: Less than half of the participants stated that they felt a deep sense of responsibility for reducing
pain and suffering in the world. Only a third reported that they
helped people who had problems or needs. In terms of priorities,
study and action related to improving the lot of the poor was at the
bottom of the list of interests. Charity or direct help to those in need,
however, came ahead of sociopolitical activism intended to change
the system and accord a real opportunity rather than temporary as-

sistance to disadvantaged people. Although half of those interviewed claimed that they try to apply their faith to political and social issues, few provided concrete evidence of doing so. For example, very few (13 percent) indicated that they are active in efforts to promote social justice and even fewer (7 percent) are involved in efforts to promote world peace. One of the greatest interests of the mainline adults was learning more about applying their faith to daily living (77 percent), followed by high levels of concern about how Christians make moral decisions (68 percent), but there is then a further drop in the number of those who would like to know more about Christian perspectives on social and political issues (41 percent). Only a third of respondents wanted to examine lifestyle in light of the world's poor, and a fifth was interested in more study about peacemaking and social justice activities. When asked to characterize their own political orientations, 21 percent identified themselves as liberal, 30 percent as moderate, and 49 percent as conservative (Benson and Eklin 1990, 11; *Effective Christian Education* 1990, 44, 46, 47).

What do these findings mean? In considering the Search Institute study, Eugene Roehlkepartain concludes that most church members have been unmoved by mainline denominations' heavy emphasis on peace and justice issues and that such initiatives may in fact have been counterproductive (1990, 497). Others, comparing the voting records and political views reported by self-identified mainline Protestants on various national surveys with denominational positions, have even less charitable interpretations. A. James Reichley, for example, cites data from 1984 exit polls of mainline support for Ronald Reagan's presidential candidacy as evidence that there is a significant disparity between the orientation of denominational staffs and leadership and that of membership, which he attributes to the development of bureaucratic structures and processes that enable liberals to control the mainline churches (1985, 274–81). Using similar voting data, Robert Booth Fowler claims that, with some exceptions — in particular, liberal positions on abortion and the environment and vague support for peace — the gap between liberal Protestant clergy and intellectuals and the laity on policy issues is great and increases at higher levels of denominational decision making. Like Reichley, he explains this divergence by the selective processes of lay recruitment to leadership positions within the denomination (1989, 92–94).

My own interpretation is quite different. To begin with, in view of the personality factors that influence Americans' voting patterns, exit polls probably do not provide an appropriate source of data about church members' views on issues or their beliefs about the appropriate role for the church. Moreover, the samples for these public polls include large numbers of people who identify themselves with denominations in which they do not have active memberships. In contrast, denominational surveys exclude such nominal members and probably overrepresent more active members who are more inclined to participate in mail surveys. A second important consideration is that few of the mainline denominations have made a concerted effort either to undertake a serious and effective educational program relating to these issues, or even to inform members regularly about denominational positions voted by judicatory bodies. Low or uneven interest in social concerns reported in the Search data, for example, may be more related to the inadequacy of Christian education, broadly conceived, than to any other factor. Corroborating this, only 14 percent of the adults reported that their congregations get members involved in peacemaking and social justice activities, and 43 percent indicated that the congregation provides opportunities for members to engage in community service (Benson and Eklin 1990, 49). In contrast, excluding respondents who were unsure, between six and seven of every ten Presbyterian elders and pastors and 83 percent of the members interviewed for the Presbyterian Panel Report indicated that in the past year their congregation had held one or more study groups that dealt with Christian responsibility and social concern (Presbyterian Panel Report 1988, 15), which possibly accounts for the difference in emphasis between Presbyterians in the Search Institute report and the denominational survey. The style of mainline political ministries, which at times borders on formulating policy statements as an end in itself, indicates that these denominations do not invest sufficient resources in inculcating a sense of identity and vocation. Finally, I think that the surveys basically identify apathy, rather than active disagreements, as the major problem. This low level of participation and commitment, apparently analogous to pervasive civil privatism, is a significant problem for many dimensions of church life, not just political ministry.

INCARNATING COMMITMENTS
IN THE LIFE OF THE DENOMINATION

Efforts to incarnate the beliefs of the community in its lifestyle, priorities, and structures constitute the second dimension of political ministry. The significance of this process of community formation and reformation derives from the very nature of Christianity as a lived truth expressed more appropriately as an ethic of character rather than as intellectual doctrine. An ethic of character tells not so much what to believe or do but who to be. Rather than focusing on rules, situations, and right action, it is concerned with questions of character, virtue, and "being" (Lebacqz 1985, 75–78). Stanley Hauerwas describes the church as a community of character which forms and shapes the lives of its members in decisive and distinctive ways. Everything the church is and does, including liturgy and worship, according to Hauerwas, is a form of religious education. Herein members learn the story of God and God's will for their lives and receive the ongoing training necessary to be faithful to the kingdom. He characterizes the church as a social ethic, namely a community where God's truth is spoken and lived (Hauerwas 1985, 186).

The Church as a Social Ethic

This conception of the faith community as a social ethic or a community of character seeking to incarnate its fundamental beliefs first and foremost in its own life approximates the self-understanding of the historic peace churches but not of the mainline denominations. Mainline churches have been oriented more toward imparting correct beliefs or dogma, whereas sectarian communities have concerned themselves more with lifestyle than theology. As John Richard Burkholder has commented, the central emphasis of the classic sectarian stance "is in living the faithful Christian life, rather than on holding correct theology" (1988, 11). This has made for very different styles of political ministry. Mennonites and some of the other historic peace churches traditionally focused inwardly on the faithfulness of the believing community. In the twentieth century, Mennonites have developed more in the direction of the Society of Friends with a political witness more explicitly balanced between incarnational faithfulness and service to the world. In contrast, main-

line churches' ministry of the Word and involvement with the world
have translated into a heavy emphasis on formulating policy positions
and expressing these views within the public arena. They assume
that their primary task is to transform the world, forgetting that
their members need to be the first line of repentance and conversion. The ineffectiveness of Christian education programs and the
relative absence of effective congregational programs of service and
witness described above is indicative of the problem. This neglect
of community formation and reformation unintentionally creates a
kind of hypocritical double standard by which standards of ethics
and justice that mainline churches are preaching to the world are
frequently not exemplified in their own structures and lifestyles.
Moreover, as the experience of the more sectarian churches shows, it
results in mainline denominations losing one of their most effective
approaches for transformation, the power of example of an alternative community.

The Church and Economic Justice

There are, of course, exceptions to this typology. Mainline churches
have developed programs and initiatives to promote community reformation, but these efforts are often short-lived. One example is the
concern with justice in the church economy reflected in a study paper entitled *Christian Faith and Economic Life* prepared for the United
Church of Christ. To be able to manage faithfully the resources of
the earth and enable all members of the human family to satisfy
their basic needs, the paper identifies three levels of change that are
necessary: first, conversion to a new vision of economics in which
God is at the center, not at the periphery; second, the reconstitution and renewal of communities defined by shared religious values
and commitments and bound together by a sense of mutuality; third,
the design, advocacy for, and management of a more just economic
system (Chapman [Smock] 1987, 37). The section on community formation identifies five areas in which the church's corporate economic
life can promote economic justice — in its being, educational mission, stewardship of resources, employment practices, and service
ministries. And the paper asks of the church: How does the church
value money, how does the church obtain its money, and how does
the church spend its resources? It observes that

> justice ministries, particularly on such matters as economics, cannot be
> divorced from the example which the church sets for its own members
> and for the wider society. A church which preaches a gospel of eco-
> nomic justice but pursues an economy of self-centeredness undermines
> its message. Similarly a church which advocates on behalf of the poor
> but invests most of its funds in elaborate church buildings is uncon-
> vincing or even hypocritical. If the church fails to incarnate principles
> of economic justice in its own practices, it can neither make disciples
> of its members not conduct an effective ministry of transformation in
> the economic system of which it is a part (Chapman [Smock] 1987, 41).

Actual patterns of church economy within the mainline denominations, however, approximate an economy of self-centeredness
rather than a commitment to justice and sharing. Judging from the
language in the pronouncement on this subject eventually adopted
by the United Church of Christ General Synod and actual practices within the denomination, the concern of the paper summarized
above with conversion, community formation, and the economy or
internal life of the church apparently reflects the orientation of the
drafter/editor, myself, more than the church for which it was written. Most mainline Christians seemingly conceptualize the church as
a voluntary association existing primarily for the benefit of and service to its members forgetting that they are a people called by God
into a partnership of service and transformation. In their conduct,
the members, particularly those from privileged backgrounds, tend
to resemble the rich Christians of Corinth whom Paul so strongly
criticized for eating and drinking too much while their poor brothers and sisters were left hungry (1 Cor. 11:20–22) rather than the
house church in Jerusalem whose generous and sacrificial sharing is
described in Acts.

Annual compilations of financial data by the National Council of Churches indicate that members of mainline churches are
not generous in their giving to congregational finance and church
benevolences. Relative to more conservative and evangelical groups
whose members are generally less affluent, mainline congregations
receive considerably lower levels of financial support. The discipline
of church tithing, still practiced by many evangelicals and conservatives, is more exceptional in mainline churches. Of the moneys
contributed, the bulk remains within the local congregations to be
spent on building maintenance, salaries, and programs for mem-

bers. When churches invest in mission outreach, they usually prefer local projects even when there are greater demonstrable needs elsewhere. Most denominations set minimum percentage standards for budget contributions to the ministries and institutions of the wider church, yet the majority of mainline congregations routinely fail to meet these voluntary goals. Beset by declining membership and rising costs, congregations and regional bodies are disposed to retain an even greater proportion of their total revenues, creating an ongoing funding crisis for national agencies that has deprived many programs, including and particularly those related to political ministry, of an adequate level of support.

Although many of these denominations have policies on matters related to the internal church economy, the decentralized nature of the polity results in a situation that resembles a market-driven, free enterprise system with few initiatives to equalize or redistribute income. Congregations raise their own finances, determine their own budgets, and set their own conditions of employment, including salaries, in virtually all mainline denominations regardless of their constitutional structures. Typically, therefore, wealthier congregations and judicatories have more abundant resources than congregations and judicatories ministering in depressed areas with greater problems. In responses to a letter my office sent to more than twenty-five finance and administration officers in mainline Protestant denominations asking them to indicate how their denomination shares its resources, including how ministerial salaries are determined and funded, only one denomination had a process to deal with redistribution among regional bodies other than salary support for some groups of clergy. Reflecting on these issues, the treasurer's office in one of the denominations commented, "The sharing of resources within the denomination is a complex [process] with a variety of criteria which include theological, economic, political, and pragmatic elements. I would be hard pressed to claim that economic justice is the most paramount of concerns."

In contrast, Protestant church polities/economies in other countries have set and implemented denomination-wide policies to assure more equitable standards. One example is the salary structure of the Evangelical Church of the Union in Germany which uses civil service scales. It includes differentials reflecting educational background, experience, and skills, but does not depend on the wealth of the congregation or the economic status of the region. The United Reformed Church in the United Kingdom has a uniform salary that is adjusted according to the life situation and family needs of individual clergy. In the United States, however, clergy are often treated like a commodity to be sold to the highest congregational bidder, and clergy who dedicate themselves to serving congregations and/or ministries providing lower levels of remuneration are regarded as less successful than those who make it to the top of the salary scale.

Spending patterns within mainline denominations suggest that political ministries have a relatively low priority. Policy statements underscoring the urgency and importance of various issues generally have not generated appropriate levels of investments of denominational funds. Although most mainline churches have a church and society division, their budgets and numbers of staff tend to be relatively small, particularly when compared with the more traditional church maintenance and mission divisions. Examples from the United Church of Christ, the denomination with the most liberal/progressive reputation, attest to this underfunding. Of the $15,000,000 to be distributed to national agencies in the 1991 United Church of Christ central budget, the Office for Church in Society received $762,524 (5 percent of the total), the second lowest of any of the national instrumentalities. When added to the funds designated for the Commission for Racial Justice, the total increases to $1,813,872, still only some 12 percent of the total (Office of the Treasurer 1990). Whereas several of the other national instrumentalities have additional sources of income from endowments that supplement this central budget funding, the Office for Church in Society and the Commission for Racial Justice do not. Other national instrumentalities that engage in justice, peace, and human rights ministries provide only limited funding. The United Church Board for World Ministries, for example, had a total budget of $13,462,306 in 1989, of which only $3,061,062 came through the central budget. In 1989 the United Church Board for World Ministries' World Issues Office, which works closely with the Office for Church in Society, received less than $200,000 for program and grants, a figure that was reduced by one quarter in 1990. Allocations within other budgets increased the grants and investment in advocacy and human rights programs by perhaps $50,000. The major share of the Board's budget went to more traditional mission work overseas (United Church of Christ 1989).

Like the United Church of Christ, the Presbyterian Church has also published a series of resources dealing with lifestyle and stewardship, one of which, *Congregational Life-Style Change for the Lean Years*, addresses the significant issue of institutional reform to develop church structures more consistent with justice, stewardship, and community. Recognizing that institutions do not necessarily change to reflect the evolving faith commitments of members, the study seeks to identify ways to model a pattern and style of organization that affirms people engaged in a faith pilgrimage and dares, through open, nonhierarchical decision making, to take institutional risks. It makes the significant point that the community of faith is not simply condemned to live with institutional patterns that are conformed to the bureaucratic structures of contemporary society. There is an option to cast off the corporate model and to substitute something more appropriate for the church. The collection of articles is not so much a how-to or a specific blueprint as a set of theological guidelines or concerns to inspire and facilitate a process. It characterizes the journey toward a new way of life and corporate existence as difficult but not grim. The authors note that sacrifices frequently bring an abundance of compensations as we are born into a new life and identity (Hessel and Wilson 1981, vi–xxi). Much like the United Church of Christ's *Christian Faith and Economic Life*, this document has unfortunately remained a think piece rather than an action guide, an expression of the views of its authors rather than a denominational commitment to reevaluate and reform church structures. And several years after it was published, when the two branches of the Presbyterian church reunited the restructuring venture had the same predilection toward a corporate model.

Affirmative action commitments constitute one significant area in which the mainline churches have actively sought greater consistency between denominational policies and practices. Many denominational agencies, particularly those on a national level, have sought greater racial, gender, and ethnic balance in staff recruitment. The relative success of this policy has changed the character of national staff, perhaps explaining in part the local churches' feeling of distance from national structures. Assemblies and synods have tended to set distribution ratios for delegates that have brought far greater numbers of women and ethnic and racial minorities into the decision-making mainstream, displacing white males who formerly predominated to a far greater extent than their numbers warranted. There has also been sensitivity to the need for diversity in electing candidates to the boards of national instrumentalities and, in some cases to the highest offices of the denominations. This development, too, has possibly brought a measure of discomfort to the membership. Despite these significant denominational commitments, local churches remain among the most segregated institutions in American society.

The corporate responsibility ministries of the mainline denominations, some of the most successful ventures to bring greater consistency between social justice principles and financial management, exhibit the tensions between efforts for economic justice and tendencies toward institutional maintenance. In the late 1960s many mainline denominations with financial investments began to make policy commitment to balance social values and social justice, as well as security and yield, in the investment of funds. As they developed their policy bases, social responsibility in investment generally had three components: an activist shareholder approach, monitoring investments and raising issues with corporations in the portfolio; the establishment of social criteria precluding certain types of investments that contravened fundamental church policies; and reservation of a portion of the portfolio for lower-yield, higher-risk investments that supported positive social goals or enhanced community economic development. Of these three thrusts, mainline denominations have been more inclined toward implementing shareholder activism, working in coalition with other religious investors. Initiatives have been coordinated through the Interfaith Center on Corporate Responsibility, an umbrella organization with both Protestant and Catholic participation, on a wide range of issues. They addressed corporate operations in South Africa and other repressive societies, equality in the workplace, fair salaries and safe working conditions in overseas subsidiaries, environmental impact, dependence on military contracts, and human rights standards for bank loans. The initiatives have contributed to corporations' acknowledging a wider responsibility to society. Despite the denominational policies mandating such shareholder activism, however, Protestant involvement has generally been limited usually to part-time involvement of a single staff person in mission agencies. Pension boards holding the bulk of the investments in mainline denominations have been inclined to provide neither funding nor staff time. Moreover agencies that do participate tend to provide only a fraction of the amount of funding and staffing they invest in financial management. When various of the denominations have adopted policies restricting certain kinds of investment, generally by adding limitations on investments related to South Africa, nuclear weapons, and dependence on military contracts to the traditional exclusion of investments in corporations producing tobacco and alcohol, the relatively autonomous finance committees and money managers overseeing agency and/or denominational investment have been extremely reluctant to comply. Many of the pension boards have, at least initially, refused outright. Implementation, to the extent it has occurred, has often required heroic efforts, even legal action. Most Protestant institutional investors also have been less inclined than the Catholic orders and dioceses that are also members of the Interfaith Center to explore actively alternative/program-related investments.

TRANSFORMATIONAL MINISTRIES

In the third dimension of political ministries, the church moves from its focus within the community to ministries of service and transformation in the world. Worshiping a God whose being is expressed in action, not contemplation, the faith community cannot long postpone its ministry of healing, serving, and transforming the creation. Called by a God who empowers and goads humanity to act for the sake of justice, compassion, and peace, the expression of faith comes in parallel efforts to convert the community to faithfulness and to confront injustice, oppression, and violence in the wider society. Because the relationship between the three dimensions of political ministry is more interactive than sequential, each building on and contributing to the others, one stage flows into the others. But the interactive and multidimensional character of political ministry also means there are fundamental cautions. To leap from belief to advocacy without intense efforts within the community to seek an encounter with the living God or to make foundational understandings of faith a lived truth, the pattern in mainline churches, violates the conception of political ministry delineated in this study.

Chapter 2 repeated Jon Sobrino's definition of faith-related political involvement as "action directed toward structurally transforming society in the direction of the reign of God by doing justice to the poor and oppressed majorities, so that they obtain life and historical salvation" (1988, 80). In this characterization, Sobrino underscores the need for fundamental structural change rather than policy alternatives. For Sobrino, as in the Jesus model, the motive force behind these initiatives for structural change, the critical mark of the presence of the kingdom, comes through doing justice to the poor and oppressed, those to whom and for whom Jesus ministered. God's preferential option for the poor provides both a challenge and a concrete standard for political ministry. The challenge to the faith community is to open itself to the poor, their pain, their life situations, and their needs. Even more, it requires the faith community to do so with a sense of interconnectedness and solidarity with those who suffer. Translated into a concrete standard, the option for the poor requires the churches to assess existing and proposed policies, as well as institutions and entire systems, in terms of their impact on the poor and disadvantaged. Beyond policy analysis, the structural dimension entails understanding the systemic causes of poverty and working to change institutions and processes that consistently disadvantage other sectors of the population while they benefit the affluent and powerful.

The discussion in previous chapters set other conditions for political ministry. It stressed that the political witness of the church should reflect the church's central beliefs and be embodied in the church's own institutions and practices. Transformational ministry should also relate to subjects on which the church has a relevant contribution to make. In engaging in political ministry the church should do so as a community involving a broad base of membership. This necessitates careful reflection and focus on a narrow range of significant issues. This style of political ministry assumes that the church has a distinct identity as a political actor with an agenda related to its other ministries.

Mainline churches, however, do not follow this model. They engage in peace, justice, and human rights advocacy, but not in transformational ministries. Assuming the givens of the existing economic, social, and political system, their major thrust is to correct or ameliorate the worst inequities. Consumed by a wide range of immediate policy issues, mainline political advocates rarely raise fundamental, systemic concerns. The church's lack of a clear identity as an alternative community standing apart from the world makes it difficult to formulate an alternative vision. Although the mainline churches frequently speak on behalf of the poor and disadvantaged, they do so more often from a sense of social responsibility than from a feeling of solidarity or connectedness with their suffering. When it comes to acknowledging responsibility, repenting for the injustices and inequities of the system, mainline Christians often forget that they are part of the problem.

Mainline political ministries related to service and advocacy, although varied, have tended to be characterized in the following seven ways.

1. Peace and justice advocacy takes place relatively autonomously, apart from other areas of church life, thus weakening its spiritual basis and discouraging broad-based participation. Even when denominations devote considerable time to articulating theologies relevant to public policy, there is such a functional disconnection between the committees that write these statements and the staff members that engage in advocacy that often the two activities are little related. Similarly, Christian education programs, particularly the syllabi developed by national staff, rarely apply biblical themes to current issues and problems. Because advocacy is separate from other areas of church life, service and transformation have been conceived as unrelated. This has had the consequence of casting service ministries in a charitable or ameliorative role. The understanding of service as a short-term, immediate response to moderate effects rather than to eliminate causes, has discouraged systematic analysis of the roots of the pain, poverty, and injustice and hindered the churches in making connections between the prevalence of suffering and the need for structural changes in society. Given the vastly greater investment in service ministries over advocacy initiatives, mainline churches are attempting to bandage the wounds of the world rather than to transform society, to lighten the burden of chains rather than to remove them.

2. Much of the emphasis within mainline political ministries has been on clarifying positions on a wide range of social problems

and public policy issues without specifying whether such pronouncements are intended for members, the general population, or policy
makers. These initiatives dominate the gathered life of the church at
synods, assemblies, executive councils, and instrumentality meetings,
possibly to avoid more divisive theological and polity discussions.
There seems to be something of an inner dynamic, almost compul-
sion, for mainline churches to speak to the world on virtually every
subject in the public domain. Reciprocally, there is pressure on these
denominations from many groups within and outside the church, as
well as in the global Christian community, to address particular crises
and issues. The absence of political parties and effective public interest groups responsive to human need and justice concerns time and
again has raised the banner — if not the church, who? if not now,
when? This preoccupation with policy positions may also reflect the
Protestant emphasis on the Word and the assumption that somehow,
once again, it will be made flesh. Denominational politics additionally encourages specialized agencies and interest groups to seek to
have resolutions voted as a way to gain attention for their concerns,
educate the denomination, increase their own status and power, and
accord legitimacy to efforts already under way. Very likely the issue
focus is also a legacy of the "mainline" or "establishment" status
that these denominations have long held, conferring an assumption
of significance to their views. And in many of the denominations
the pattern of adopting public policy resolutions without expectation
that such decisions will affect denominational priorities or redirect
staff energies away from more traditional forms of ministry eliminates the discipline of limiting such actions.

Considerable issue proliferation results from this practice, usually without a clear sense of priority among the various concerns. It
is not uncommon for a national synod or assembly to act on ten
or more subjects with social and political implications. Since these
bodies meet every one-to-four years, mainline churches develop an
enormous compilation of social teaching on diverse subjects over
time. The decentralized nature and regional organization of their
polities relative to political ministries also ensure that at any one
time a particular denomination very likely has a wide range of peace,
human rights, and justice concerns pursued by various units, often in
an uncoordinated manner, possibly even with inconsistent positions.
Added to this melange, much of the advocacy work of national staff is

conducted through ecumenical coalitions, thus expanding considerably the total number of issues in which the religious community has an interest. On those occasions when specific denominations identify priorities on which to focus, their efforts are then supplemented by an ecumenical division of labor that assigns issues not being covered by one denomination to others. In dealing with so many issues the churches often sacrifice quality, the possibility of making a real difference, for quantity, providing a religious witness for the sake of having the churches' concerns noted.

This issue-oriented advocacy is problematic. The very relevance of the mainline denominations to the political process comes at the risk of their irrelevance for the long-term transformation of society and their members. It has discouraged a structural and systematic orientation dealing with fundamental causes rather than symptoms of injustice and inequity. Even if the churches were somehow to achieve all their various public policy goals, they would still not have institutionalized a more just, equitable, or participatory political or economic system. At a time when many people have begun to raise major questions about the adequacy of the political process and institutions, mainline churches still envision themselves as political actors within the system rather than an alternative community standing apart from it, evaluating it, and offering proposals for basic changes.

For a church to address the world from an explicitly religious basis, referring to fundamental faith principles, is quite different from the current pattern, which is often to deal with a wide range of complicated technical and specialized issues in which the application of moral principles is debatable and members are less likely to understand the rationale for church involvement. Relating to this question is the distinction made by the National Conference of Catholic Bishops between universal moral principles and/or formal church teaching and the prudential judgments that apply these principles to specific issues (1983, pars. 9–12). Sometimes the discussion has centered on the competence of the church to address such matters. Most, perhaps all of the churches, have considerable expertise in their staff and members, but it is possible to question the appropriateness of investing the prestige and energy of the churches in policy ministries where their moral and spiritual authority are weak and their members are discouraged from active participation.

3. In translating faith principles into policy prescriptions, the political witness of mainline churches has been dedicated to serving the needs of the poor, the unfortunate, and the oppressed and promoting the integrity of the creation and welfare of the global society. Institutional self-interest plays a much less important role, and churches almost never represent the narrow economic or political interests of members. Self-interested lobbying, to the extent that it occurs, is generally confined to such issues as church-state relations, clergy and church tax exemptions, and regulations governing the various social welfare institutions that the churches operate. These concerns, however, constitute but a minor part of the work and are often pursued by representatives of pension boards and other parts of the church that do not normally engage in advocacy. The churches' access to and standing within the policy process, as well as with their own constituency, often reflect the extent to which their claims to speak on behalf of the groups lacking a voice are well grounded. As the next chapter will detail, mainline churches' participation in a global Christian community often means they represent the perspectives of overseas partners, thus adding an authentic and significant perspective to foreign policy debates. It has, however, been far more difficult for predominantly middle-class churches to develop ongoing links with the poor in their own country. Solidarity with the poor, a theme reiterated in mainline writings on economic justice, has yet to be translated into effective political initiatives based on ongoing consultations, institutional linkages, or the kind of partner relationships forged with overseas churches. Further, mainline churches are more inclined to speak for the poor than to engage in complex and time-consuming initiatives to empower the poor to speak for themselves.

4. Mainline denominations tend to implement effectively only a limited number of the policy actions that their bodies adopt. This evaluation applies to their uneven record of educating and informing members, incarnating principles within the life of the denomination, and developing appropriate strategies to influence public policy. Some of the incidents that have caused the greatest dissension within these denominations have resulted from members learning about positions their church has adopted from secular media without understanding the basis for the decision. In many cases, the beginning and end of a synod or assembly resolution is the writing of a letter to communicate the action to the relevant public body or official.

Why does this happen? Many policies are adopted for the sake of recording the church's response to the signs of the times or having a policy base on a particular issue, and not for the purpose of developing a meaningful program. The complexity of the process of writing, distributing, evaluating, and voting these positions in most of the denominations so preoccupies committees, staff, and boards that it deters implementation. Since much public policy work is done in coalition with other churches and groups, consultation and coordination on issues and strategies is complex and time-consuming, sometimes almost becoming an end in itself. Organizationally, most denominations have clearer lines of authority and processes for developing policies than for implementing them. The decentralized nature of the polity, segmental organization of national agencies, and fragmentation in the structure discussed earlier inhibits staff so inclined to coordinate efforts on specific issues at different levels of the denomination. Many of these policy statements are written in such a way that they do not specify implementation processes for congregations. Research has shown that calling on churches to undertake specific activities, rather than to be concerned in the abstract, considerably enhances prospects that they will respond (Royle and Bolin 1983). Issue proliferation without a designation of priorities in itself may overwhelm staff, clergy, and laity alike, so that they do not know where to begin. The translation of policy into effective action involving several levels of the church is more the exception than the rule. It usually requires a special set of circumstances, such as a deep and pervasive sense of outrage, a clearly recognizable religious rationale, a widely shared recognition of a crisis, and/or the mobilization of a key activist constituency within the denomination with a strong commitment to the issue.

5. Mainline political ministries have concentrated on immediate, short-term policy changes through legislative instruments, rather than major long-term reorientation of attitudes, priorities, or institutions. Eight years of responding to the escalating policy outrages of the Reagan administration contributed to this tendency, because it left the religious community and other progressive public interest groups in a defensive position, constantly on the alert to

prevent or mitigate destructive policy initiatives. A misplaced sense of their own establishment status and power may also incline these denominations toward a legislative focus as the easy way to achieve their objectives, rather than investment in the more difficult tasks of organizing their members or seeking to empower disadvantaged groups. To enable them to pursue legislative advocacy, many mainline denominations have Washington offices with staffs monitoring legislative developments, lobbying on the hill, often doing so ecumenically, and seeking to mobilize church members to express their views on particular issues. Additionally, many of the denominations publish newsletters, hold advocacy seminars and public policy training sessions, send legislative alerts to politically conscious members, and issue background information papers on public policy issues. Several, including the United Church of Christ, the Presbyterian Church, and Interfaith IMPACT for Peace and Justice, an ecumenical advocacy organization, have developed networks to facilitate educating members and contacting them at critical points in the legislative process to express their views. In the case of the United Church of Christ, this peace and justice network reaches 14,000 members organized on a state and congressional district basis. Plans call for the Presbyterian network to incorporate over 100,000 members of the church. Other denominations have chosen to invest in the Interfaith IMPACT effort to organize ecumenically on a congressional district basis.

This disposition and the heavy investment of staff and resources in the legislative process, however, have tended to conform these denominations to the political system rather than to challenge it from the standpoint of their faith. It has also served to encourage them to engage in a dangerous flirtation with congressional power brokers that contradicts Jesus' teachings on power. The advocacy initiatives of these churches have been rendered generally reactive and captive to the secular Washington agenda, the dynamics of interest-group lobbying, and an unimaginative incremental issue approach. This, in turn, has contributed to mainline advocacy ministries' having a secular character. Issue analyses and alerts to members, such as the materials prepared by Interfaith IMPACT and the United Church of Christ, for the most part could be sent by any liberal secular group. In lobbying within a pluralistic secular political system, the church community has opted to underscore the similarities rather than the differences between itself and other public interest groups. That the Catholic bishops would award a leading public relations firm a multimillion dollar contract to promote opposition to abortion is a logical but unfortunate outcome of accommodation to secular political styles.

Assessments of mainline churches' legislative advocacy tend to be mixed. One of the more balanced secular treatments of the subject, Allen Hertzke's *Representing God in Washington*, concludes that "the interactive, collective activities of religious lobbyists play an important role in enhancing the representativeness of American policy" (1988, 154). The author argues that church lobbying organizations, by articulating values beyond narrow self-interest and representing a broad constituency, partially compensate for the pervasive fragmented elite-based organizations focusing on particularistic interests that dominate the American political system. Because the mainline churches' lobbying groups, in contrast to other political actors, see themselves as representatives of voiceless, hard-to-organize citizens, he credits them with forcing elites to address otherwise unarticulated needs and values (Hertzke 1988, 206). Acknowledging that many major Protestant churches are international institutions with relief agencies, missionaries, development programs, and members scattered across the globe, he identifies this international network as serving as a lobby resource that provides mainline denominations with special information and in certain cases unique access to policy makers (Hertzke 1988, 111). He does not, however, give the churches such high marks for effectiveness on domestic issues. My own perspective is that the public policy work of the churches has been an important contribution to the public policy process, but at the expense of developing a more appropriate and focused church political vocation.

6. Mainline churches have an unstrategic approach to political ministry. This disposition reflects the absence of a concrete vision of a more just, compassionate, and peaceful society as well as the lack of long-term goals and a plan for the denomination to achieve these objectives. It also reflects a failure to undertake systematic social analysis, to base strategies on models of society reflecting actual power dynamics, or to invest in carefully designed long-term initiatives with appropriate tactics. There are many similarities between the unstrategic character of mainline ministries and the orientation of other activist churches that seemingly tend more toward preaching to the world than changing it. *The Kairos Document*, a theological comment on the political crisis in South Africa, although acknowledging the policy commitment of the English-speaking Protestant denominations to justice and change, severely criticizes their superficiality, failure to engage in social analysis, and reluctance to undertake effective political action. The document also castigates these denominations for their inadequate understanding of politics and political strategy (Kairos Theologians 1986, pars. 3:1–3:3), charges that apply equally well to their mainline counterparts in the United States.

Commenting on the United States Catholic bishops' economic pastoral *Economic Justice for All* (1986), Larry Rasmussen characterizes it as "softly utopian," a feature he traces to the unwillingness or inability to deal adequately with issues of power. Like the bishops, mainline Protestants' political ministries both underestimate the power of social sin to frustrate desired social progress and overestimate the power of evangelical and educative means to effect the common good (1989, 134–35). Despite reference to human proclivities to sinfulness, mainline statements ring with an optimism sometimes bordering on a utopianism about the possibilities of achieving fairly substantial social reform with relatively little effort. Rasmussen attributes these unrealistic expectations to the inadequacies of the models or lenses through which these faith communities view society (1989, 137–40).

In addition to employing social analysis and developing adequate models, Christian political ministries involve organizing to overcome or offset entrenched constellations of power, something which churches generally are not inclined to do. Such efforts to plan strategically a series of initiatives with carefully crafted tactics to work toward a set of clear-cut objectives are necessary in a complex, multitiered representative political system. Moreover, organization requires establishing a coalition of commitment and imparting the motivation and skills for group members to participate in the campaign for change. That mainline churches have a more spontaneous approach reflects their traditional style and heritage, their inadequate appraisal of the obstacles, their short-term horizons akin to those of others in American society, and their general lack of organizing skills.

7. All of the factors discussed above shape advocacy as a specialized ministry in which a relatively small group of staff, members of boards, and various groups of activists within churches engage in this mission on behalf, but not with the ongoing participation, of the wider church. Although broader involvement does occur on some issues, this is more the exception than the rule. As noted in the Lilly/Search Institute study, 72 percent of mainline adults reported that they had never marched, met, or gathered with others to promote social change; 52 percent had never donated time to helping the poor, hungry, and sick; and 78 percent had never engaged in promoting social justice (*Effective Christian Education* 1990, 26). This low level of involvement in advocacy and service reflects participation patterns in virtually every aspect of church life, including attendance at worship and church education programs. To be mainline has become synonymous with lack of serious commitment, with the church imaged as a voluntary association catering to individual members rather than as a community dedicated to partnership with a God of peace, justice, and compassion.

Processes of leadership selection and policy-making within the mainline denominations tend to develop an activist core at various levels of the institutional church who have a stronger commitment and a greater disposition toward a justice and peace orientation than the majority of members. This pattern occurs in many other types of organizations and is characteristic of church structures in other countries as well. Writing from a South African context, Charles Villa-Vicencio suggests that such a faithful minority, inspired by the "dangerous memory" of the teachings and ministry of Jesus of Nazareth, often coexists on the margins of churches, most of which are more inclined to compromises with the existing political and economic order. Villa-Vicencio links the role of this community, or alternative church, with the ability to hear and respond to the cries of the oppressed (1988, 5).

That the views of clergy, staff, and church leaders tend to be more activist and progressive than the typical member has given rise to allegations bordering on accusations of conspiracy by some analysts who disagree with the content of these policies and/or the political involvement of the mainline churches. Some assume that activists are self-promoted into leadership and representational roles, thus skewing the policy-making process. Others go further, claiming that denominations intentionally manipulate the composition of delegates to synods and assemblies.

My interpretation of this pattern stresses the strong correlation between three formative influences — serious study of scripture and theology, participation in service and advocacy, and knowledge of and involvement in the wider church beyond the local congregation — and the kind of faith commitment that translates into a strong political ministry. Thus an activist inclination is likely to reinforce the mindset of those members also inclined toward a role outside the local church. Conversely, selection into a wider church role provides exposure to national and global church ministries and many educational opportunities that tend to socialize a person to a very different type of perspective. In a United Church of Christ survey of members in the Indiana-Kentucky Conference, for example, familiarity with the wider church was associated with the belief that the church should take an active role in society. People who said that they were more familiar with the work of the association, the conference, and the national bodies were more supportive of involvement in social issues than were those less familiar. Likewise, those who were more active in their local churches were more inclined to be supportive than the less active respondents (Royle 1989). Although regular church attendance is often thought to go along with conservative views, in a Lutheran survey frequent attenders held views more favorable to connecting faith and politics than those who attend less often (Office for Research, Planning, and Evaluation, 1990).

In survey after survey of mainline Protestant denominations, the recurring tendency for clergy to be more favorable to church social action, make more connections between faith and politics, and hold more liberal views on most substantive issues than laity is likely to be related to similar factors. The profession probably attracts many persons who are more socially concerned and activist in temperament. Seminary education, ongoing involvement in the life of the local congregation, biblical and theological reflection, participation in service and advocacy ministries, and awareness of the ministries of the wider church then reinforce these tendencies. Ministers' social networks and life experiences therefore strengthen their allegiance to the church's core values, including an understanding of the church as dedicated to God and God's creation, whereas the socialization experiences of members tend to shape values and

expectations more consistent with a self-interested conception of
the church as a voluntary association serving its members (Wood
1981, 3).

I believe that the current pattern is untenable, not because
decisions are framed by unrepresentative bodies, but because mainline churches are deficient in socializing/educating members to their
core values and explicitly developing policy statements from this
biblical and theological foundation. Moreover, the kind of de facto
division of labor between the publicly oriented leadership and staff of
national agencies and the privately centered local church, sometimes
producing attitudes bordering on mutual suspicion, is inimical to the
integrity and reformation of the denomination. National staff who
scrupulously follow denominational policies and often invest their
lives in their jobs nevertheless feel very distant from member congregations, assuming that it is their role to minister on behalf of,
not to empower local church members. Indeed, at least some have
written off the possibility of local churches' understanding the problems of the world or responding appropriately, and thus rationalize
their focusing on the faithful remnant, those church members with
commitment to political activism. Conversely, many members of local
congregations steadfastly ignore the very existence of the denomination of which they are a part, refusing to read denominational
publications, ignoring judicatory actions, disclaiming responsibility
for addressing peace and justice issues, and assuming the worst of
the national staff members who have dedicated themselves to serving the denominations. Since partnership with the God of peace and
justice mandates commitment to peace and justice, the future faithfulness as well as the integrity of the churches require widening the
range of involvement and mutual support for political ministry at
each level of church life.

Chapter Four

Changing Context
of Political Ministries

I n the past two decades the political ministries of the mainline Protestant denominations, and to some extent the Catholic Church as
well, have responded to a series of major cultural, theological, ecclesiological, and political shifts. Three of these developments that will
be discussed in this chapter are (1) changing patterns of religious
affiliation with a concomitant "disestablishment" of the mainline
Protestant churches, (2) the emergence of a global Christian community, giving rise to a more international perspective, and (3) the
growing recognition that humanity confronts major crises affecting
the future of the earth and the human community, about which the
church cannot remain silent. Each of these by itself might have reshaped the identity and role of the churches. Together they have
brought these denominations to the threshold of a redefinition of
their character and mission. For reasons that will be made clearer in
this chapter, much of the initial adjustment to the new environment
and experimentation with new ministries has occurred in the political sphere. At some points the interconnectedness between these
new challenges and opportunities and the recasting of the political

role of the churches have been explicit and intentional, but at other points less conscious and clear.

THE DISESTABLISHMENT OF THE MAINLINE CHURCHES

Journals and newspapers almost daily chronicle one or another aspect of the various crises of membership, identity, purpose, and finances that confront contemporary mainline churches on both an individual and an ecumenical level. *The Wall Street Journal* delights in writing what fortunately has been the premature obituary of the National Council of Churches. Denominational newsletters report shortfalls in budgets and painful cuts in programs and staff. *Christianity and Crisis* and *The Christian Century* publish frequent articles raising questions about the future of liberal Protestantism. One denomination after another has considered or attempted a reorganization and relocation as a means to overcome these problems. A report to the Governing Board of the National Council of Churches, prepared in the spring of 1989 by a special committee of fifteen religious leaders, summarizes the situation as follows:

> The crisis in the Council and in the communions cannot be understood apart from the domestic and international context in which we live. Neither the churches in the NCC, nor even the entire Christian community enjoy or expect the privileged status and moral authority they once took for granted. The religious community, now more pluralistic, is only at the threshold of mutual understanding. These bodies experience forces such as racism, sexism, secularism, and nationalism not only as serious threats to humankind but also to their own institutional welfare (Committee of Fifteen 1989, 1).

Reconfiguration of the Religious Landscape

Wade Clark Roof and William McKinney's seminal study, *American Mainline Religion: Its Changing Shape and Future* (1987), documents many of these trends and suggests that a new American religio-cultural order is now in the making. Arguing that the formerly dominant Protestant churches have lost the power and influence they once wielded in the religious, cultural, and political spheres, they conclude that the mainline denominations no longer occupy the center or mainstream and describe them as playing a more modest role in a fragmented and pluralistic religious landscape. According to Roof and McKinney, the established "culture-religion" that had sustained the normative faiths of most Americans and to which the mainline churches had once made a notable contribution, has lost its ability or authority to set norms. In the 1980s, therefore, the consensus disintegrated as groups and forces competed with one another in a system that had no strong religious center. In characterizing the major Protestant churches, they also compare them unfavorably with white conservative Protestants, black Protestants, and Catholics, who they claim have more cohesive bonds, a greater sense of vitality, and higher levels of commitment, discipline, and dynamism.

One indication of decline for Roof and McKinney and others are the data that indicate that the major Protestant churches affiliated with the National Council of Churches have several million fewer members than they did twenty-five years ago. Liberal Protestant churches (which Roof and McKinney somewhat arbitrarily identify as the Presbyterians, Episcopalians, and United Church of Christ) have been losing members since 1960 and now constitute only 8.7 percent of the total population. Moderate Protestant bodies (the churches Roof and McKinney describe as a product of nineteenth-century America — the Methodists, Lutherans, Reformed, Northern Baptists, and Disciples of Christ) peaked about ten years later and now account for 24.2 percent. In contrast, Catholics (25.0 percent), conservative white Protestants (15.8 percent), and black Protestants (9.1 percent), as well as those with no religious preference (6.9 percent), are increasing their membership, Catholics at a somewhat lower rate than in earlier periods (Roof and McKinney 1987, 82–96).

What accounts for this pattern? Roof and McKinney and others attribute much of the reconfiguration to changing demographic patterns. Mainline denominations tend to have an aging membership with a low birth rate and a high death rate. Although these churches continue to attract people who are switching denominational membership, formerly a sign of upward mobility, they do so at a reduced rate. Even more significant, the proportion of younger members, particularly males, who have withdrawn from any type of church involvement, is higher in mainline churches than in conservative churches (Roof and McKinney 1987, 182–85).

Legacy of the 1960s

More fundamentally, Roof and McKinney relate the loss in membership, status, and influence of the mainline Protestant churches
to a series of profound cultural, religious, and social shifts dating
from the 1960s. Like historian Sydney Ahlstrom (1975, 603–16),
they understand the civil rights struggle, the assassination of a president, and the war in Vietnam to have had significant implications
for religious as well as political life. They argue that the upheavals
of the 1960s induced a growing privatism, a focus on individual self-
fulfillment, and greater religious experimentation. Simultaneously,
greater mobility and a decreased sense of rootedness contributed to
an erosion in the role of the family in religious socialization and a
weakening of ascriptive or inherited loyalties. These changes have
resulted cumulatively in a phenomenon they describe as religious
"voluntarism," a sense of having a wide range of religious options
unrelated to past commitments and a greater willingness to change
religious affiliation to suit personal needs. They claim that this privatized religious culture, with its demand for immediate and intense
religious experience, favors evangelical and fundamentalist faiths
and oriental religions. Conversely, such a disposition disadvantages
mainline churches, which have a more institutional, intellectual, and
activist orientation (1987, 40–63).

They argue, in addition, that these events and the sharper
generational conflict they induced eroded the old civil faith that
once unified Americans and conferred a sense of national values and
purpose. This had devastating consequences for the churches most
affirming of the American culture and highest in socioeconomic status, the liberal Protestant denominations (1987, 20–21). Churches
that retained distance from the culture by cultivating distinctive
lifestyles and beliefs, however, did not suffer comparable declines
in religious participation and institutional support (1987, 20–21).
In somewhat of an overstatement, Roof and McKinney attribute
much of the plight of contemporary mainline churches to their
too-close relationship with the "American way." They portray these
denominations as so wedded to the beliefs, values, and behavior of
the dominant culture that they became virtually indistinguishable
from it. Describing liberal mainline churches, particularly during the
1950s peak in membership, as a kind of "culture-religion" captive to

middle-class values, they assume that they were therefore unable to sustain a strong transcendent vision. The authors' consistently negative critique of these denominations also portrays them as unable to forge a meaningful interpretation of modern life (1987, 22).

To underscore the significance of the situation, Roof and McKinney characterize the mainline or formerly dominant churches as confronting a third "disestablishment" that has relegated liberal Protestantism into a minority voice and made it one player among many in a more truly pluralistic environment (1987, 239–40). They equate these developments with two earlier reconfigurations of the American religious landscape: the legal disestablishment of Congregationalists, Presbyterians, and Episcopalians at the end of the colonial period and the incorporation of Catholics and Jews into the religious center during the first part of the twentieth century. To illustrate the loss in status and power of the mainline denominations, McKinney in an article contrasts President Dwight Eisenhower's 1958 trip to New York City to lay the cornerstone of the National Council of Churches' new headquarters building with George Bush's decision to pay a courtesy call on Jerry Falwell, rather than the general secretary of the NCC òr the presiding bishop of his Episcopal Church, before announcing his candidacy for the presidency in 1988 (1989, 465).

Others go beyond Roof and McKinney to ask whether the low-church Protestants who make up the core of the religious Right have become the new political establishment. Gary Wills, for example, identifies the election of Jimmy Carter as a turning point in American political history because Carter was the first president whose religion was not "cool" and "mainline." Wills notes that Carter's defeat was even more significant in political terms. It turned on his loss of the evangelical and fundamentalist vote to Ronald Reagan who, in contrast to Carter, openly embraced the political agenda of the religious Right. Wills also points out the efforts of George Bush, a preparatory school Episcopalian in background, to cultivate Jerry Falwell and other evangelicals and to portray himself as a born-again Christian (Wills 1989, 24–26). Yet the decline of the religious Right as a national political force after the 1988 presidential election suggests that these assessments were at least premature, if not erroneous.

Although other religious historians and analysts dispute some aspects of Roof and McKinney's analysis, they concur that mainline

Protestantism is in decline. Robert Handy (1984) dates the second disestablishment far earlier. According to Handy, the Protestant era in American life — the period in which the mainline churches provided a measure of inspiration and direction — came to an end during the 1920s. Although familiar perceptions and goals continued to influence many people, he maintains that the consequences of disestablishment were evident in several areas of the country, particularly the Northeast, after 1940. Handy views the postwar religious revival of mainline churches' peaking in the 1950s, the period that Roof and McKinney use as their baseline, as an aberration in the trend toward religious pluralism (1984, 185–91).

The Role of Religious Education

In identifying the causes for the decline of mainline Protestantism, there is both broad agreement and difference in emphasis. Dorothy Bass, for example, although concurring with much of Roof and Mc-Kinney's demographic analysis, believes that the main deficiency of liberal or mainline Protestantism has been educational, their failure to transmit the meaning and excitement of Christianity from one generation to another. According to Bass, liberal Protestantism has become confused and tentative about appropriating and conveying the Christian tradition. She cites the virtual biblical illiteracy of adult church members, the weakness of children's religious educational curricula, the devolution of denominational religious journalism into a public relations activity, and the near disappearance of a religious presence in higher education. Accommodation to the culture has been one result of the weakness of mainstream Protestant educational strategies. "Among those whose roots in tradition are weak, the ideas and experiences that can keep persons faithful in the midst of an unfaithful society are eroded, and the illusions of the dominant culture take hold" (Bass 1989, 11). Much of her analysis is corroborated by the Search Institute/Lilly Endowment study of six major Protestant denominations cited in the previous chapter. This report concludes that of all areas of congregational life, involvement in Christian education programs has the strongest ties to a person's growth in faith and denominational loyalty, but it also documented the pervasive absence of effective programs and the low rates of participation in the congregations sampled (Benson and Eklin 1990).

Political Factors and the Clergy Crisis

Like Bass, Donald Miller faults the religious education programs of the 1960s and 1970s as contributing to the decline of mainline Protestantism, but also cites other explanations. Miller mentions Dean Kelley's research that attributes the differences between the membership growth of conservative churches and the membership loss of the mainline denominations to the failure of liberal churches to place high demands on their members in terms of moral and lifestyle prescriptions. He also considers several other culturally related factors: the growing individualism that has weakened the compelling character of sources of external authority: the increasingly therapeutic orientation of American culture, inclining psychologists and psychiatrists to assume roles formerly held by clergy; and the emergence of other types of voluntary associations performing some of the traditional roles of churches. Attributing much of the responsibility for the decline to the role and character of liberal clergy, Miller discusses three aspects of the "clergy crisis," claiming that liberal clergy who are too progressive alienate many in their constituency; liberal clergy exposed to seminary education dominated by a therapeutic philosophy tend to be more concerned about expressing feelings than cultivating community or understanding the Christian tradition; and, by not concealing their own theological doubts and questions, liberal clergy encourage some church members to seek the certainty of more conservative forms of religious participation (1986, 201–19).

Miller's discussion of the clergy crisis in liberal Protestantism as one of several factors contributing to the decline in membership bears some similarities with the less nuanced claim of Richard John Neuhaus, that the political role of mainline denominations has been a major cause of their current problems. As noted earlier, Neuhaus, a neoconservative political thinker, has castigated mainline churches both for their past unquestioning identification with American political goals and programs linked to social and economic betterment and for their more recent criticism of American policies (1984). Like other neoconservatives, Neuhaus believes that religion does and should play a central role in validating American political culture, institutions, and policies. His unrelenting attacks on the mainline churches reflect his concern that by abdicating their culture-sanctifying role the mainline churches have left a dangerous vacuum.

To what extent have progressive clergy and radical social action policies alienated members and driven them from mainline denominations? In assessing claims made by Miller, Neuhaus, and others, there are no "exit polls" that provide even semidefinitive answers, but available data suggest that contemporary political ministries reflect rather than precipitated the changed status of these churches. On the side of those who argue that political involvements have been a problem, various of the surveys discussed in the previous chapter do show differences in the attitudes of clergy and lay members on political issues, the clergy across denominations consistently inclined to greater activism, and there has been vocal opposition within these denominations to some of the official policies voted by synods and assemblies. That the disagreements with these positions have precipitated mass withdrawals or significant denomination switching, however, cannot be substantiated. Careful statistical analyses, such as the work of Roof and McKinney, do not support the contention that middle-aged members are leaving mainline churches in significant numbers, fleeing from controversial social action stands. Membership loss has occurred primarily among young adults, a group in apparent rebellion against all forms of institutional religion: 59 percent of nonaffiliates in American society are less than thirty-five years old, the highest percentage of any age group (Roof and McKinney 1987, 154–55). Other data cited by Roof and McKinney indicate that those who drop out of church participation are considerably more liberal than those who retain their religious affiliation (1987, 222). Far from being perceived as existing on the political fringe, the church is viewed as a symbol of conventionality by most members of society (Roof and McKinney 1987, 222). To attract the membership constituency lost to secularism, particularly the better-educated and more affluent members of younger groups, mainline denominations would therefore have to break more decisively with their heritage and become less, not more, conventionally mainstream.

Moreover, the same surveys that exhibit discrepancies between clergy and lay members on political and social issues more significantly reveal membership support for peace and justice ministries, particularly when such initiatives are based on a biblical foundation and/or core Christian values. Most members of mainline churches appear to expect and to accept active political ministries as a component of their denominational heritage. Survey results cited in the previous chapter, for example, point to considerable membership support despite low levels of participation. Even when policies or stands taken on specific issues generate controversy, most members seem willing to tolerate disagreement if the leadership and decision-making processes are viewed as legitimate and/or these decisions are grounded in core values (Wood 1981; Presbyterian Panel Report 1988; Office for Research, Planning, and Evaluation 1990).

The Role of Political Ministries

To assert that political ministries have not been a major factor precipitating membership losses or changes in status and power does not mean that the political role of mainline churches has not been problematic. In making these judgments, however, it is very important to differentiate between substance and style, between the understanding that political ministries constitute a central component of an ethical, social, and incarnational faith, and the inadequate manner in which mainline denominations have conducted their political witness. As noted, the model of political ministry developed in this study differs significantly from the patterns of political involvement in mainline churches. The critical evaluation of mainline political involvement in the previous chapter underscores this point. A changed approach, particularly one that was more consistently faith based and grounded in the life of the faith community, would very likely have quite a different result. Political ministries involving more dialectical initiatives to convert simultaneously the faith community and the world to greater righteousness, compassion, justice, and peace could very likely be a major source of religious renewal.

In evaluating the impact of political ministries it is also important to recognize that the very language of decline and disestablishment reflects establishmentarian assumptions that value large memberships (even if nominal), fancy buildings, elaborate programs, and access to the centers of political power — characteristics that have not historically been marks of Christian faithfulness or vitality. Others view the trends that Roof and McKinney refer to as the "disestablishment" of the mainline churches more hopefully as conferring new possibilities for a more authentic and faithful role. For those who mourned the captivity of these mainline churches to American culture and the established order, such a loss of majority status and influence constitutes a prerequisite for these churches to lose the world and rediscover their identity and true mission. There is a long tradition of Christian thinkers that have questioned the close and comfortable relationship of religion, culture, society, and politics in the United States, believing that it was detrimental to the churches. *The Church Against the World*, coauthored by H. Richard Niebuhr, Wilhelm Pauck, and Francis Miller in 1935, presents one of the strongest expressions of the point of view that the Protestant church is/was fundamentally threatened by its close identification with Western culture, nationalism, economic systems, political ideologies, and worthwhile social causes. This concern is as relevant today as it was when the book was published.

A New Consciousness

Chroniclers of the "disestablishment" also err in underestimating the impact of internal developments that have made mainline churches less inclined to opt for establishment status. The analyses delineated above for the most part conceptualize disestablishment as the confluence of a changing culture, socioeconomic system, and political process, with static churches unable to adjust to shifts in their environment. In some sense, however, these denominations actually have come closer to "abdicating," because many of their leaders and at least a significant cross section of members no longer identify with the white, European, and patriarchal norms or the view of the United States as a beacon and blessing to the world that went with being part of the establishment. The upheavals of the 1960s were more than an external historical divide. They had a profound internal impact on many mainline Christians, particularly the socially concerned and sensitive members likely to be actively involved in political ministry. These events disillusioned many Americans, motivating them to question fundamental assumptions about their country, its institutions, and their own place within it. More specifically, the civil rights movement brought one of this country's greatest sins into the open, the contradiction between theoretically subscribing to egalitarian values and principles but in practice engaging in racial discrimination. As the first American war to be considered illegitimate by significant sectors of the population, including eventually the official position of most of the mainline denominations, the Vietnam War was considered a second serious betrayal of the American heritage. Moreover, the American role in Vietnam came to be seen as part of a pattern of illegitimate intervention and domination. And as mainline churches became more sensitive to the needs and problems of the poor and disadvantaged, they also became more aware of the extent to which the economic and political systems were weighted against their interests. Eventually the Reagan administration's nuclear policies, militaristic tendencies, and favoritism for the rich created something of a *kairos*, a time of crisis and challenge, for these denominations.

Mainline denominations currently are also more diverse in their leadership and self-understanding and therefore less inclined to be establishment-oriented. Mobility of their members and the subsequent weakening of denominational ties have meant that denominations are less likely to be relatively homogenous enclaves defined by class, race, national origins, and regionalism. The changing social location of the mainline churches and the leveling of some of the historic differences among denominations have created an openness to rethink denominational priorities, orientations, and policies. A commitment to greater diversity within the churches has also brought more women and representatives of racial and ethnic minorities into leadership positions, many of whom are less comfortable with conformity to establishment norms and place a higher priority on justice commitments than did the "old boys" networks of white males that formerly monopolized decision making. The significant growth in the number of women ordained to the full ministry, particularly for those mainline Protestant denominations in which female seminarians now constitute 40 percent or more of students, suggests a religious revolution in the making whose import has yet to be fully discerned.

Yet although leaders of mainline churches may now feel uneasy with some aspects of their historical roles, they are not consistently antiestablishment in their orientation. The erosion of the traditional American civil religion and the concomitant loss of status and influence for the mainline churches has cast them into a "postestablishment" role that they neither self-consciously sought nor fully understand or embrace. Although leaders of these denominations sense a major shift, they are not inclined to be reflective or analytical about the implications. They are more disposed to focus on symptoms than on the underlying causes and to seek "quick fixes" through relocating, restructuring, or merging than to raise fundamental questions about what it means to be a faith community at the end of the twentieth century. Staff of mainline denominations are more likely to hearken nostalgically for the "good old days" when their establishment position made them arbiters of national life, rather than to welcome the freedom or opportunities for religious creativity in their new situation. Even when critical of policy directions of incumbent administrations, mainline denominations have not reimaged themselves as the minority, prophetic, and servant community that John Howard Yoder (1984) identifies with a post-Constantinian outlook. Pushed out of the political center, they have begun to define new roles and modes of ministry that are somewhere in between the bondage of the establishment and the freedom of the radically committed minority.

This movement away from establishment status, nevertheless, has been a major precondition and catalyst for a redefined political ministry. A more autonomous relationship to the American political and social system has conferred freedom to ask fundamental questions. Mainline denominations have begun to cultivate an alternative consciousness and to learn to perceive reality through the lenses of those excluded from the mainstream. Relative disestablishment has enabled these denominations to respond to new situations and demands, key among them the dynamics of a global Christian community and the *kairos* of a potential nuclear holocaust and profound injustice.

As might be expected in a transition of such monumental import, however, mainline churches have not fully adjusted to the new context in which they function. Sometimes mainline churches distance themselves from the power structure, but at other points church representatives assume that they still have mainline status and access to the centers of political decision making. There are even occasions when these denominations seem to be attempting to do both at the same time. This divided consciousness affects and pervades their political ministries.

INCREASED GLOBAL CONSCIOUSNESS

From the 1960s onward, mainline Protestant churches, as well as the Catholic Church, have been increasingly integrated into a global Christian community. The Second Vatican Council (1962–1965) marked the emergence of an international Catholic Church no longer shaped solely in the image of European theology and culture. By 1951 the World Council of Churches was beginning to reconceptualize itself as more than a Western council of churches, and at its Conference on Church and Society in 1965 roughly half of the participants came from Two-Thirds World countries (Drimmelen 1987). Christians in Two-Thirds World countries, once perceived to be on the margins of the faith, now constitute an overwhelming majority that will increase during the twenty-first century.

This development raises fundamental questions about the character of the church, its mission, its theological emphases, structures, understandings of the world, and relationships between its member churches, perhaps unequaled since the early centuries of the Christian movement. The global character of the church is itself an important development for a religion that theologically has affirmed the oneness of the human community but structurally has either been regional or national in character and consciousness. Moreover, the global church of the third millennium of Christianity is coming to consciousness as a church of the poor, anchored in the suffering, struggles, and needs of those who live amid poverty, economic injustice, or political oppression. Within this global community mission is no longer solely a "one-way enterprise," directed from Western churches to Asia, Africa, and Latin America, but has become a more balanced and equal partnership between the former missionary-sending churches and the now-independent churches they helped to establish.

This global Christian community challenges theology and mission to function within a more universal context. Just as the oneness and interconnectedness of all people have increasingly become an economic, political, and environmental reality, faith within a world church has to recognize the responsibility of Christians for the destiny and future of God's creation and the welfare of all of God's people. A document entitled *Kairos Central America: A Challenge to the Churches of the World*, based on biblical and theological reflection on the political situation in their region by Central American Christian leaders, states the matter clearly:

> It is no longer possible to be a Christian shut up in the narrow confines of one's own community, or country. Today the only way to be consistent in our Christianity is to be taken seriously our historical responsibility with regard to our world neighbors. The cosmos is our home. The world is our family. The peoples are our neighbor. The world is our responsibility (1988, 102).

To be Christian from a global perspective is to be poor and at risk. In global power terms, it is to return to a status akin to that of Christians in the early centuries of the church.

The Challengers

Two-Thirds World Christians struggling to find their own voice, formulate their own models, and articulate their own theologies have provided a new source of energy and dynamism, fundamentally transforming what it means to be Christian. By shaping and expressing an understanding of the gospel and the role of the church from the perspective of the poor, they have recovered the prophetic trajectory in Christianity. By conceptualizing the gospel as a message about saving the world, not just individuals, they have helped focus on the promise and task of redeeming the whole of the human community with its political structures and economic and social arrangements. By identifying Western church structures and theologies as products of a particular culture, they have stripped them of their pretenses to be universally normative. By giving voice to the needs and aspirations of the millions of Christians hitherto on the periphery of the consciousness of American churches, they have challenged these denominations to a more inclusive and sensitive conception of mission. By vesting Christianity with more evangelical fervor and greater relevance to the great issues of the day, they may be contributing to a global Christian revival movement.

The inclusive, egalitarian, destabilizing vision of Two-Thirds World Christians, however, has met with some of the same opposition as did the ministry it perhaps best approximates, the Jesus movement/community. Contemporary equivalents of the Pharisees, Sadducees, and Roman governors ensconced in the Vatican, Western churches, White House, and conservative think tanks have responded to this theological threat to the status quo in much the same way as their predecessors, labeling Christian proponents of change unacceptable, deviants, revolutionaries, and cryptocommunists. An alliance between a conservative pope and the largely reactionary Curia intent on restoring central control and conformity to a narrowly interpreted dogma has threatened innovations in global Catholicism that had made the church more responsive and relevant to situations of poverty and oppression. Conservative political forces intent on maintaining the global balance of power and privilege have identified exponents of liberation theology, black theology, feminist theology, and the church of the poor as a radical challenge and responded by conducting a form of low-intensity conflict against them. Such groups as the neoconservative Institute for Religion and Democracy and the Ethics and Public Policy Center exist primarily for the very purpose of attacking progressive Two-Thirds World churches and their supporters within the mainline denominations. Typically, they categorize any theological critique of the current order as a distortion and politicization of the gospel, insinuating that Marx and Lenin, not Jesus Christ, are their sources of inspiration. Neoconservative writers also impugn the ability of these Christians to speak on behalf of the poor, suggesting that capitalism is more responsive to their needs (see, for example, Weigel 1989, 65–67).

A Global Appeal to Mainline Churches

Staff and members of mainline churches who have participated in ecumenical meetings or who have spent time overseas relating to Two-Thirds World churches frequently begin to view theological, ecclesiological, and social issues through new lenses and adopt a more global perspective. As the situation of the poor and oppressed becomes a more definite priority, they become aware of the First World biases shaping many of their assumptions about religion, the church, and the world. In such a context it no longer seems legitimate to evaluate the morality and efficacy of policy and institutions in terms of the benefits that accrue to those already privileged. An analysis of injustice and poverty in structural terms often sensitizes First World Christians to the extent to which policies of their own governments disadvantage the poor and are in some cases a contributing factor in pervasive oppression.

The creation of a new kind of global Christian community in which mainline Protestant churches become equal participants rather than senior partners, attuned to the experiences, needs, and suffering of the churches in Africa, Asia, and Latin America, has had major implications for political ministries. Many Two-Thirds World churches operate within very unjust and oppressive situations in which religious bodies constitute one of the few sources of independence and effective opposition to dehumanizing conditions. The magnitude of the injustice, violence, and poverty has led church leaders in many of these countries to acknowledge that they are living amid a *kairos*, described variously as a moment of truth or emergency, that makes special demands on the church. Heeding the cries of their people, courageous religious leaders have engaged in strenuous efforts to bring about systemic changes through political ministries, often at great risk. As Archbishop Romero of El Salvador once commented, "Religion held with deep conviction leads to political involvement and tends to create conflicts in a country like ours where there is a crying need for social justice" (quoted in Sobrino 1988, 81). But these appeals for justice and reform are often met by violence. The assassinations of Archbishop Romero and many less well known Christians in other Two-Thirds World countries; frequent imprisonment of religious leaders in South Africa, the Philippines, and South Korea; mass disappearances of lay leaders in many Central American countries; "salvaging" of church members in the Philippines; severe restrictions on the operations of church agencies in El Salvador and elsewhere; accusations of communist inclinations directed at church human rights ministries chronicling abuses by the military and government forces in other countries — these are some of the penalties imposed on churches and their leaders when they demand change.

Two-Thirds World Christians are sustained in their initiatives for freedom and justice by deep faith and by support from churches in other parts of the world. Political involvement for these Christians often constitutes an expression of spirituality and discipleship to a God of peace, justice, and liberation. Their hope, not optimism, that God's kingdom of righteousness will eventually overcome the principalities and powers, inspires their efforts. This is evident in a collection of the meditations of Dom Helder Camara, for twenty-five years the archbishop of Olinda and Recife in northeastern Brazil, the poorest and least developed region of the country. His ministry on behalf of the poor and oppressed resulted in one ostensible defeat after another, and his *Hoping Against All Hope* expresses the faith at its source:

> Hope without risk
> is not hope,
> which is believing
> in risky loving,
> trusting others
> in the dark,
> in the blind leap
> letting God take over.
> (Camara 1984, 4)

Archbishop Desmond Tutu's statement to the Eloff Commission investigating the political role of the South African Council of Churches when he served as its general secretary provides a second important example. The South African government threatened to disband the South African Council of Churches and silence the witness of the church. The archbishop responded by reminding his government inquisitors that

> God's purposes are certain. They may remove a Tutu; they may re-move the South African Council of Churches, but God's intention to establish His Kingdom of justice, of love, of compassion, will not be thwarted. We are not scared, certainly not of the Government, or any other perpetrators of injustice and oppression, for victory is ours through Him who loved us (1983, 188–89).

Such situations of risk and suffering often prompt Two-Thirds World churches to appeal to churches in other parts of the world for assistance. In contrast to past generations, when requests for aid from overseas churches were primarily for money and personnel, embattled Two-Thirds World churches are now likely to request political initiatives. This is particularly the case in the relationship with the American churches because of the decisive role of United States foreign policy in supporting many of the political regimes oppressing these Christians. In responding, the mainline churches serve as the agent or political proxy of their partners, representing their plight to the American people and government and calling for policy changes or interventions on their behalf. This role has given rise to a new activism in foreign policy advocacy by many mainline churches, based on an agenda shaped by the priorities and needs of other churches within the global Christian community.

Four types of initiatives exemplify the process by which the global church expresses its recognition that a suffering church has a moral and political claim on the whole body of Christ.

1. North American church and human rights organizations have learned from experience that a quick response to human rights violations can be critical. Immediate recognition and condemnation of the arrests and disappearances of Two-Thirds World church leaders, pastors, and lay workers, and appeals for due process or release, often determine whether such prisoners or victims disappear permanently, are severely tortured, or are treated in a more responsible way. The sense of a worldwide community monitoring the situation may also deter or reduce the incidence of such abuses. This has led to the formation of many formal and informal human rights networks through which persecuted churches can relay critical information about human rights violations to partner churches, knowing that these denominations and ecumenical organizations will respond quickly with appeals to the responsible governments or to the United States government to intervene. Such networks have functioned between churches and ecumenical organizations in South Africa, Namibia, Chile, the Philippines, El Salvador, and other countries, as well as various denominations and ecumenical organizations. The Human Rights Office of the National Council of Churches, a critical point for monitoring abuses and alerting relevant staff in member denominations, for example, has links to more than one hundred human rights organizations operating in Two-Thirds World countries and Eastern Europe. Once such urgent-action messages are received, the counterpart peace, justice, and human rights networks within several of the denominations forward appeals for action to members. In a severe emergency, ecumenical or denominational delegations also visit the disturbed area as an act of solidarity. The hope is that their presence will be a source of protection for endangered churches. On one such mission to El Salvador during a period of heightened repression in early 1990, I was told by several church leaders that the urgent-action response of the American churches during the preceding months had saved many lives. The delegation's very presence in El Salvador, according to a Salvadoran cleric, represented for him the reality of the global Christian community.

2. Another type of political witness occurs when, in response to appeals by endangered churches, the American church constituency offers prayers, moral support, and mobilization to assist them. One such example is the Stand for Truth Campaign mounted by American churches in the spring of 1989 in response to the escalating attacks on the South African religious community and the urgent appeals by South African church leaders for support. In February 1988 the South African government outlawed seventeen major democratic organizations, including the Congress of South African Trade Unions and the United Democratic Front. Churches immediately challenged the bannings and marched on Parliament in Cape Town. That action marked a new phase in church resistance to apartheid, prompting heightened repression and persecution. The headquarters of both the South African Council of Churches and the Southern African Catholic Bishops Conference were destroyed, even larger numbers of church staff and ministers were detained, and assassinations of key church leaders were attempted. To respond to requests by the South African church, major Protestant denominations, several evangelical organizations, and the United States Catholic Conference formed a South Africa Crisis Coordinating Committee to build spiritual union and solidarity between local congregations in the United States and the church and people of South Africa through prayer, reflection, and study. A campaign beginning on Pentecost Sunday then led to two days of lobbying, worship, and witness in favor of comprehensive economic sanctions in commemoration of the thirteenth anniversary of the Soweto massacre in mid-June. Supported by churches throughout the world, the Stand for Truth Campaign in South Africa went on to become a major factor sparking the possibility of meaningful change in that country.

3. A third type of initiative relates to appeals from Two-Thirds World churches to religious bodies, asking them to seek changes in United States foreign policies that are harming their countries. Such requests reflect the trust and sense of partnership on both sides of the relationship in pursuing God's peace and justice, an energizing and inspiring bond that I have had the privilege to experience. These appeals for action come in a variety of ways: through pastoral letters and other formal statements by church bodies; through bilateral, ecumenical, or informal consultations between American and overseas churches; through letters, cables, and faxes. The advent of fax technology particularly has enabled frequent and rapid communication between church institutions across the continents. They are most valuable in sensitive situations, because such messages are less likely to be intercepted by oppressive political regimes. Sometimes the requests are very specific and direct. At other times they deal with the general direction and impact of United States foreign policy in a particular area. In times of crisis the flow of cables, faxes, and letters permits a high degree of international coordination and collaboration.

These direct ties with suffering religious communities, as well as the ethical nature of the issues, account for the keener focus on these communities and the energy many denominations have invested in opposing the United States' foreign policies. Major efforts have been expended particularly to protest U.S. foreign policy in Central America, including frequent delegations to Nicaragua and El Salvador, mailings to church members, coordinated lobbying in Washington, marches, rallies, prayer vigils, and occasional civil disobedience. South Africa has been the second focus of intense congressional lobbying, constituent mobilization, and campaigns to put pressure on corporations and banks to withdraw from South Africa and cut their ties with the apartheid regime. Persistent appeals from churches in the Philippines, South Korea, and Chile have been relayed to policy makers through mainline denominations. They petition the United States to reduce support and/or military assistance to those repressive regimes that violate human rights and to provide economic rather than military aid. Mobilization of church constituencies has also occurred on a number of global economic issues. To respond more effectively, several of the denominations have developed justice, peace, and human rights networks.

Although the churches have not transformed United States foreign policy, they have played a significant role in selective issues. Studies indicate that religious groups are viewed by House members as key sources of information on foreign policy issues (Hertzke 1988, 113). The mainline churches' international connections have enabled them to become one of the most effective foreign policy peace and justice lobbies in Washington speaking on behalf of a global constituency. The churches, more than any other group, restrained military intervention in Central America and mobilized opposition to military aid. In the case of South Africa, church initiatives have been significant in sustaining the antiapartheid movement, developing support for economic sanctions legislation, campaigning for corporate withdrawal, and supporting passage of municipal and state regulations that penalize corporations operating in South Africa.

4. Another approach has been to hold ecumenical forums and bilateral church meetings to explore jointly major problems and consider ways to address them. There have been, for example, at the request of the National Council of Churches in Korea, a series of dialogues with member churches in the National Council of Churches in the United States and the Canadian Council of Churches to discuss peace, democratization, and reunification of the Korean peninsula. Complementing these initiatives, there have been denominational partnerships dealing with peace and justice issues. The World Council of Churches has also played a central role in widening these deliberations to the global Christian community, which has included their sponsoring a major consultation in Korea that was one of the first public meetings to address reunification. In the absence of other channels, the World Council of Churches has also been instrumental in facilitating contacts between churches in North and South Korea.

Increasingly, Two-Thirds World Christians evaluate the nature of their relationships with First World churches in terms of the response to such requests. *The Road to Damascus* (1989), for example, makes explicit this linkage. It states that Christians in the seven countries represented by the writing group (El Salvador, Guatemala, Korea, Namibia, Nicaragua, the Philippines, and South Africa) will assess the faithfulness of First World sisters and brothers in terms of whether they support efforts to create a more just world. Writing within the context of a perceived *kairos*, or moment of crisis, the Damascus theologians identify a fundamental conflict between Christians who side with imperialists, oppressors, and exploiters, and Christians who follow the true gospel of Jesus Christ. They challenge First World Christians to elect solidarity with the true God, the God of the poor who is angry about injustice in the world, through commitment to Jesus' mission of liberation to the downtrodden.

Just as in the case of disestablishment, mainline denominations have made only a partial adjustment from First World dominance to partnership within the global Christian community. The development of a global Christian fellowship, one of the most visible signs of God's presence and activity in the world today, has barely touched the institutional life and membership of mainline churches. The division of labor in mainline polities that places overseas mission activity almost exclusively within national agencies means that staff and directors of these agencies have been the primary actors involved with these global relationships. Political advocacy initiatives educating and mobilizing significant church constituencies have been the major exception in reaching out to a cross section of members. Commitments to support Two-Thirds World church leaders' struggles for human rights, freedom, and democratization have been translated into political ministries directed at governments and multilateral agencies. Yet rarely have they resulted in a meaningful sharing or redistribution of resources from First to Two-Thirds World churches or in greater participation by Two-Thirds World partners in decision making in mainline church institutions. The El Escorial Consultation, held in 1987 and sponsored by the World Council of Churches, envisioned a discipline of ecumenical sharing in the church and the world in which the global Christian community become "members of one body, bearing one another's burdens and sharing together in God's gift of life for all" (World Council of Churches 1989, 27) That vision remains elusive.

DEFENDING GOD'S CREATION: THE RENEWAL OF JUSTICE AND PEACE MINISTRIES

Future generations may look back on the 1980s as a time of *kairos* for the global church and for the American church in particular. *The Kairos Document*, written by a group of South African lay leaders and theologians, opens with these words:

> The time has come. The moment of truth has arrived. South Africa has been plunged into a crisis that is shaking the foundations and there is every indication that the crisis has only begun and that it will deepen

and become even more threatening in the months to come. It is the KAIROS or moment of truth not only for apartheid but also for the Church and all other faiths and religions (Kairos Theologians 1986).

Their statement has broad applicability beyond South Africa. In the global Christian fellowship a moment of *kairos* for one part of the community is shared by all. But beyond the challenge posed by the apartheid system in South Africa and other situations of extreme injustice in the Two-Thirds World, many churches have begun to wrestle with their fundamental responsibility for preserving God's creation and providing all members of the human community with the basic necessities of life. In confronting the darkening valley of potential nuclear destruction, First World Christians have come face-to-face with the realities of the principalities and powers in much the same way as Two-Thirds World Christians when dealing with dehumanizing systemic injustice and poverty. Speaking God's word of life in the midst of administrations obsessed with instruments of death has recast political ministries in a more prophetic role. This has emboldened some of the mainline churches and the United States Catholic Conference to begin to deal with other fundamental issues of structural injustice.

Ironically, it was the Reagan administration's policies, more than any other factor, that called forth this religious renewal. The Reagan regime's inclinations toward a more militaristic and interventionist foreign policy reawakened the religious peace movement, just as its strategic option on behalf of the affluent engendered stronger faith-based concern with the ethical implications of economic policies. Although the world had lived with the possibility of annihilation since the advent of nuclear weapons, the seemingly cavalier attitudes of the Reagan administration vested the unthinkable with a greater plausibility. Suddenly the very future of the creation and the prospects of future generations seemed threatened. By advocating the possibilities of fighting and winning a nuclear war, the Reagan government brought churches, as well as other groups, to confront the fate of the earth. In diverting massive resources from welfare benefits and productive investments into a new arms race, the administration challenged churches to express its solidarity with the poor. By seeking to subvert independent Two-Thirds World governments while supporting so-called friendly authoritarian regimes, it precipitated a more activist foreign policy advocacy on the part of the religious community.

The Call for Change

The perceived threat to the future of creation and to the dignity of persons inspired major Protestant denominations and the Catholic Church in the United States to delve within to revitalize and recast peace and justice ministries. Of less importance in the 1970s, peace and justice issues became a priority in the 1980s. Development of public theologies addressing these issues was one response. The intensification of public policy advocacy, sometimes in the name of the denomination, was another. A willingness to begin to address structural issues and to evaluate the adequacy of institutions as well as policies was a third. In several denominations the call for public policy changes was part and parcel of a reexamination of church programs and structures to consider making them more consistent with the demands of a God of peace and justice.

The writing of a series of pastoral letters on peace and economics represents a major turning point in the political witness of the churches. Such pastoral letters have precedents, particularly in the hundred-year history of the social encyclicals of the Catholic Church. Nevertheless, their timing, crisis orientation, public processes of formulation, and relatively radical policy recommendations provide them with a special character. In some ways the systematic biblical foundation, the empirical analysis, and the detailed public policy proposals of the United States Catholic Conferences' pastorals on peace and the economy have more in common methodologically with some of the Protestant documents than with papal encyclicals. The similarities between the major Protestant and Catholic papers demonstrates that since Vatican II the Catholic Church has become a full partner in ecumenical discussions — although not yet fully participant in ecumenical organizations — in the United States.

The Peace Pastorals

The 1980s, the decade of the peace and economic pastorals, opened with the adoption of a major report by the 192nd Presbyterian General Assembly in 1980 entitled *Peacemaking: The Believer's Calling* that reassesses the concept of peacemaking and the direction of United States foreign policy in light of a biblical and confessional faith and a markedly changed situation in the world. In 1980 the Tenth Biennial Convention of the Lutheran Church in America also approved a major policy statement *Economic Justice: Stewardship of Creation in Human Community* (Tenth Biennial Convention of the Lutheran Church in America 1980). However, it was the decision of the National Conference of Catholic Bishops to appoint a committee of five bishops, chosen to represent a diversity of opinions, to draft an encyclical letter on peace that marked the turning point in the public character of the pastorals. The bishops' drafting committee held a series of fourteen public meetings to interview a broad spectrum of specialists, including theologians, political scientists, and government officials, with very diverse views. They issued two intermediate drafts, each with a request for comments and criticisms. Responses to the first draft alone amounted to some seven hundred pages. The second and third draft revisions reflected some of the reactions to the first draft. This public process culminated in a meeting of the entire body of bishops to revise and approve the final draft in May 1983. Commenting on this remarkable initiative, the ethicist Roger Shinn notes that "never before in the history of the US had a church body developed a social policy with so much public participation and attention" (1988, 225). Although the Protestant denominations did not have the resources to mount as elaborate a process or the ability to command as much attention, they too appointed committees representing diverse perspectives, held hearings (although more likely to be denominational in character), disseminated drafts for response (again, more often within their constituencies), and sometimes voted final texts in their highest judicatory bodies.

Entitled *The Challenge of Peace: God's Promise and Our Response*, the Catholic Bishops' peace pastoral opens with an acknowledgement that the world is at a moment of crisis because nuclear war threatens the existence of the planet. The bishops explain that the nuclear age is an era of moral as well as physical danger. Ours is the first generation since Genesis with the power to virtually destroy God's creation (1983, par. 3). Writing from the perspective of the Catholic faith, the bishops consider the letter as an exercise of their teaching ministry. According to the bishops, Catholic teaching on peace and war has two purposes: to help Catholics form their consciences and to contribute to the public policy debate about the morality of war, and to address the wider civil community, that is, members of other religious communities and all people of good will who make up the polity (1983, par. 16).

Other denominations — the United Church of Christ (General Synod of the United Church of Christ 1985), the Presbyterians (General Assembly Presbyterian Church (U.S.A.) 1980; 1988), the Methodists (United Methodist Council of Bishops 1986), and the Lutheran Church in America (Twelfth Biennial Convention of the Lutheran Church in America 1984) among others — also wrote major theological documents that underscore the discrepancy between the faith vision of *shalom* and the assumptions of current public policy. Like the Catholic bishops, they begin with a sense of urgency and emergency. The United Methodist Council of Bishops, for example, whose document *In Defense of Creation* was published in 1986, states that confronted with "the darkening shadows of a threatening nuclear winter" they have risen to the defense of the creation — all of the creation, "air and water, trees and fruits and flowers, birds and fish and cattle, all children and youth, women and men" (1986, 11). There is a consensus among the drafters of these statements that the possibility of devastating nuclear exchanges and the overwhelming destructiveness of even conventional weapons require fundamentally new approaches to issues of war and peace. Each of them rejects the use of nuclear war and nuclear weapons. Like the Catholic bishops', the Protestant peace pastorals question the morality of deterrence theory, reject just-war theory as inapplicable to the realities of nuclear war, and condemn a military-based economy devoted to destruction and death. *In Defense of Creation* argues that the moral case for deterrence, even as an interim ethic, has been undermined by an unrelenting arms escalation, by the license it provides for perpetual hostility between the superpowers, and by the contradiction between the assumed rationality of decision makers and the absolute terror of annihilation. In its place the Methodist bishops articulate an ethic of reciprocity shaped by a vision of common security that would result in states acting together in agreed stages to eliminate their nuclear weapons (1986, 14–15). The Protestant documents also tend to condemn any first use of nuclear weapons, endorse a halt in manufacture and deployment of such weapons, and call for international negotiations leading to nuclear disarmament. Several support independent initiatives to promote trust and facilitate disarmament.

The various peace pastorals affirm the role of the church as peace maker, identifying at least four major dimensions. The first is to articulate a biblical vision and ethical principles and perspectives on peace to members of their denominations, society, and policy makers, and thereby to transform the terms of the debate on policy issues. Second, convinced that decisions on these issues go beyond military and political considerations and involve fundamental moral choices, the pastorals call for a moral transformation. The Catholic bishops' pastoral letter on war and peace, for instance, concludes with a ringing call to conversion. Third, and following from the dimensions described above, the pastorals state that the church has the responsibility, indeed the obligation, to draw policy implications from biblical and ethical teachings. Several denominations, the Methodists and the United Church of Christ in particular, go beyond expressing policy alternatives to call on members to organize and advocate promotion of these positions. Fourth, besides calling on the churches and their members to work for peace, the pastorals also underscore the importance of the churches serving as an alternative community to model the principles of peace to the world. The pronouncement "Affirming the United Church of Christ as a Just Peace Church" and the accompanying study documents, for instance, discuss the transformation of the church as well as public policy initiatives (Thistlethwaite 1986).

Although the various peace pastorals question fundamental assumptions underlying foreign and military policy, and by doing so place the mainline Protestant denominations and the U.S. Catholic Conference on the cutting edge of policy debates, they do not offer a comprehensive peace theology or challenge conventional assumptions about the nature of war and peace. Their biblical analysis and theological principles in regard to the nature of peace are applied primarily to nuclear policy and to the arms race, not to the full range of ethical policy issues determining whether contemporary societies choose life or death, blessing or curse. They fail to go beyond the destructive symptoms to challenge the national security state orientation that gave rise to nuclear terror and the obsession with instruments of death. Only two, the United Church of Christ (General Synod of the United Church of Christ 1985) and the Methodist Church (United Methodist Council of Bishops 1986, 40), call for the elimination of war as an instrument of national policy. Despite the consensus that just-war criteria are not applicable in a nuclear age, the documents basically accept the validity of the just-war approach. Although they flirt with nuclear pacifism, they do not find pacifism or active nonviolence a potential inspiration for a new theological orientation relevant to the main body of Christians. Nor do they advocate heroic or unconventional responses to the *kairos* of nuclear destruction. For example, after an extensive study process within the denomination of a document encouraging nonviolent resistance as an instrument of peacemaking in the nuclear age, the Presbyterian General Assembly approved a policy statement that recommends respect and emotional support for individual or congregational initiatives, but does not encourage them (1988, 26–27).

The Economic Pastorals

As paeans to capitalism became virtual idolatry of the market, and tax reforms and economic policies of the Reagan administration became the functional equivalent of a strategic option on behalf of the rich, the various economic pastorals followed. These public theologies of economics, each the product of an independent denominational initiative, appear to be a response to four factors. First, a severe recession in the early 1980s significantly increased unemployment and poverty, the burden falling disproportionately on racial minorities, women, and children. During the recovery later in the decade, economic growth primarily benefited the already affluent, reinforcing and aggravating the gap between the rich and poor. Second, policies of the Reagan administration that redistributed income in favor of the already affluent and weakened or eliminated the so-called safety net protecting the poor and vulnerable appeared to abrogate the New Deal social contract that committed the state to institute progressive social welfare legislation and to promote the common good of all sectors of society. The Reagan rhetoric of blaming the victims and extolling the virtues of untrammeled free enterprise further challenged the religious community to respond. Third, a series of crises in the global economic system undermined the economic prospects of most poor countries and underscored the absence of effective international mechanisms or institutions for resolving common problems. As the gap between degrading poverty and dazzling wealth became ever more pronounced and Two-Thirds World debtor countries in Africa and Latin America experienced significant losses in income and living standards which took a terrible toll in human suffering, the religious community was propelled to connect its faith heritage to global economic trends. Fourth, the visibility of poverty and suffering shown so clearly by the mass media of our time, made it even more imperative that the religious community not remain silent. As the homeless wandered American streets and sought shelter in public buildings, it became difficult to sustain the argument that economic growth would resolve the problems of poverty. The specter of famine and death in Africa recorded by television cameras gave silent voice to the "least of these," the brothers and sisters with whom Jesus so closely identified. And once again the conscience of the church was confronted by a Savior who warned in the parable of the great judgment: As you do not feed the hungry, shelter the homeless, welcome the stranger, minister to the infirm, "truly I tell you, just as you did not do it to one of the least of these, you did not do it to me" (Matt. 25:45).

Although some of the Protestant denominations' statements on the economy came earlier, the Catholic Bishops' *Economic Justice for All* (National Conference of Catholic Bishops 1986) again received the most attention. As its drafting committee held public hearings and the bishops debated various drafts, the religious community changed the dynamic of the public debate on economic policy. The Catholic efforts were paralleled or followed by independent initiatives in many Protestant churches, including the United Church of Christ (Chapman [Smock] 1987; General Synod of the United Church of Christ 1989), the Episcopal Urban Bishops (1987), and both the Northern (Advisory Council on Church and Society 1985) and Southern Presbyterians (Office of the General Assembly 1984) prior to the reunification of the denomination, all of which sought to reinstitute moral and religious concerns in an economic system seemingly captive to the tyranny of economic forces. The Christian Church (Disciples of Christ) also issued a study paper on the impact of economic systems on the Two-Thirds World (1987).

Grounded in a faith vision, the various economic pastorals typically review and analyze major scriptural passages emphasizing God's concern for economic justice and people's accountability for the economic dimensions of their lives. Many focus on themes in

Jesus' ministry — his announcement that he had come to bring good news to the poor, his identification with and ministry to the poor and exploited, his demanding teachings on wealth and poverty, his sharp criticisms of exploitation and indifference to suffering. From these broad biblical mandates, they frequently draw a set of middle-level axioms or principles of economic justice. These biblical lenses are then used to evaluate contemporary economic institutions and policies and to recommend reforms to enable these systems to conform more closely to biblical norms.

There is considerable diversity among these pastorals' specific foci and formulations, yet there is also a striking similarity in the articulation of Christian principles of economic justice. Most specify that a faith-centered economics has a special responsibility to the poor, the weak, and the people at the margins of society. Many emphasize the importance of community and the need for economic systems to promote and sustain such communities. The concept of human rights and freedom articulated in these documents is broad, citing economic as well as civil or political rights as essential to maintain the dignity of human life. The Episcopal bishops' biblical test of the justice of any economic system, for example, is whether it affirms every person's "divine right" of access to a reasonable and nutritious diet, decent shelter, adequate medical care, freedom of worship, and the opportunity to participate in shaping the society in which he or she is placed, equipped with sufficient education and training to do so (1987, 2). Concerned to protect the integrity and viability of the creation, several of the pastorals underscore the responsibility of contemporary societies to protect the interests of future generations. Many stress the need for participation and inclusiveness in both the economic and political systems and point toward fundamental reforms to establish greater economic democracy.

Several of these documents attempt to reconceptualize economics. Identifying the term economics from its two Greek roots as "the law or management of the household," a United Church of Christ study paper, *Christian Faith and Economic Life*, states that economics in scripture and Christian tradition, far from being confined to the allocation of scarce resources or the analysis of prices and wages, "relates to the management of the household, God's household of creation and the household of the human community." It goes on to remind members of the denomination that "among Christians the sphere of economic concerns encompasses issues central to the well-being of the individual, the integrity of the community, and human faithfulness to God's intentions and mandates" (Chapman [Smock] 1987, 4). The Catholic bishops similarly remind their readers that "every perspective on economic life that is human, moral, and Christian must be shaped by three questions: What does the economy do *for* people? What does it do *to* people? And how do people *participate* in it?" (1986, par. 1).

In issuing a call to personal and societal conversion, the churches stress that the pursuit of greater economic justice constitutes a faith imperative. The Presbyterian Church's *Christian Faith and Economic Justice*, for example, states that "as Christians we are called to look at the economy and at particular economic systems and situations not only in light of the economic data and analyses available to us, but also in light of God's promise to establish justice on earth and the divine demand that we seek and do justice in our common life" (Office of the General Assembly 1984, 19). These various public theologies of economics also recognize that the church has a special responsibility and role in this effort to expand the life opportunities of the poor and oppressed and to transform economic systems to better reflect biblical norms of economic justice. As noted in the United Church of Christ study paper, "The church and its members have the right, indeed the obligation to serve as God's instruments in identifying injustices and calling on society to conform better to God's intentions" (Chapman [Smock] 1987, 420).

The restoration and revitalization of the biblical and theological mandate has reoriented these churches to pursue an economic justice measured by the treatment of the poor and disadvantaged, and not the aspirations of the middle class or the affluent. Refocusing on the poor leads to a devastating critique of current economic policies, but less often to an examination of the underlying structures that produce and sustain poverty. Most of the economic pastorals note the persistence of significant poverty in the United States even in times of relative prosperity. They express concern and sometimes outrage about the increasing gaps between the poor and the rich, the growing concentration of wealth, and the lessening of society's commitment to support and assist its least fortunate members in this country. Many of the pastorals point out that far from being shared equitably, the burden of poverty falls disproportionately on blacks, Hispanics, Native Americans, women who head households, and children, and draw conclusions about patterns of institutional discrimination. And they do more than just analyze data. Various economic pastorals engage in what the Episcopal Bishops describe as the prophetic responsibility to become "a conscious channel for God's judging word on those societal arrangements and economic decisions that cause pain and injustice" (Episcopal House of Bishops 1987, 11).

Awareness of the desperate situation of some of the poor and the massive dimensions of the problem result in the churches' recommending major public policy initiatives. The Catholic Bishops have developed proposals to overhaul the social welfare system and create full employment. The Episcopal Bishops call for an expansion and reform of income supports and an improvement in public-sector delivery of human services. The United Church of Christ advocates adoption of an economic bill of rights that will provide a national guaranteed minimum income level, ensuring every person access to adequate food, clothing, and shelter.

Reflecting the increasing global perspective of these churches, many of the economic pastorals consider the nature of economic relations within the international economy. Several undertake an analysis of global economic trends, finding the increasing gap between the desperate poverty of the majority of people in the world and the affluence of the advanced industrial economies to be deeply disturbing. Aware of the existing technological ability to eliminate hunger and poverty, they fault the developed countries, particularly the United States, for failing to do more. Some refer to the discrepancy between the ability and willingness to alleviate suffering as a moral outrage. They note the precipitous decline in living standards and per capita incomes in African and Latin American countries as a result of expenditures for debt servicing and repayment. *Economic Justice for All* acknowledges that interdependency in the global economy translates into dependence for developing countries (National Conference of Catholic Bishops 1986, 122). Most of the papers that deal with the global economic system advocate major policy reforms to improve the terms and conditions of trade for Two-Thirds World countries, increase availability of finance on more favorable terms, reduce their debt burdens, and improve access to technology and resources needed for development. A few go beyond these measures to call for global economic institutions that will better reflect a shared sense of responsibility toward all members of the human community and facilitate initiatives to resolve common problems.

Although the economic pastorals represent a major contribution toward a prophetic witness, they also have limitations. To begin with, they illustrate the strengths and weaknesses of drafting theology through a committee process reflecting the pluralistic character of the mainline denominations and Catholic church. In the case of several of the Protestant denominations, drafting committees representing a wide spectrum of backgrounds and/or ideological positions were deliberately chosen in an effort to be representative of the diversity of the church. The dynamics of such a committee inclined it toward compromise rather than coherence or insightfulness. The drafting and study processes, often several years in length, had the advantage of facilitating debates within major constituencies of the various churches. That the churches followed such a participatory process and encouraged reflection and reformulation undoubtedly provided greater exposure for the issue and stronger standing for the documents when they were finalized (Blank and Chapman 1989). As often happens within these churches, however, the complex multiyear study processes also activated many groups with greatly varying interests and views. The intensity of the debates and emotional reactions to the economic pastorals was at a considerably higher pitch than those produced by the peace pastorals, suggesting that they challenged members in a far more personal way. In some cases these discussions clarified positions and led to consensus on critical issues. The very effort to be inclusive and responsive, however, also meant that the final drafts incorporated many perspectives. A section written to satisfy one constituency or set of needs may be inconsistent with or even contradict another.

The economic pastorals also tend to respond to structural problems with inadequate public policy approaches. Like other initiatives in the political ministries of mainline churches, the documents concentrate more on short-term policy changes through legislative instruments rather than long-term transformation of economic institutions or systems. Although the analysis in several of the documents acknowledges the structural nature of the problems with which they are dealing, when it comes to proposals they fall back to moderate and discrete public policy changes. This tendency to focus on short- or medium-term public policy initiatives unfortunately diverts attention from the fundamental issues of ethics and justice being raised. It also means that there is a major imbalance between the categorical nature of the faith mandates presented, the urgency of the situation, and the moderation of the proposed solutions. As Paul Camendisch notes,

> Seldom do the proposals for change seem congruent with the radical character of the gospel challenge or with the disturbing descriptions of massive human suffering arising from hunger and malnutrition, and from unemployment, much less with the descriptions, sometimes bordering on the apocalyptic, of the numbers of children living in poverty. If such profound problems do not call for an alternative economic system, one would at least expect proposals for significant changes in the existing one, some plan for altering the motivating spirit of present structures, or, at the very least, an analysis suggesting that the present problems are aberrations in a system that can and should be set right. But these are not forthcoming (1987, 72).

As noted in the previous chapter, the lack of a strategic orientation characterizes much of the churches' political ministry. The pastorals were a response to the escalating policy outrages of the Reagan administration, but not a commitment to embark on a long-term effort toward major economic changes. Once they were issued, little activity followed, either within the church or within the public policy arena, to maximize their impact. Most of the church advocacy in Washington on economic issues, in fact, proceeded as if the pastorals had never been written. At best the pastorals became efforts to introduce another voice into the public policy debate, but certainly not blueprints for mobilizing denominational constituencies, empowering poor and marginalized communities, or transforming the world to make it more consistent with biblical vision of economic justice.

Although the economic pastorals generally recognize that economic justice has three levels or dimensions of concern — individual faithfulness and lifestyle, the economy of the congregation or of the church, and public policy — the balance is heavily skewed toward public policy. There is, too, an apparent reticence in applying the principles of economic justice, as identified in the documents, to the life of the church. *Economic Justice for All*, for example, devotes 20 paragraphs out of 365 to the challenges to the church.

The text on the church as an economic actor states that "all the moral principles that govern the just operation of any economic endeavor apply to the Church and its agencies and its institutions; indeed the Church should be exemplary" (National Conference of Catholic Bishops 1986, par. 347), but it never deals with the contradictions between the norms of justice and participation stated in the document, and the structure and practices of the Catholic Church. The United Church of Christ's pronouncement on "Christian Faith: Economic Life and Justice" constitutes the major exception to these trends. Its Proposal for Action, approximately half as long as the pronouncement it accompanies, focuses on the economy of the church, but the failure to invest meaningful resources or staff time raises questions about the denomination's inclination to implement the proposals (General Synod of the United Church of Christ 1989).

Few of the churches, Catholic or Protestant, have mounted serious efforts to disseminate or implement the pastorals. Far more time, energy, and attention was vested in the writing process than in promotion of finished products. This may reflect a dissipation of interest, the sense of urgency and commitment waning over the years. It is also undoubtedly related to the patterns of political ministry noted in the previous chapter; mainline churches characteristically tend to focus on word rather than deed, policy formulation over action. The result has been that the economic pastorals, like the peace pastorals, have not received the considered attention in their own churches that might have enabled them to become instruments of religious renewal. Only the U.S. Catholic Conference has invested a major sum to prepare study resources and develop a network of economic pastoral educators. Yet although their several hundred thousand dollars is considerable when compared with the absence of budgets for this purpose in most Protestant denominations, it is certainly insufficient for the task of truly reaching the people in the pews. Like many other public policy statements prepared by mainline churches, the pastorals by default have become the property of staff and small activist constituencies. As the decade closes there is a growing possibility that the documents and the peace and justice vocation they embody may become forgotten or discarded as preoccupation with the relocation of denominational headquarters and restructuring of denominational and ecumenical institutions draws energy away from these commitments.

In the final analysis, the consensus in the pastorals on the faith-mandated option for the poor is never translated into a program for enabling the predominantly white middle-class denominations and churches for which they are written to join in solidarity with the poor or for empowering the poor to take control of their own destinies. As documents written almost entirely for and by those who are privileged by the current economic order, they rightfully state the need for conversion and commitment to change, even at the risk of forfeiting economic advantages. Yet they fail to detail the lifestyle changes and actions necessary for their congregations, if so motivated, to cross this threshold. Although the strength of *Economic Justice for All* lies in its consistent emphasis on the themes of empowerment and participation, its weakness is that it offers few concrete recommendations on overcoming marginalization and powerlessness. If the economic pastorals, like the public policies they address, were to be evaluated by the criteria of the Catholic Bishops, that they be judged "in light of what they do for the poor, what they do to the poor, and what they enable the poor to do for themselves" (1986, par. 24), they would receive mixed reviews at best.

EVALUATION

Mainline Protestant denominations confront a challenge to respond simultaneously to a series of complex and fundamental shifts in the religious, cultural, political, and economic context in which they operate, each of which has major implications for their identity, conception of mission, political role, and base of membership and support. In the past generation, and particularly during the 1980s, they have dealt, sometimes simultaneously and sometimes consecutively, with the effects of three major discontinuities: the erosion of their mainline religious status and prerogatives, the emergence of a global Christian community shaped by the needs and perspectives of Two-Thirds World Christians, and the recognition that their own government, as well as many others, was pursuing policies that threatened the future of the earth and the welfare of key sectors of society. Cumulatively, these changes have tended to accelerate political involvement and shape political ministries in a critical mode.

It may be helpful at this point to evaluate the extent and direction of the changes in the political ministries of the mainline churches during the decade. There were, of course, many points of continuity with the trends identified in the previous chapter. Many traditional modes of operation still shaped their political witness. In contrast to the model of political ministries put forward in chapter 2, in which efforts to reform and transform the world rest on the twin bases of an explicit faith foundation and structures and lifestyles consistent with the faith community's vision of peace, justice, and righteousness, the mainline churches continued to focus primarily on changing the world and not themselves. Engaging in political ministries that focused more on policy formulation than implementation, they were still characterized by issue proliferation, the relative absence of a strategic approach for achieving their objectives, and an overemphasis on short-term legislative changes rather than a longer term reorientation of attitudes, priorities, or institutions.

What was notable, however, was the degree of change. Far more often than in the past, mainline churches began to raise fundamental questions related to the identity and vocation of the faith community. At least in the peace and economic pastorals the churches spoke from a biblical and theological foundation and addressed society in a far more prophetic manner. Moreover, various policy statements, if not sustained initiatives, recognized more clearly the need for the church to incarnate its faith commitments. Particularly on foreign policy issues, the mainline churches shed much of their characteristic caution and moderation and began to challenge their members and government; a number of church leaders engaged in civil disobedience and invited their members to join them. Although mainline denominations were far from achieving true solidarity with the poor, they at least began to contemplate moving in this direction. Their advocacy agenda increasingly and explicitly promoted policies benefiting the poor, rather than their more affluent constituents. As these denominations began to speak more frequently in the name of the institutional church, they developed a greater sense of self-awareness and a more clear-cut identity. And as they began to shed their establishment character, they had greater scope to experiment, albeit within the bounds of institutions responsive to their predominantly middle-class memberships.

These developments have reoriented the political ministries of the mainline denominations in a countercultural direction. Just as the mainline churches began to move beyond culture-religion and political liberalism, the political mood of the country became more conservative. While these denominations tried to articulate a new vision of global integration based on partnership, the country engaged in a decade-long immersion into nostalgia for the era of American supremacy as a means of avoiding the unsettling realities and complexities of a more pluralistic world. Just as the denominations were articulating a new vision of public responsibility and solidarity with the poor, the cultural movement predisposed people toward greater individualism, preoccupation with self-fulfillment and advancement, and apathy.

These opposing trends have made the transition and adjustment of the mainline churches all the more difficult, but by sharpening the distinctions between the church and the world, they may provide the impetus for a church renewal movement. In a much-quoted book originally written almost two decades ago, *Why Conservative Churches Are Growing* (1986), Dean Kelley suggests that cultural exclusivity, strong bonds, and a comprehensive interpretation conferring meaning and purpose to life fostered and sustained the growth of such churches. In contrast, Roof and McKinney point to the weakness of group bonds in mainline Protestant churches, describing congregations as "religious audiences" — rather than communities — with low attendance, lack of vitality, and an excess of doubt and uncertainty in matters of faith (1987, 86–87). Although this characterization is something of an overstatement, it contains an element of truth. Thus the dissonance between the mainline churches and the larger society may carry within it the seeds of a redefinition of role and identity.

However, these profound and complex changes have affected American churches quite unevenly. Not only is the perspective of the mainline denominations out of keeping with that of the conservative and fundamentalist groups that continue to affirm an America-first vision of the world and yearn for the security of traditional values and social arrangements, there is also great diversity of perspective within each of the mainline denominations. Those who have consciously confronted and responded to the new religiocultural and political context still represent a minority, a disproportionate number of whom are national staff, lay leaders, directors of national and regional agencies, intermediary judicatory officials, and activists within the denominations. Most church members remain immersed in the life of the local congregation, relatively unaware of or uninterested in the issues with which the national staff deal or the global church in which they operate. For every member and group within a mainline denomination who has gone beyond the frontier of a cultural Christianity legitimating the political system and culture there are many others either upholding the traditional synthesis or frustrated and angry with the loss of meaning and security. For each person within a denomination who has spent time in a Two-Thirds World country participating in church programs or who has had an opportunity to interact with Christians from other countries engaged in mission to the United States, there are countless others who have not had such transforming experiences. And just as economic injustice is perceived very differently by those advantaged by current economic policies and those who suffer, power and influence may seem to be a protection from even the perils of nuclear war.

Like the white members of the English-speaking churches of South Africa about which Charles Villa-Vicencio writes (1988), middle- and upper-middle-class members of the American mainline denominations have generally been too firmly trapped in the benefits of the system in which they function to evaluate objectively its deficiencies, too comfortable within the existing order to identify fully with those disadvantaged by its arrangements. Thus far disestablishment, globalization, and revitalization of peace and justice ministries have not so much changed the consciousness of the majority as they have considerably increased the size, radicalized the perspective, and mobilized the activist communities within the mainline churches. This trend has exacerbated tendencies, noted in the previous chapter, for advocacy ministries to involve a small core of activists at various levels of the church, leaving the majority of members supportive at best in the abstract but uninterested in direct participation. At the close of the decade, with denominations responding to the assumed dissatisfaction of the silent majority, relocation and reorganization threaten to become substitutes for serious efforts at renewal of the institutional church.

These trends point to critical horizons of discussion, reflection, education, and transformation within each of the denomina-

tions. Although Roof and McKinney locate the future of liberal
Protestantism in the ability to celebrate its past heritage (1987, 240),
such a strategy seems more like the religious counterpart of the national penchant for nostalgia. Since the world will never again be
the same, the church can ill afford to be anchored in its past. The
need for major adjustments, many of which are already substantially
in process, is a given. Moreover, to be true to its fundamental character as "a people called," the religious community must respond
to perceived divine initiatives within its own time and place. The issue is how such adjustments to a fundamentally changed world can
become the basis for a new and vital faith.

Chapter Five

Into the Future

Today the major or mainline Protestant denominations confront a series of challenges, the response to which is likely to shape their character into the future. Literature cited in previous chapters has focused on such issues as decline in membership (particularly in the younger age groups), decreases in availability of funds and resultant staff and program cuts, and ideological disagreements between liberals and conservatives over church policies. However, I believe something far more profound is at stake. These churches seem to be experiencing something akin to a corporate identity crisis, reflecting a lack of clarity and the absence of shared understandings about the nature of faith, the possibilities for meaningful community life, and the role of the church in society. Thus the task ahead is the reformation of these denominations amid a crisis of meaning, values, and commitments that has some analogies to the situation of the early Christian community within the Roman empire two thousand years ago and of the church at various historical turning points.

MAINLINE *KAIROS*

To place the current situation in a more theological context, the
mainline Protestant denominations confront a *kairos*, a decisive, critical moment, a time of opportunity, a crisis hour. This present *kairos*
(the word comes from the New Testament) challenges them to a
partnership with a God of justice, peace, and compassion.

The Internal Tensions

Tracing their heritage to Reformation theological and political con-
figurations, the mainline denominations are no longer being sustained by the perceived relevance of their traditions to contemporary
life, the salience of the social, economic, and ethnic identities that
once constituted their membership bases, or the effective education
and socialization of members. The lack of maturity and weak commitments to faith have made many mainline members into lukewarm
or social Christians. Congregational autonomy and an absence of a
strong sense of community and common purpose have diminished
possibilities for implementing meaningful programs and projects.
Decisions of higher judicatory bodies, even when scrupulously based
on correct procedure, tend either to be ignored or treated at most
as advisory, a kind of menu from which other parts of the denomination can pick and choose. There is an intrinsic inconsistency or
contradiction between the public, ethical, activist, and social change
orientation that these denominations at least nominally affirm, and
the private and self-interested character of their congregations that
function primarily as voluntary organizations to benefit and serve
their own members. This split personality has given rise to public theologies in which the church is understood as a community
serving God's mission to heal, reconcile, and restore *shalom* to the
creation, and to institutions and practices in which such ministries
are accorded low priority. It has also contributed to tensions between
local congregations that are focused inward and the more inclusive
levels of the denominations attempting to respond meaningfully to
injustice and pain in the world.

    Complicating these internal tensions are ambiguities and con-
tradictions about the social role and influence of these churches.
Historically, these denominations have tended toward an unreflec-

tive identification with American culture, political and economic systems, and aspirations. The social position and relative economic well-being of many of their members have also meant that through much of American history mainline churches have functioned as part of the establishment, even while they are disposed to seek reforms for major injustices. However, changes in the religiosocial landscape during the past fifty years, particularly during the post-Vietnam period, have displaced these denominations from the cultural, religious, social, and political center. Their internal changes (documented in the preceding chapters) have also rendered them less suitable for an uncritical, culture-affirming role. Moreover, the development of a greater global consciousness through relationships with churches in Two-Thirds World countries and the revitalization of their peace and justice ministries have brought the leadership and a cross-section of their membership to raise fundamental questions, at least about major policy directions and perhaps about the adequacy of American institutions. Yet although these groups no longer fit within the establishment mold, they have not reconceptualized their fundamental understanding of the church as a prophetic or an alternative community. The denominations therefore remain suspended between an establishment identity and an opposition role, divided between members with a congregational orientation who affirm the benefits of the status quo and those with a wider understanding of the church and its responsibilities who seek fundamental change.

The Critical Moment

As the South African Kairos Theologians have noted, the present *kairos* is both a challenge to decisive action and a gift of grace and opportunity (Kairos Theologians 1986, chap. 1). God's call for conversion represents an opening in history, a brief moment when it is possible to transcend the past, redefine the present, and create a new and more faithful future. This theological turning point vests the faith community with new powers of discernment. It offers a chance to restore community bonds and an opportunity to reconstitute its corporate life. Ironically and paradoxically, the very depth of the crisis within the mainline churches provides great creative possibilities for a new and vital future different from their past character. The loss of status and influence of these denominations as they pass from the mainline to the sideline, far from being something to mourn, can enable these churches to regain their true vocation as an alternative community with an alternative consciousness dedicated to serving God.

I believe that the *kairos* has three dimensions, reflecting the three components of political ministry. First and foremost, the *kairos* relates to the articulation of the fundamental beliefs and clarification of the vocation of these faith communities. Whom or what do mainline Christians worship? What is their conception of God? Will they affirm the biblical and theological traditions that disclose a God of peace, justice, and compassion ever seeking to transform the creation? Or will they be tempted by representations of the divine as holy, removed, and transcendent, more desirous of elaborate worship than righteous action, accepting of and legitimating the injustices and inequality of the existing political order? Will the faith community called together in Jesus' name remember and emulate his announcement that he had come to bring good news to the poor and liberation to the captives, and model its ministry accordingly? Are the members willing to take the risk of his invitation to be followers? Will they accept the Gospels, particularly the three Synoptics, as disclosing the paradigm of God's relationship to humanity, with all that entails?

A related question is, will the members of these mainline churches be able to affirm and express tangibly in their lives that God is the ultimate source of being, purpose, and meaning? God-centeredness entails a fundamental and sustained level of individual and corporate commitment of the type referred to as discipleship. As the term implies, it means placing God at the center of life with a priority over all other relationships and commitments. To acknowledge the God of scripture as the ultimate source of being, purpose, and meaning is to temper the claims of all other loyalties and to measure them against this faith standard. It means accepting partnership with God's efforts to nurture, judge, renew, and transform the creation as the fundamental purpose in life. Reciprocally, it also precludes compartmentalizing life into a religious sphere for God and other segments for secular purposes. And having no God before the true God requires turning away from the idols of contemporary society — the materialism, consumerism, and preoccupation with success, status, and power.

The second dimension of the *kairos* is the development of the will and ability to strive for a correspondence between the nature of God, God's intentions for humanity, and the nature of life in community. As noted, in its better days the faith community took its basic comprehension of God, not secular institutional models, as the beginning point in shaping its norms and institutions. When God's people have endeavored to be faithful to their calling they have sought to pattern communal life and structures in the image of God's righteousness and compassion (Hanson 1986, 468). Applying this mandate to the present would mean a far greater focus on the quality of faithfulness in the internal life of the faith community, something very different from the institutional maintenance approach current in most churches. It would restore a balance between fundamental beliefs as expressed in doctrine and pronouncements and as incarnated within the community. And it would entail far more strenuous efforts to shape mission and ministry in the world from basic faith principles. To do so effectively would require the development of participatory processes to make and implement a series of corporate decisions. These would be based on the community's vision of faith and fundamental beliefs to redefine the nature of their community life and structures and to articulate the character of their commitment to the creation. Restoration of the church as a community of faith communities would also involve establishment of new structures and modes of relationship within the denominations that integrate levels of the church and specialized structures, reduce bureaucracy and hierarchy, and educate and empower local congregations.

The third dimension of the *kairos* is a broad-based commitment to partnership with and for God, with and for others, and for the future through engaging in ministries of transformation and service. I believe that among the outcomes of such a reformation would be a movement well beyond the political advocacy now characteristic of the major Protestant denominations to more authentic ministries of service and transformation. Only an alternative community dedicated in all facets of its own life to God's *shalom* can undertake something approximating a prophetic ministry. Such a faith-centered approach would establish the primacy of theological and biblical principles as a source of inspiration and guidance, and as the basis on which the faith community would evaluate secular institutions, programs, and actors. Positioning the faith community to espouse programs and reforms that systematically benefit the poor, the weak, and those without a voice, political ministry requires that members of a predominantly middle-class church would be willing to make sacrifices and to share effectively with others. It assumes that the church, rather than aspiring to be part of the establishment, would understand itself as an alternative community challenging injustices, inequities, and violence. Cognizant of its own weakness, however, the faith community would act very selectively and strategically, carefully making serious long-term commitments to fundamental change.

Although I acknowledge the complexity and magnitude of the changes I have in mind, I believe that there are historical precedents for such a transformation of the church community. Much of the history of the church has been a dialectic between the dynamics of institutional maintenance and reform. As Christianity moves into its third millennium becoming a global faith, with a majority of its adherents living in the poverty, oppression, and the social turmoil characteristic of Two-Thirds World countries, it may be that historical conditions will once again give rise to a significant reconceptualization of the faith. The vitality of Two-Thirds World churches and the debates initiated by the various forms of liberation theology may presage a far-reaching realignment within the global Christian community. Relationships with Two-Thirds World churches have already provided one of the most significant trajectories for change in many of the major Protestant churches, and a more authentic and inclusive partnership reaching out to a wider circle of churches could possibly help to spark the renewal. The experience of North American Mennonites in changing from a relatively withdrawn, sectarian type of community, defined by an ethnic identity, into a peace church involved in the challenges of the contemporary world, suggests the possibility of such an intentional transformation (Redekop and Steiner 1988). The United Congregational Church in South Africa is now beginning a major renewal of the type advocated here.

As preceding chapters indicate, the major Protestant churches do not yet acknowledge this call to conversion and transformation. Even as they embrace the rhetoric of change, the leadership of these churches continue to be wedded to the basics of their mainline, establishment heritage. Rather than engaging in a searching analysis about the state of the faith and the vitality of their communities, they

are looking for quick fixes through such mechanisms as relocation
and restructuring. Those within these churches who are cognizant of
the situation seem more inclined to mourn the loss of power and influence that went with establishment status than to choose to become
an alternative community.

To allow the moment to pass will result in an immeasurable
loss for the churches and for the gospel. The Kairos Theologians
quite appropriately refer to the poignant passage in the Gospel of
Luke in which Jesus, arriving in Jerusalem, wept over the city, antic-
ipating the imminent tragedy of its loss and destruction "because you
did not recognize the time of your visitation [*kairos*] from God" (Luke
19:44). Distracted by their own institutional maintenance issues and
immersed in longing for a political saviour, Jesus' contemporaries
could not recognize the things that made for peace. There are still
grounds for hope, at least, if not for optimism, that some within the
mainline churches, perhaps a smaller and more coherent group, will
respond to the opportunity of this moment. The remainder of this
chapter looks into a future that would enable communities to begin
the process of renewal and transformation.

THE TRANSFORMATIVE POTENTIAL
OF SCRIPTURE

How is it possible to begin a process of conversion, to initiate the
kind of bonding that constitutes a "partnership of service and freedom with and for God, with and for others, and for the future"
through which we become part of God's love affair with the world
(Russell 1979, 23)? American churches have tended to have two approaches. Conservatives and fundamentalists focus on doctrine and
personal morality. They stress acceptance of a literal understanding
of scripture, framed by a a very unbiblical conception of inerrancy,
and adherence to behavioral standards that frequently have more
to do with nineteenth-century culture than with biblical norms. The
demands of the conservative churches and their strictures have the
advantage of conferring meaning for some, particularly those seeking an escape from the relativism, diversity, and ambiguity of modern
life (Kelley 1986). Yet their narrow conception of faith and their in-
tolerance limit their appeal. Liberal or mainline churches preach and

teach a more complex and nuanced conception of faith that lacks the biblical centering of the conservatives, the experiential qualities coveted by many Americans, and the assurance of the conservative and fundamentalist. Although the liberal approach incorporates service and social response more fully than the conservative, it does not have a compelling theological vision that links these themes to core beliefs.

I would like to propose an alternative approach. Like many conservative Christians, I believe that in shattering something, the essential ingredient for individual congregational change and renewal, the agent of transformation is likely to be scripture. Unlike the literalism and formalism so characteristic of the conservative approach, though, the approach I have in mind would employ scripture within today's context, using an interactive process to enable the text to speak to contemporary culture and social situations and to suggest courses of action. Such a methodology would be consistent with the nature of the Bible. Scripture does not provide a systematic theology based on a set of universal principles that can be rigidly applied to all ages and peoples. The Bible is the testimony of a series of communities called across the centuries to journey with and toward a God of peace and justice, rather than a normative rule book; a guide for relating to God in community, rather than a fixed content (McFague 1987, 43). Biblical communities shared a vision of divine purpose that extended over the entire span of time and space, yet each generation of the community of faith received new insight into that purpose as it applied the vision to new historical circumstances (Hanson 1986, 4). We are called to do the same. In coming to scripture with questions and perspectives drawn from one's own culture and context, it is possible to unlock new meanings, to unfold new dimensions in the text.

Some methodologies unlock and enhance the transformative potential of scripture more than others. I believe that a participatory, interactive group process, in which members of a community together explore, discuss, and interpret scripture, relating the text to problems and issues they confront in their lives, can best serve as an instrument of a contemporary community's redefinition of its fundamental beliefs and vocation. Paulo Freire's discussion of the nature of education as an instrument of self-discovery in his *Pedagogy of the Oppressed* (1984) captures much of the dynamics of the process I have in mind. He distinguishes between two modes of teaching: the traditional relationship of an active teacher and passive students, and a liberating or participatory approach that enables each member of the group to engage directly and become a subject, rather than an object, of the process. In the former, knowledge is considered to be a gift bestowed by the all-knowing teacher on pupils considered to be "empty vessels" needing to be filled with knowledge. In the latter, the leader provides a framework for thinking and stimulating participants to consider a common problem and find solutions. All members of the group are active in analyzing, suggesting, deciding, and planning. Biblical study is much enhanced by such a participatory and dialogical group approach.

See, Judge, Act

See-Judge-Act is one method with a participatory, contextual, and application-oriented approach to scripture that has been employed very effectively in South Africa, Brazil, the Philippines, and other Two-Thirds World countries to initiate a process of spiritual and political transformation. The three-part exercise first asks participants to assess (See) who they are as a church, through undertaking a social and ecclesial analysis of the context in which they live. It encourages them to ask questions about the collective identity of the community and the nature of the social, economic, and political systems in which it functions. The second stage (Judge) involves an intensive study of selected biblical texts to understand better God's intentions of who they should become. In the third stage (Act) participants formulate an action plan, delineating what the community will do to transform itself and make a difference in the world.

The experience of the United Congregational Church of Southern Africa, an English-speaking Protestant denomination whose roots are in British and American congregationalist mission, illustrates the potential of the See-Judge-Act method as a central component of intentional initiatives to renew and transform denominations. In 1987 the leadership of the United Congregational Church began an exploration of the implications of *The Kairos Document,* a theological comment on the political crisis in South Africa. The Kairos Theologians' denunciation of the state theology of the Dutch Reformed Church, characterized by the theological justification of apartheid with its racism and authoritarianism, had little relevance for the denomination, given its history of opposition to the system. But the document's critical treatment of the "church theology" of the English-speaking churches had a profound impact. Although acknowledging the policy commitment of these denominations to justice and to change, *The Kairos Document* severely criticized their superficiality, failure to engage in social analysis, and reluctance to undertake effective political action (1986, par. 3:1–3:4). Underscoring that the *kairos*, the moment of truth for South Africa, called for a response from Christians that was biblical, spiritual, pastoral, and above all prophetic, the document stressed the need for a return to the Bible to search the Word of God for a message that was relevant to the situation (1987, par. 4:1).

Responding to *The Kairos Document*, the United Congregational Church's leadership engaged in intensive scriptural study, using the See-Judge-Act method. It had an electrifying effect, reshaping their sense of identity and vocation. The See-Judge-Act biblical study method was again used at a ministers' convocation in January 1989. These processes resulted in the United Congregational Church's launching a pastoral plan entitled *Hearing the Bible Today* as the basis for renewing faith and action. At its center is the development of See-Judge-Act Bible study groups at every level of church life. Beginning with preparation of materials, the denomination is training five thousand resource people, the equivalent of three to four persons per congregation, to serve as facilitators. Just as the elected leaders and ministers in the denomination were brought to a new understanding of the imperatives of their faith, the hope is that the denomination-wide biblical study will enable members to have new clarity on their journey as a people of God (United Congregational Church of Southern Africa 1989).

I believe that the initiation of denomination-wide study processes based on the See-Judge-Act method, with congregations exploring a clarification of their fundamental beliefs and vocation through interaction with central biblical texts, could be a critical element in the conversion of mainline churches. My hope that non-traditional approaches to studying scripture may provide an opening to a more authentic and mature faith comes from my own personal faith journey and, even more, from my observance of the transformative potential of biblical study during my years of residence and travel in Two-Thirds World countries. I have witnessed groups grappling with the texts time and again in a variety of cultures in such a way that it illumined their own situations, modified and deepened their faith, and enabled members to take the initiative to change their lives. The discovery of the God of compassion, love, and justice typically then empowered their own efforts to pursue social and political change. And in those few situations where See-Judge-Act has been introduced to North American groups, it has evoked similar responses.

Ecclesial Base Communities

A recent book on the progressive church in four Latin American countries (Nicaragua, Brazil, El Salvador, and Peru) documents the critical role of biblical study in sustaining the ecclesial base communities so central to the struggle for social justice and freedom in these countries. Ecclesial base communities, as the name implies, are small faith communities, typically of fifteen to twenty-five persons, most or all of them poor, at the base of the society and the church. Almost always organized by pastoral agents — bishops, priests, nuns, or lay people trained and commissioned by the church — one of the fundamental goals is to foster a more meaningful spiritual life in the absence of sufficient clergy to serve such communities. In reviewing the data on base Christian communities in Latin America, Scott Mainwaring and Alexander Wilde, the editors of the study, characterize the base communities as generally more religious in a conventional sense and less political than most analysts have claimed. It is their view that most people join these communities not out of a desire to change the society but out of religious inclination. Thus the communities spend most of their time praying and engaging in Bible study. Affective concerns, such as developing ties of community and solidarity and forming friendships, are also of interest. Despite initial nonpolitical motivation, however, participation in the discipline of the base communities and in their biblical study often lead members to an awareness that the Christian faith requires a commitment to social justice and human rights. Although the way that people translate this realization into action varies considerably, depending on their political situations, there is a consensus among them that the pursuit of social change, political commitment, and political participation are legitimate, indeed essential, expressions of religious faith (Mainwaring and Wilde 1989, 2–8).

Alvaro Barreiro's moving study of basic ecclesial communities in Brazil, based on data from reports written by the communities, reveals many of the same themes. Basic ecclesial communities described in this work are located within and on the outskirts of urban areas or remote rural communities and live under conditions of extreme deprivation and socioeconomic neglect. Yet even in such situations of poverty and misery the gospel can convert and liberate these communities. As Barreiro notes,

> there are times and circumstances in the history of the Church when the gospel is heard and accepted as the good news of the kingdom, in its original newness. On such occasions, the gospel demonstrates its force for liberation and salvation, giving sight to blind eyes, opening deaf ears, untying mute tongues, and stirring and converting consciences and hearts. All this occurs when "the poor hear the good news" (Luke 7:22). When the good news is preached to the poor, in a pure, free, and fearless manner, it kindles in them the fire of hope, transforming their lives. This is what is happening in thousands of Basic Ecclesial Communities (Comunidades Eclesias de Base — CEBs) scattered throughout all of Brazil (1982, 1).

Barreiro documents the manner in which the basic ecclesial communities enable the poor to hear the good news and then to make the transition from knowledge received to knowledge discovered. Central to the process is study of the biblical texts that underscore God's love and concern for the poor. The poor, the oppressed, those who have lacked a voice in the affairs of the world, then begin to understand that in the divine economy, far from being inconsequential, they have infinite worth. Through studying the Gospels, particularly that of Luke, they discover a Messiah in solidarity with the poor who proclaimed that the poor were the privileged recipients of the reign of God. In the base communities those whom the world counts as low and contemptible become, through God, the conveyors of the new existence in Christ (Barreiro 1982, 42).

Barreiro characterizes the process through which these communities relate scripture to their lives as "evangelical liberation." It is based on three means of pastoral action: intimately entering into people's poverty, struggle, and hope; liberating education through consciousness-raising and human development programs; and prophetic denunciation of injustices and oppression (1982, 29). He notes that preaching the gospel to the poor means specifically preaching the reality of the love of God, a love that brings salvation-liberation for each one of them and their communities from the concrete state of oppression in which they find themselves. Liberating education, rooted in the concrete realities of people's lives, entails raising consciousness of specific injustices — expulsion of squatters from the land, exploitation of farm hands on large estates, intrusion of an arbitrary and authoritarian government prone to severe human rights violations, illiteracy, disease, and lack of jobs, schools, and hospitals — in order to prompt the people to begin to organize to promote change (1982, 30–31). By vesting the members of these communities with a new sense of worth and meaning in their lives, the study of the gospel also enables members to create new types of human relationships and to undertake shared projects and programs to address their problems. Formerly lacking a capacity for initiative, the poor now participate actively and consciously in the analysis of their situation, interpretation of the gospel, selection of goals for shared undertakings, and the identification of tasks to attain their objectives. Giving witness to their faith, the work of the people is done unselfishly as a service dedicated to the community's welfare.

Although the proclamation of the good news to the poor cannot be identified with a specific sociopolitical program, it does have strong political implications. As Barreiro notes, "What the CEBs (Base Ecclesial Communities) want to do is to make a reality 'here and now' of the process of liberation begun in a totally irreversible manner by Jesus" (1982, 28). That process of liberation entails taking a critical position toward the oppressive realities of these communities, denouncing these situations as contrary to God's love and intentions (1982, 31). Breaking down the dividing walls of hostility, the gospel unites people into new communities with a capacity for initiative and collective action, some of which is political in character. It instills courage, hope, and consciousness of human dignity leading to new demands. All of this constitutes a constant, disturbing, scandalous challenge to the status quo within both the society and the church. It is little wonder therefore that repressive elites in Brazil have considered the base communities a threat, whether or not they engage in direct political activity.

The Power of Scripture

What is it, then, that enables the Bible to have such a transformative potential? Johann Baptist Metz attributes this power to scripture serving as the repository of "a dangerous memory of freedom." According to Metz, memories such as this, contained in certain strands of the biblical tradition, particularly in the Exodus narratives and in the Gospels' promises of the kingdom of God, can be claimed by particular communities. Such memories of the freedom of Jesus and the call of God to all people to be subjects before God can inspire Christian communities' sense of dignity, lead Christians to a critique of what is commonly accepted as plausible, and empower those who challenge oppression (Metz 1980, 69, 89, 90). Building on Metz's concept of "dangerous memory," Sharon Welch identifies base Christian communities, black churches, and women's collectives as principal bearers of these dangerous memories. She suggests that the memories inspire a form or expression of resistance within these communities that is often imagistic rather than analytic. She describes the expression as one of protest, hope, and vision that motivates political action (1985, 42–43).

I prefer to speak more simply of the power of certain passages within scripture to bring the individual and the community to an encounter with a God of compassion, peace and justice. Within the Hebrew Bible and the New Testament are some of the most inspired texts ever written, evoking divine visions of a new creation, a kingdom recapturing the just peace of the *shalom* order, a reconciled and redeemed humanity in which friendship and love displace enmity and hatred. Far from an abstract utopia, these ideals come as the goals and intentions of the Creator and Redeemer of the universe, the One within and beyond everything that is or will be. Counterbalanced with these texts of hope and liberation, is the poetry of anguish, the cries of pain and suffering human and divine, over injustice and oppression. I believe that God's presence and will come forth most powerfully in the expressions of solidarity with the suffering and in the divine refusal to accept brokenness as the human condition. Although the poor and those excluded from the mainstream have historically been more open to God, I believe that others can also gain these sources of inspiration, albeit with somewhat different responses and consequences. My hope stems from the power

of the texts to address all sectors of society and to elicit a partnership in two directions, with God incarnated in the person of Jesus
of Nazareth, and with the human community ever waiting to be
made new.

Walter Brueggemann points to the ability of biblical texts to
effect change through stimulating and inspiring the social imagination (1978). The encounter with the divine, with another order
of reality, is characteristically expressed in poetry, in images, rather
than descriptively in prose. Poetry, particularly divine poetry, can
reach a deeper, more fundamental level of being than can theology,
dogma, or literal, one-dimensional, descriptive modern prose. The
images and symbols of poetry are able to transcend and shatter the
presumed world by substituting the powerful vision of another reality, God's proposed world, and to inspire the community of faith
to reach toward that new creation. Poetry and prophecy go hand in
hand throughout the Bible. The poetic/prophetic imagination offers the key means by which God's agents time and again challenge
and oppose the injustice of the dominant reality and offer the higher
reality of the biblical vision in its place.

Suffering and oppression often render their victims open to
such images of promise and hope, but what about those who are comfortable, complacent with the way things are, seemingly resistant to
the biblical mandate for change? I think that potential for recep-
tivity to alternative futures tends to be more complex than is often
assumed. In contemporary affluent societies most people remain un-
fulfilled, yearning for greater meaning and purpose. Overwhelmed
by the complexity of the world, distracted by consumerism, numbed
by actual and potential violence, many people have lost the capacity to feel, to respond, to envision a different world. To lack social
imagination may be more problematic than to tenaciously hold fast
to the status quo. Biblical texts can provide the inspiration, the energy to motivate people to take the risk of working toward a new
future.

Moreover, in complex societies many individuals and communities live with double identities, as oppressed and as oppressors,
benefiting from and disadvantaged by the status quo — although in
very different balances depending on social, geographic, and racial
factors. To note this dual identity is not to claim equivalence with
those outside the mainstream in any way or to absolve middle- or

upper-class Americans from responsibility for intentional or unintentional complicity with structures of injustice. It does, though, increase the possibility that even comfortable Christians have an experiential basis for hearing and responding to the cries for justice that arise from the many varieties of injustice — economic, political, sexual, religious, and cultural.

Several feminist theologians have written about this dual vision, or standing, in relationship to white middle-class North American women. In her book *Justice in an Unjust World*, Karen Lebacqz holds up a mirror to herself and discovers that, on the one hand, it reflects a white, middle-class, middle-aged American woman who can never presume to know the pain of the black woman or Native American man in the United States, the Jew in Christian society, the desperately poor in Latin America, the disenfranchised in Africa, the landless peasant in Korea, the wheelchair occupant who cannot climb the cathedral steps in France. Yet Lebacqz also realizes that as a woman who has suffered at the hands of patriarchy, she has had experiences that enable her at least to try to see reality from the perspective of the oppressed. Although oppressions differ, each is a possible window to injustice and, therefore, to justice (1987, 12–14). The implications of Lebacqz's insight can be further generalized. Few people have not experienced injustice. To use Lebacqz's formulation, although injustices differ enormously in intensity and significance, each provides a possible insight into the broader reign of injustice in which we live. One of the potentials of scripture is to enhance this sensitivity and foster a sense of identity and community with all who suffer.

The path from scripture to understanding to action, for those who basically benefit from the status quo, is likely to be quite different from the dynamic for those who suffer. In a culture fundamentally antithetical to a faith-centered life, with an ethic of selfish individualism and excessive consumption, biblical lenses offer one of the few means to destabilize expectations and to challenge those comfortable with existing arrangements to question society's norms and values. To come to faithfulness, such groups have to understand that their values, lifestyles, and the systems that support them, exist at the expense of others and thus contravene essential dimensions of the *shalom* vision. They have to hear the words of rebuke in scripture and respond by accepting responsibility, providing redress, and working for greater justice. In contrast, the poor begin with a perception of injustice and return to the Bible for assurance that God did not intend humanity to live in systems which impoverish and oppress the human community. For "haves," immersion in the peace and justice trajectory of scripture provides a means of escaping determination by the culture, values, and institutions shaping the community's situation and identity. For "have-nots," the same passages contain the seeds of another form of liberation, an empowerment to reject the dehumanizing culture and oppressive systemic arrangements. These respective forms of liberation precede and give rise to active engagement in efforts to transform and change policies, institutions, and systems.

COMMUNITY FORMATION
AND REFORMATION

The importance of community formation and reformation has been one of the central themes of this study. As the faith of the "people of the way," Christianity's truths require embodiment in the life and structures of the community. Just as members of the early Christian community expressed their faith through their life together, contemporary Christians cannot pursue a sustained relationship with God apart from such a vital faith community. *Ekklesia* implies both a calling out from the world and a calling into new forms of relationship, captured best perhaps by the term partnership. Such community and lifestyle considerations do not, however, represent a turning inward at the expense of mission. Christian communities permeated with the presence of Christ are partnerships in service in which the members live, not for themselves, but for others, particularly those experiencing suffering and injustice in the world. As Letty Russell notes, *koinonia* (partnership, participation, communion, community) and *diakonia* (service) belong together (1979, 75). By definition, partnership involves growing interdependence in relation to God, persons, and creation, so that the individual as well as the group transcends itself, moving constantly in interaction with ever-wider sets of communities (Russell 1981, 29).

A Community of Communities

As in all partnerships, the development of community at various levels of the church requires commitment and common struggle, possibilities and limitations. A partnership in Jesus Christ, the relationship described in the New Testament as *koinonia*, the gift of the Spirit, has an already/not yet character "for although in Christ we are already made partner with God, ourselves, and one another, we are still in the process of becoming partners in all relationships of our lives, and we do not yet experience the full expression of this participation in the New Creation" (Russell 1981, 23). Partnership is provisional, tentative, open-ended — an ongoing process initiated by God. Despite human sinfulness and limitations, it recognizes and builds on human potential for compassion, love, justice, and relationship. With and through God these capabilities provide the basis for progress toward partnership. Selfishness and self-centeredness, however, inhibit partnership from ever becoming fully realized.

Identifying community as the commanding matrix for the spiritual life of both Israel and the early church, chapter 2 conceptualized the church as a community of church communities. Inspired by Paul's metaphor of the church as the body of Christ (1 Cor. 12:12–26), it imaged the church as very different from a series of institutions or a collection of voluntary associations catering to the individual needs of members. In the model of the church as a community of faith communities, members would share in both the communal intimacy and the face-to-face relationships of a primary community. This could be a faith group akin to a base Christian community, a house church, or a congregation and would be organically linked to more inclusive levels of their denominations and to the wider church. Like parts of a body joining to perform certain tasks, constituent primary communities — the focus of faith interpretation, embodiment, mission, and witness — would group and regroup into ever-more inclusive partnerships of communities, orienting their lives toward God to participate in the in-breaking of the divine order into the imperfect structures of this world. Although regional and national structures would continue to exist to facilitate and coordinate mission initiatives and projects requiring larger-scale organization, there would be a bottom-up rather than top-down dynamic. Consistent with the image of the church as the body of Christ, the more inclusive levels of this church organization would seek to serve and empower the basic communities to increase and enhance participation, not to perform mission on their behalf nor to dominate or direct their institutional lives.

Mainline Protestant churches, however, do not conceptualize their churches as a community, and there are many structural and attitudinal factors that inhibit the development of community within and between mainline churches. Ecclesial analysis in chapter 3 identified some strengths, particularly the decentralized location of their polities within congregations and the absence of effective hierarchies, but also many serious problems. The voluntary association model of congregational life casts the church as a service organization dedicated to fulfill the needs, both spiritual and social, of its members as individuals, not as a community-building and facilitating institution. Lacking a mature and intense faith, most mainline Christians consider participation in community life, shared activities, service projects, and advocacy to be optional. They lack an intrinsic bonding relationship with each other, let alone with more inclusive levels of their own denomination, the global Christian community, or the human family. In place of an organic linkage, wherein each part of the church cooperates with and is accountable to the other, mainline denominations have a more layered organization, a division of labor with very weak connections between the various levels. A pattern of voluntarism inheres, each level selectively choosing which programs, decisions, and staff functions of more inclusive bodies with which it will associate, sometimes ignoring them altogether. Divided within, neither the congregation nor the more inclusive levels of the church have the doctrinal uniformity, similarity of worldview, ideological consistency, or social ties that once compensated for the absence of effective organizational linkages. Special-interest groups have proliferated at all levels of the denominations, many of which are bent on winning support for their views regardless of the costs to the community. Functional specialization, particularly at the national level, establishes each agency, sometimes each office, as a separate fiefdom. Although these denominations are tied together by a variety of representative structures for policy-making and governance, local congregations tend to feel that they are not consulted, informed, or invited to participate in a meaningful way.

Confronting formidable obstacles, some of which were discussed in chapter 2, community formation at the congregational level requires some preconditions to make progress possible. Among the most critical are consensus on fundamental beliefs and a faith-based commitment to community life. Biblical models of inclusiveness also underscore the need for congregations to incorporate members of a variety of economic, social, racial, and ethnic backgrounds. These criteria, however, do not reflect the current composition of mainline congregations. Mainline congregations tend to be social, economic, racial, or ethnic ghettoes with little social and economic diversity and low motivation for inclusiveness. Conversely, because neither traditional doctrinal differences nor contemporary statements of faith and policy seem to play a major role in selection of congregational or denominational membership, there are a wide range of theologies and political orientations. Such ideological proliferation causes ongoing conflicts and divisiveness, making it difficult for many churches to agree on any kinds of programs. At regional and national levels, disagreements between visions of a public, socially oriented church model and a private, voluntary organization model threaten to tear denominations apart. Some of the most vicious disputes arise over the implementation of policies duly adopted by judicatory bodies.

Community formation, as well as institutional formation and reformation, require more theologically selective and more racially, ethnically, and economically inclusive bases in reconstituting congregational and, then, denominational membership. What I have in mind is that each congregation go through an intensive participatory process, defining its fundamental beliefs and its sense of the churches' vocation. This process would be repeated at more inclusive levels of the denomination. Core beliefs and commitments, once defined, would become the grounds for affiliation. Congregations would then be composed of members with basic theological affinities, and Christians interested in the kind of intense commitment to biblical mandates and community life envisaged here would be grouped with other like-minded people. Taking seriously the biblical model of community, such strenuous Christians would as a matter of priority seek out others of similar disposition. They would look particularly among the poor, the disadvantaged, and the racial and ethnic minorities in order to incarnate biblical norms of compassion and sharing and to emulate God's concern and priority for the poor and oppressed. As denominations redefined their charters, congregations would then review their affiliation, realizing that to confirm membership in a denominational grouping under such circumstances is to take very seriously the mutual responsibility of belonging to a community of faith communities.

This process would not be fashioned as an "inquisition" or an "alongside" theological exercise of the type in which many mainline churches now engage. Rather, it would be based on the recognition that there are very significant contemporary differences in fundamental theological and church orientation that deserve to be articulated as the basis of congregational and denominational life. Many of these have little to do with the traditional doctrinal formulations that once constituted the historical divisions between Catholics and Protestants, or among the various Protestant denominations. This new process would, in addition, acknowledge that commitments to community, formation of institutions in light of beliefs, and articulation of and participation in ministries can be viable only among people with a common vision. One major divide might be that between Christians who, through their theological orientation, affirm the interpretation of biblical themes outlined in this study, and those who do not. Another might be between those with a community orientation and those with a more individualist and personalist approach to faith, and a third between those who understand the church as first and foremost serving as God's partner/instrument to transform the creation and those who are more inclined toward a voluntary society model.

Although I realize that the vast majority of mainline Christians would not be able to make the kind of commitments envisaged here, I am very hopeful that there will be a sufficient basis for at least one major denominational grouping. I am also assuming that the process of biblical study outlined above would be a major means of conversion, augmenting the number of people so dedicated. Such a community would undoubtedly gradually attract and convert others. Further, the reconstitution of serious teaching ministries could also make a difference over time, possibly changing churches from within. Faithfulness, however, has always had to do more with the quality of community life than with numbers. To have a more coherent, active, and authentic faith community would far outbalance the disadvantages of a reduction in the size of the membership.

As mentioned above, the vision of the church as a community of faith envisages bonds of interrelatedness and accountability between congregations forming denominations, and beyond denominations, to the whole of the global Christian community and the human family. How, then, does such a sense of bonding emerge? Again, I would like to point to biblical study as a beginning. Processes of denominational redefinition would also contribute to these goals by making membership a more conscious decision on the grounds of faith and by encouraging members to be more aware of being part of wider communities. A more intentional teaching ministry would undoubtedly have such an objective.

Learning to Be Community

Of the various strategies, learning to be part of a wider community by acting on that basis is perhaps the most effective. Community contacts, exchanges, and projects can enable communities at various levels of a denomination — and across denominational and national frontiers — to come to know and make commitments to one another and to build such a sense of belonging to wider communities. Some of the most promising and creative mainline programs already have this as their objective. They provide opportunities for voluntary service in other regions of the United States and overseas, arrange for intercongregational exchanges across geographical areas, facilitate various types of partnership pairings of congregations and regional groupings, and enable missioners from other countries to come for extended periods to participate in American churches in a form of reverse mission. Contacts with Christians from other cultures struggling to express and incarnate their faith in situations of extreme poverty and oppression particularly have energized, transformed, and reordered many American congregations.

For mainline denominations to change from their present patterns to engage in the type of partnerships envisioned in this model of the church as a community of faith communities also requires a major reform of the manner in which these churches are organized and operate. The dynamics of such a reformation would include greater consistency between the faith principles and values the churches espouse and the institutions and priorities that shape their collective lives together. Taking seriously Jesus' teachings on power, community, and responsibility would entail the dismantling of hierarchies. Commitment to an ethic of justice implies fashioning a church economy based on such principles. Incarnating compassion, connectedness, and sharing would result in the formulation of new budget priorities. And the support and institutionalization of all of these reforms would be enhanced by the recovery of the churches' teaching ministry.

Reconstituting denominations so as to be more consistent with Jesus' vision of an inclusive community in which there are neither oppressors nor oppressed, rulers nor ruled, means dismantling the institutions and bureaucracies borrowed from corporate America. Such corporate models with their specialization, elaborate structures and processes, and hierarchies are incompatible with the vision of the church as a radical democracy based on the full equality and shared involvement of all believers. Superimposed on the relative or complete autonomy of local congregations, these corporate models also do not work very well. The model I am proposing would recognize the congregation as the basic unit of church life and seek to build a relational system. It would envision relationships between levels of the church as partnerships between communities at differing levels of inclusiveness but of equal status. To promote participation and involvement, regional and national staffs would have facilitating and enabling roles. Intermediate judicatories and national bodies would respond to initiatives from congregations and groupings of congregations. Rather than performing ministries "on behalf of" or in place of member church bodies, they would seek to educate, empower, and link communities. Such a model of empowerment over time would result in a bottom-up rather than top-down dynamic within the church.

Decentralization and participation would result in a greater demand for the development of structures of mutual accountability and coordination. Partnership implies that each unit accept basic responsibilities for making a contribution commensurate to its resources and abilities to the total ministry of the wider community. Otherwise, in displacing "ministry on behalf of" models, churches would lose their capacity to serve and transform the world. Moreover, thinking and acting globally, as well as within regional and national frames of reference, requires connections, information, and, sometimes, skills not found in local congregations.

I will therefore propose three approaches to organizing mission in a decentralized system. First, churches and other units within denominations would covenant together annually, making and perhaps then adjusting multiyear commitments. Although covenantal language is often used in mainline churches, the concept of covenant usually remains abstract, devoid of specific content. To translate covenant into an operational system of mutual commitments would emphasize that denominational membership has its responsibilities as well as rewards. Relieved of many of their current assignments, regional and national staffs, even if reduced in number, would be able to establish a grid of project and funding opportunities, focused on specific regions and needs, to facilitate coordination. Congregations in particular states, for example, could be matched with specific partners overseas to avail themselves of particular program options. They could also join those in other regions across the United States to address other needs and issues. In this model synods and assemblies would no longer focus on resolutions commenting on the "signs of the times." Instead, they would provide opportunities for biblical study and theological reflection; they would serve as brokers for project and program funding and personnel assignments. The few pronouncements debated and voted would issue from actual involvements in these ministries of service and transformation.

Fuller and more effective forms of participation also require new modes of consultation through which major decisions at all levels of the church would be identified, studied, discussed, and evaluated by the affected communities before bodies acted on them. Such a pattern envisages a closer partnership or dialogue between synods and assemblies and their constituent communities, which would combine elements of a direct and representative democracy. Such an arrangement would require selectivity and focus in the identification of issues and concerns and the investment of time, energy, and patience in the process. It would also call for new skills, likely to be only gradually realized, in relating faith to policy, listening to and respecting others (particularly those with different views), valuing and eliciting participation, reflecting and dialoguing, dealing with conflict, negotiating, and compromising. Although matters of faith cannot be defined solely by means of a vote of members, they cannot be formulated in the absence of mutual consultation and broad participation. Such a participatory process would additionally strengthen the legitimacy of the decisions reached, enabling them to be the basis for ordering the life of the wider community.

Inclusiveness of leadership to bring about a more effective sharing of power within church structures is another component of church reformation. Its affirmation of the value and integrity of all persons implies a community in which power is widely shared and in which those who have been last are accorded new opportunities to be among the first. This insight is central to the message of a document prepared by the World Council of Churches' 1987 consultation on Sharing Life in a World Community. To be a new people, members of one body, bearing one another's burdens and sharing together in God's gift of life for all, those attending the consultation committed themselves to a new value system based on a far more equitable distribution of resources and power. Consistent with this goal, the participants emphasized the need for churches to place at the center of decision making precisely those who have been excluded from secular power structures because of gender, age, economic and political conditions, ethnic origin, or disability (World Council of Churches 1989, 28–29). In recognizing the diversity of gifts in its membership, preparing for leadership those hitherto denied power, and giving those who have lacked a voice a new means to express themselves and provide service to others, churches would be following the model of the Jesus community.

Education, the Link

In the model of church renewal put forward here the recovery of the churches' teaching ministry would be critical to clarifying vocation, instilling a sense of commitment, and energizing and motivating members. Without such an investment in education, decentralization might mean withdrawal into a self-centered parochialism. Education, broadly conceived, would serve as a major linking mechanism, making partnerships possible. In some sense everything the church is and does, including its liturgy and worship, is religious education through which we learn the story of God and God's will for our lives and receive the ongoing training in the skills necessary to be faithful to the kingdom (Hauerwas 1985, 186). Letty Russell, for example, likens educational ministry to any form of serving in the name of

Christ that fosters mutual growth consistent with God's purposes.
Her characterization emphasizes its incarnational, participatory, and
service dimensions. Although in a sense all ministry is educational,
she points out that it can be more intentionally so when there is
a process in partnership whereby persons of all ages are invited to
join in God's continuing action. Thus growth in the ability to serve
others is a central dimension of educational ministry (Russell 1981,
58–59). Very much like the praxis of liberation theology, authentic Christian education requires linking study and action through
involvement in partnerships of service and commitment, partnership with God in efforts to heal the creation, and commitment to
transformation.

The Search Institute/Lilly Endowment study discussed in
chapter 3 concludes that an effective Christian education program
contributes more than any other congregational factor fostering
growth in faith. In this study, effective Christian education encompasses more than a congregation's having inspiring Sunday worship
services and offering Sunday school, church school programs, Bible
studies, youth ministry, and camping retreats — as important as these
are. Of the factors identified as promoting effective education, an educational process that not only transmits information and knowledge
but also allows insight to emerge from the crucible of experience
emerges as particularly significant. Both reflection and interpretation
of personal religious experience and involvement in the faith stories
of others contributed to this insight. Reciprocally, effective education
enabled participants to apply their faith to their own life situations
and moral decision making. According to the study findings, effective educational content blends biblical knowledge and insight with
significant engagement in global, political, and social issues, and with
issues related to cultural diversity. It creates a sense of community
in which people help each other to develop faith and values (Benson
and Eklin 1990, 54–55). Thus congregations that successfully recruit
members to become involved in community service — helping people who are poor or hungry — and to participate in peacemaking
and social justice activities are better able to promote faith development (Benson and Eklin 1990, 49). Reflecting on their data, the
two research directors suggest that educational emphasis needs to
be placed particularly on the development of caring skills through
service to others.

> The experience of serving others, through acts of mercy, compassion, or the promotion of social justice, is an important influence on the deepening of faith. . . . Some of the best education occurs in these moments of giving, of connection, of bonding to others. Service needs to be a cornerstone of educational programming, partly because it is educationally-rich, and ultimately because, as people of faith, we are called to serve (Benson and Eklin 1990, 66).

Lifestyle and Justice

Church reformation also raises major lifestyle issues. Now, as it did in the time of Jesus, living faithfully entails modeling or incarnating the norms of the kingdom of God. Recent writings have identified and argued for a variety of hallmarks of the kingdom ethic. Letty Russell (1979) and others have written about the church as *koinonia*, a living example of an effective community of sharing that prefigures the kingdom of God. The description of the early Christian community in Acts provides a model of the generous and sacrificial sharing that can accompany a strong faith commitment. A report of a 1987 World Council of Churches' consultation observes that God has given the creation to humanity for faithful use and sharing and develops guidelines for the ecumenical sharing of resources to better enable the Christian community to be a new people, "members of one body, bearing one another's burdens and sharing together in God's gift of life for all" (World Council of Churches 1989, 27). Groups of evangelicals, particularly those involved in Evangelicals for Social Action, have been major advocates that Christians be more sensitive to lifestyle considerations in order to be better able to rediscover the biblical mandates related to the option for the poor, God's will for economic justice, and paradigm of Jesus as a model for radical, costly, self-giving. A second impetus for a simple lifestyle, they note, is the pervasive poverty within the global community (Sider 1982, 23–32). Many pacifists or proponents of nonviolence, Stanley Hauerwas among them, posit that an ethic of nonviolence "is not an option for a few, but incumbent on all Christians who seek to live faithfully in the kingdom made possible by the life, death, and resurrection of Jesus" (1983, xvi). This position is supported by the Gospels, which portray Jesus as prescribing nonviolence in all social relationships, albeit an active nonviolence rather than a passive withdrawal. In a world that still did not know the things which made for peace (Luke 19:42), the response to hatred and violence he preached was a nonviolence (Luke 6:27) that constituted a means of social change and transformation rather than an ethic of perfectionism. And inspired by Jesus' teachings and example, the early church during its first four centuries opposed all violence, military service, and involvement in warfare. Finding all of these contentions and others compelling, I believe that the kingdom ethic as reflected in the life and community of Jesus of Nazareth is complex and inclusive and cannot be reduced to a single attribute.

Church reformation also means far more intentional efforts to model principles of justice in the church economy. In contrast to contemporary concepts of justice that tend to evaluate the fairness of distributions of power, wealth, and goods in accordance with relative contributions, the biblical understanding focuses more on need. Jesus' life and teaching envisage an order of justice in which every person is equally entitled to the protection of the community and no person is exempted from responsibility to others, particularly to the poor and the vulnerable (Hanson 1986, 423). M. Douglas Meeks captures this biblical ethic in his image of God as Economist who creates and empowers life against death at all levels of human existence, including arrangements for the production, distribution, and consumption of the necessities of life. To achieve justice and freedom, God's household seeks to eliminate the domination of any persons over others and the inequalities that prevent fulfillment of needs basic for each person to keep his or her calling to be God's image, child, disciple, and friend (Meeks 1989, 11).

Although such a model of transformed economic relations has inspired Christian communities through the centuries, it has usually been treated as an ideal rather than a model to emulate. The analysis in chapter 3 indicated that contemporary mainline churches do not even affirm an ethic of sharing, either within the local congregation or within more inclusive levels of the Christian community. The contemporary mainline church economy, operating according to market principles, mirrors the inequities within the larger society rather than offering an alternative model. Within the congregation, between levels of the church system, and even more pronouncedly within the global Christian community, there are few dynamics to redistribute resources and power, to assure that members and basic units of the church community have the means to live individually or institutionally.

Caught in the tension between the ideal of *koinonia* and the realities of capitalist economic systems, American churches may never attain the standard of comprehensive mutual sharing. Yet it is possible, indeed essential, for them to have a church economy clearly and recognizably different from relationships within and between government, businesses, and other secular bureaucracies. For the church to be the church requires its working toward an ethic of justice that would begin to redress inequalities of income and resources. To do so churches would need to address the issues raised in chapter 3. Of greatest priority are these: adopting fair and inclusive employment practices with equitable levels of remuneration based on consistent and uniform criteria, formulating new budget priorities that redress the emphasis on church maintenance at the expense of mission, and instituting socially responsible investment and financial management policies and practices. An ethic of justice also requires churches to begin to share and redistribute resources and power within and between church bodies so as to be able to provide those congregations and regions with the greatest need the commensurate means to undertake their ministries. Such a redistribution assumes that church economies should concentrate resources on the basis of need, not on the income levels of their members, congregations, or regional judicatories. This kind of redistribution depends on members contributing more generously than at present and congregations voluntarily sharing a substantial portion of their contributions in a central pool. In the case of affluent congregations, the percentage recommended to be contributed might be half of their members' giving. Part of this pool would then be used to achieve a greater equalization of congregational resources according to set criteria. Other major uses could be the support of special service and transformation projects, particularly in Two-Thirds World churches.

MINISTRIES OF TRANSFORMATION

A central thesis of this study is that political ministry consists of dialectical initiatives in which a community grounds its mission to the world in its own identity and beliefs, incarnates its vision of God's peace and justice in its own life and institutions, and attempts to transform the world in the image of God's kingdom. Each of these three dimensions is integral to political ministry, and each builds interactively on the other two. This tridimensional model differs from the positions of those who claim the priority of the churches' mission to the world, and of those who argue that the political task of Christians is to be the church rather than to serve the world. As the critique of the mainline denominations in previous chapters underscores, churches that depreciate the importance of nurturing the quality of their own life as a faith community tend to lack an effective basis for defining and implementing their mission and are unable to elicit strong membership support and involvement. Nevertheless, the "church first" or "church only" approach, which enjoins the church to abstain from social activism and politics for the sake of perfecting its own faithfulness and communion, one example of which is found in Stanley Hauerwas and William Willimon's *Resident Aliens* (1989), forgets that to begin to know a God of compassion, justice, and peace it is necessary to engage actively in peace and justice initiatives within God's creation. Concerned that both conservative and liberal churches are basically accommodationists, Hauerwas and Willimon quite correctly seek to challenge the assumption, prevalent at least since Constantine, that the church is to be judged by the manner in which its presence works to the advantage of the world (1989, 30). Their strategy for achieving a more cohesive and committed faith community, however, contradicts major themes in Jesus' ministry.

Proclaiming the good news of the coming of God's kingdom to the world, particularly to the poor and oppressed, Jesus and the Jesus community embodied the kingdom norms in the midst of systems dedicated to the maintenance of an oppressive Temple elite and Roman imperial political power. Yet, in addition, Jesus actively and nonviolently confronted and sought to transform the relationships of inequality and domination that were at the core of Jewish and Roman injustice, albeit through an unconventional revolution from below. The ministry of Jesus went beyond eliciting individual and community conversion, as central as these were to taking on the principalities and powers. Jesus did not confine his efforts to establishing an alternative community as the model of the redeemed creation. He sought further, within self-defined limits, to proclaim and actively bring into being the good news to the poor, release to the captives, liberty for the oppressed, and the other requirements of God's Jubilee, otherwise known as "the year of the Lord's favor" (Luke 4:18–19). The churches established in his name are called to do likewise.

The fundamental motive for transformational political ministry, within a partnership is compassion for suffering, or what Jon Sobrino describes as "love for those most deprived of life and working so that they may have life" (Sobrino 1988, 81). A political ethic based on this expression of love of neighbor harkens back to Jesus' announcement that he had come "that they may have life, and have it abundantly" (John 10:10). According to Sobrino, political love has five characteristics that differentiate it from other forms of love. It requires a *metanoia*, a turning to see the truth of the world as it is, both the visible manifestations of death and the underlying structural causes. It necessitates what he terms pity, perhaps better understood as compassion, for the suffering of the oppressed majority, comparable to Jesus' response to the multitudes. It demands an awareness of responsibility and coresponsibility for the condition and destiny of all of one's brothers and sisters. It entails a concern with effectiveness in trying to transform the situation of the poor. And, finally, political love brings the faith community to view the poor not only as objects of beneficial political activity, but also as the subjects of their own destiny and liberation (Sobrino 1988, 81–82).

Although the third dimension of political ministry most closely approximates conventional definitions of political involvement, churches are called to a different kind of politics. A major theme has been that in engaging in political ministry, particularly in the dimension of transformation, churches should do so in a manner consistent with their vocation as a people called into partnership by God. More specifically, this study has argued that political ministry should express both the foundational beliefs of a particular faith community and its sense of identity. For there to be an intrinsic connection between faith and advocacy, not merely a theological or biblical rationale tagged onto a basically secular political agenda, mainline churches would have to evaluate issues, discuss alternative courses of action within their communities, determine priorities, and engage in advocacy ministries in a very different manner than they do at present. One key element would be to start with faith as expressed in biblical and theological principles, moving then to confront issues — not the reverse. Another would be to make a much more serious and broad-based effort to educate, consult, and involve members in public policy on a religious, rather than a predominantly secular, grounding. Relatedly, churches would need to adopt an approach to advocacy that underscores their distinctiveness by addressing the political community from an explicitly ethical and religious perspective. This prescription does not preclude working in coalition with other faith communities or secular groups whose principles, strategies, and goals are similar to the churches'. It does rule out the submergence of their identity, accepting a secular rationale for the programs or actions contemplated, or the adoption of a secular political style, as mainline churches are inclined to do.

To Be the Faith Community

The point has been made repeatedly that adherence to an incarnational theology means that there must be consistency in the norms and policies that the Christian community lives by and proclaims to the world. This requirement does not so much constitute a perfectionist standard that immobilizes people of faith as it provides a reminder that it is both hypocritical and ineffective for churches to preach principles that they are not prepared to model themselves. A church whose own resources are spent primarily on maintenance of buildings and salaries cannot speak very convincingly about the need for imaginative initiatives in funding programs for the poor. Churches with homogenous congregations and white middle-class male leadership lack credibility on issues relating to inclusiveness and affirmative action. As mainline churches criticize spending priorities and the American government's failure to respond effectively to the global economic crisis, they might first examine their own denominational patterns of support for Two-Thirds World churches. Consistency between preaching and action suggests, too, the churches' need to engage in service and advocacy in a spirit of repentance, ever aware of the extent to which they, immersed in the current order, are part of the problem. It is only by gradually achieving a more faithful individual and corporate lifestyle that the churches can become instruments of transformation.

The social and covenantal character of life in a faith community also necessitates that the conceptualization and exercise of all aspects of political ministry, including service and transformation, come through a shared and broadly participatory process. Political ministry evolves as an expression of the community's life and engagement. This basic need for wide-scale involvement in the selection of issues and in engagement in advocacy has both costs and benefits. Consultation and mandate development take a great deal of time and effort. Such processes narrow the range of issues the faith community can address at any one time and, perhaps, the nature of issues appropriate for church involvement. Although the faith community can and should deal with highly controversial subjects to accomplish transformational objectives, such topics require particularly sensitive treatment to build understanding and acceptance within relatively pluralistic constituencies. Mobilization of members additionally requires a careful selection of strategies and a major investment of energy. Without such efforts the church can engage in politics but not in political ministry. Moreover, faith-based political initiatives with strong membership support can be much more effective than the dissemination of political positions or statements to political leaders on behalf of the church that do not clearly rest on a strong membership base.

To conceptualize the churches' role as an alternative community shaped by an alternative consciousness, as I have done here, underscores several points. Adherence to these biblical mandates, particularly to the vision of the just kingdom, would lead to an orientation, priorities, and objectives very different from those of secular political actors. Functioning more in the tradition of the historic peace churches than of the mainline denominations, the churches would not aim to be part of the establishment or power structure of the society. As an alternative community, the churches would position themselves as a principled critic and reformer operating outside the day-to-day realities of politics, rather than as a political actor within the system. Such a reconceptualization of the role would confer freedom for the faith community to be the faith community in the political process and would mean that the churches address the system from a position of relative weakness. This would require far greater selectivity and focus in the churches' political involvement and, thus, very difficult and painful choices.

As alternative communities, churches would also recognize the risk of the cross. Engaging in political ministry is fraught with difficulties, ambiguities, and dilemmas. That Jesus' ministry on behalf of abundant life and against the forces of death ended on a cross has major implications for political ministry. Against the hope that with and for God all things are possible is the reality that the faith communities must pursue partnership with the God of peace, justice, and compassion in a world in which the principalities and powers dominate. More fundamentally, in our age, as it did two millennia ago, to respond to Jesus' call imposes severe costs on lifestyle, priorities, time commitment, family relationships, and vocation. To proclaim God's good news is to do so realizing that there are no shortcuts to the kingdom. Jesus, particularly in the second stage of his ministry, went forward to his final confrontation with Jerusalem in the expectation of defeat, failure, and his own death. Jesus also anticipated that his followers would face severe penalties and predicted that they would be handed over to councils, beaten, and forced to stand before kings and governors (Mark 13:9). Churches seeking to speak truth to those in power historically have suffered many forms of persecution. Although few faith communities operating in constitutional democracies risk the kinds of penalties Jesus envisioned, those actively seeking God's peace and justice have to accept the likelihood of misunderstanding, criticism, ridicule, opposition, and often defeat. Yet to make a commitment is to know the joys as well as the costs of discipleship. It is to be part of the "already" while reaching toward the "not yet" of the kingdom. And beyond failure, and even death, there is the horizon of the new life of the resurrection.

Ironically, by addressing the political system from a position of relative weakness the believing community could very well develop a more effective capacity for change. A broad-based process of careful determination of priorities would likely foster greater commitment to these initiatives within the community. Specialization and focus in the churches' political witness offers the possibility of developing considerable expertise and creativity. It is also more consistent with providing for the education and involvement of a broad cross section of members. As an alternative community, mainline denominations would be freed from their lingering captivity to privilege, and such a position would enable them to move into a more complete partnership with the disadvantaged. Such a self-definition/status reversal is likely to be a prerequisite for allegiance to a kingdom vision that questions and destabilizes the injustices and oppression of the given order. It would, additionally, relieve mainline churches of their self-imposed mandate to speak to everything at the expense of actually implementing a more modest agenda. Moreover, as John Howard Yoder notes, viewing the world through the power of weakness, the faith community would be able to develop a capacity for genuine innovation, surprise, and paradox as it learns to perceive reality in a very different way. Yoder also discusses something he terms "servant strength," the power of a principled minority position as it seeks to help move the total social system (1984, 91–99).

Five Dimensions of Transformational Ministries

The conception of transformational ministries put forward here would lead to a political witness with five major dimensions: identifying social, political, and economic injustice, undertaking ministries of service and direct intervention, offering an alternative vision capable of redirecting political debate and focus, promoting significant social change, and empowering the poor and disadvantaged. These dimensions and their implications are explained as follows:

1. Identifying social, political, and economic injustice: The faith community begins with what might be termed a hermeneutic of suspicion. A commitment to biblical mandates provides a vision of society as it ought to be and, concomitantly, a standard by which to evaluate the extent to which present systems fall short of these ideals. Thus a prophetic stance emanating from a strong faith commitment invariably acknowledges the imperfection and inadequacy of all human systems, institutions, and structures, as well as the performance of their members. This is not to say that all secular authorities and systems are alike — some come far closer to approximating norms of justice than others — but to underscore the fundamental difference between the kingdom vision and the realities of the current order. This understanding protects churches from being coopted by or accommodated to the systems in which they function. To judge and evaluate secular political actors and institutions by faith standards also precludes legitimizing or giving uncategorical allegiance to any cause, political party, ideological system, or program, in the name of Christianity. Tempering and relativizing the claims of secular authorities, the primacy and priority of faith has led Christian communities from its earliest days in times of crisis to reject certain demands of governments. It is not an accident of history, therefore, that the text of the Barmen Declaration issued in 1934 by the Confessional Synod of the German Evangelical Church as an act of resistance to the demands of the Third Reich begins with an affirmation of John 14:6, "I am the way, and the truth, and the life."

Such a prophetic critique, however, is neither an end in itself nor a cause for inaction. Noting the ambiguity of Christian political obligations, a recent book by Glenn Tinder (1989) argues that Christianity implies a categorical skepticism concerning political ideals and plans. His overwhelming sense of human sinfulness produces a kind of paralysis. In his writing, pessimism about fallen humanity leads to inaction, a waiting for God in history that advocates political passivity. What I have in mind is quite different, something closer to Walter Brueggemann's view of prophetic ministry. Brueggemann defines prophetic ministry as nurturing, nourishing, and evoking a consciousness and perception alternative to the consciousness and perception of the dominant culture. Such an alternative consciousness, according to Brueggemann, serves to criticize and thus help to dismantle the dominant consciousness. Beyond rejecting and delegitimating the present ordering of things, however, it also energizes persons and communities by its promises of another time and situation toward which the faith community can move (Brueggemann 1978, 13). Partnership with a compassionate God and love and solidarity with suffering humanity impel the faith community to go forward, aware of both human limitations and the responsibility to serve as an agent of beneficial change. To depend solely on God is to abdicate a partnership relationship and to assume a conception of the divine out of keeping with the interpretation offered here. Moreover, Tinder's reflective passivity can only be a prerogative of the privileged, not a strategy for the suffering.

For churches to be able to identify and document specific social, political, and economic injustices, as well as to evaluate institutions and systems, research and social analyses are critical. Identification and documentation often require on-site visits to gather data, such as the fact-finding missions central to human rights ministries. Relationships of trust with the affected communities and membership within global networks also provide ready access to critical information. Social analysis, however, goes beyond such case study work to evaluate systematically the patterns of inequality and injustice and to attempt to assess the underlying causes. Defining social analysis "as the effort to obtain a more complete picture of a social situation by exploring its historical and structural relationships" (1983, 14), Joseph Holland and Peter Henriot advocate using social analysis in conjunction with theological reflection preliminary to planning and action. To analyze social reality or obtain a cross section of a system's framework at a given moment in time, they assess a number of society's elements, among them the historical dimensions of a situation, its structural components, the various divisions (including classes) of society, the power structure, and the multiple levels of the issues involved.

2. *Undertaking ministries of service and direct intervention:* Called to minister to and bind up the wounds of the suffering, churches have a central role in offering concrete examples of compassion, sharing, inclusiveness, justice, and nonviolence. To do so they need to undertake projects that express tangibly the love of God and neighbor. These would be of three types: service projects, in which church members work with the suffering; pilot projects that offer new models and ways to organize community life; and high-risk initiatives of direct engagement in situations of conflict. Within the context of political ministry, such a ministry of service would differ significantly from traditional charity. The programs envisaged here are based on the recognition of an interconnectedness in creation that bonds even the most comfortable and secure with those who suffer. Undertaken on a community basis in partnership between providers and receivers, they would encourage those offering the assistance and care to treat victims as full human beings rather than as objects of pity. So that its initiatives would not create and perpetuate dependency, the partnership in service would include those being served in all phases of planning and execution. It would also accord them opportunities to serve others. To go beyond ameliorative ministries that deal primarily with symptoms, the programs would link service with social analysis and advocacy in order to address fundamental causes of inequality and exclusion.

Churches also need to be centers of healing and wholeness through direct involvement with those who suffer brokenness and injustice. Such immersion, based on person-to-person contacts, has been among the most creative trajectories of such groups as Witness for Peace and the Fellowship of Reconciliation as well as some of the missions sponsored by the National and World Councils of Churches. As a form of incarnational ministry, the Fellowship of Reconciliation has organized delegations in a variety of situations of actual or potential conflict to share the risks and pain of the people and attempt, through its presence, to contribute to the resolution of conflict. It has also facilitated person-to-person programs across national boundaries designed to eliminate traditional feelings of enmity. The Witness for Peace works by stationing groups, sometimes for a few weeks or for considerably longer periods, on the front lines of violence. Its members' presence as observers in solidarity with the potential civilian victims often lowers, sometimes even prevents or eliminates, fighting in the areas in which they are located. The National Council of Churches has also sent delegations of solidarity and accompaniment to witness to the concern of the American church community and to afford greater protection to vulnerable groups. This peacemaking model has wide potential application in both international and domestic contexts, particularly in the midst of drug wars, racial and ethnic tensions, and disasters of various types. The actions of such volunteers for peace and justice would provide a greater tangible sense of commitment than policy statements or legislative advocacy.

3. *Offering an alternative vision capable of redirecting political debate and focus:* Addressing the political system from the perspective of faith mandates, the churches would attempt to redirect public debate and refocus the range of options under consideration toward more just and meaningful change. In a political system fragmented by special interests, the churches would reach toward expressing concern for the welfare of the human community and, beyond that, solidarity with the integrity of the created order. Credibility based on consistency, expertise, and commitment would enable the churches to offer an ethical and principled point of view often absent in consideration of vital issues. Focused on the common good, they would seek to counterbalance the prevalent inverse correlation between the significance of a decision and the amount of public debate. And the churches' social analysis could provide the concrete data to raise fundamental questions about injustices and biases in the social, economic, and political systems.

By engaging in political ministry from a kingdom perspective the churches would be able to envision long-term possibilities for transformation beyond the scope of the secular political groups. Significant efforts to express the kingdom vision, however, require the formulation of concrete alternatives through new models and proposals. This entails something far more specific than abstract theological conceptions and more constructive than criticisms of the inadequacies of the present system. Today it is far easier to identify the limitations of current structures and institutions than to offer proposals for a fundamentally more just, peaceful, and compassionate order based on new relationships of responsibility, mutual accountability, and sharing. Churches have a particular responsibility to be centers of visioning and creativity. They could do so either by drawing from their own membership through a kind of religious think tank or by establishing the free space in which others can work, much as the churches in Eastern Europe did prior to the recent democratic realignments. Ecumenical initiatives would be able to reflect the orientation and strengths of the global Christian community. In some cases the churches might also sponsor the work of other research institutions or provide platforms for the proposals of other groups.

How specifically might the churches attempt to refocus debate? I have in mind something on the order of what the mainline churches began when they issued their peace and economic pastorals, yet with a more strategic and intentional design that would not make the drafting an end in itself. It would entail formulating a range of proposals based explicitly on faith principles, possibly by a group working within a visible public arena. Hearings and a study process within the community might be used strategically to gain attention. Once such a paper or proposal was issued, the churches would need to facilitate significant public debate of the recommendations. They would also need to organize ways of promoting new directions, a step that was neglected when the peace and economic pastorals were issued. Obviously, such a process must be used carefully and selectively. Moreover, the churches would have far greater credibility and impact if they were to work ecumenically with a series of parallel denominational study processes and involvements.

4. Promoting significant social change: At several points this study has referred to Jon Sobrino's definition of faith-related political involvement as a contemporary rendering of the transformation themes in Jesus' ministry. According to Sobrino, it consists of "action directed toward structurally transforming society in the direction of the reign of God by doing justice to the poor and oppressed majorities, so that they obtain life and historical salvation" (1988, 80). In this characterization Sobrino underscores the need for fundamental structural change rather than incremental policy alternatives to transform systems of injustice. Systemic oppression, such as racism, sexism, and class exploitation, the result of institutional processes often subtle in nature which consistently benefit some and disadvantage or deprive others, cumulatively leads to relationships of domination and exploitation. Because systemic oppression can be sustained without deliberate acts of malice or the intention to harm others, it requires not just changes in individual behavior but the transformation of institutions and processes to restore equity and justice. For Sobrino, as in the Jesus model, the motive force behind these initiatives for structural change, the critical mark of the presence of the kingdom, comes in the condition of the poor and oppressed, those to whom and for whom Jesus ministered. The structural implications of such a commitment are staggering in a global system whose arrangements and structures, both on an international level and in most countries, concentrate resources, income, and power, thus depriving the majority of the means to live. Sobrino also realizes that no matter how drastic the structural transformation, within our lifetime, and likely for all the future, the kingdom will always be now and not yet. Such recognition, however, does not preclude the possibility of significant progress toward the goal of greater justice.

Such efforts to bring about structural reform require confession and repentance, with the faith community recognizing that it is itself part of the reign of injustice. To fail to acknowledge church members' shortcomings is to forget Jesus' admonition, "You hypocrite, first take the log out of your own eye, and then you will see clearly to take the speck out of your neighbor's eye" (Luke 6:42). Membership in societies whose norms and institutions are not consistent with God's intentions have made Christians victimizers as well as actual or potential victims of injustice. Regarding the situation in El Salvador, Sobrino's home, American citizens, whose government, preferring the security and benefits of an unjust status quo, has supported and armed an oppressive elite and sustained a brutal civil war, bear a responsibility. Similarly, the affluent lifestyle of most people in the North rests on rules of exchange in the global economic system that cumulatively disadvantage poor countries seriously. Yet North Americans' comfortable life experience frequently mutes or numbs them to the realization of their own complicity in and benefit from the present unjust ordering. For people of faith, however, there can be no neutrality, no repudiation of responsibility, no legitimate withdrawal in the midst of a world of suffering.

Love and compassion for those without the means to life, sometimes described as the preferential option for the poor, provides both a challenge and a concrete standard for political ministry. The challenge to the faith community here, as in other dimensions of community life, is to open itself to the poor, their pain, their life situations, and their needs. It demands a compassionate vision of society from the perspective of the poor and powerless. And, even more, it requires the faith community to act with a sense of interconnectedness and solidarity with these who suffer. Such a partnership, based on a relationship of equals with shared commitments and undertakings, between a predominantly comfortable middle-class church and the poor and disadvantaged itself represents a major undertaking.

Translated into a concrete standard, the option for the poor requires churches to assess existing and proposed policies, as well as institutions and entire systems, in terms of their impact on the poor and disadvantaged. Each policy under consideration, every item of proposed legislation, all institutional changes should be judged as to whether they will improve the lives of the poor. Beyond policy analysis, the option for the poor has a structural dimension, which includes understanding the systemic causes of poverty and working to change institutions and processes that benefit the affluent and disadvantage other sectors of the population. It also means preparing and convincing the "haves" to be willing to relinquish power and resources so others may have abundant life.

In promoting such structural change the faith community confronts a series of dilemmas. Its status as an alternative community, marked by weakness rather than power, juxtaposed with the enormity of the task constitutes the first of these. Then, the mandate to use means compatible with faith principles eliminates many of the conventional strategies relied on by secular political groups. It precludes, for example, not only fraud and deception but also the elitist approach of imposing change from above. A conception of power as servanthood and empowerment is inconsistent with the direct seeking and holding of political office. Such dilemmas, however, can be the impetus for greater creativity in identifying alternative approaches. Moreover, the churches live in hope, a hope not borne of optimism that there are quick fixes or easy paths to peace and justice, but of the realization that their efforts are grounded in a partnership with a God whose Spirit remains forever present and active in the creation.

What kinds of approaches would be consistent with moving society toward the kingdom, albeit in very small, incremental steps? I have in mind long-term, patient, and persistent initiatives to promote very selective and specific changes. Initiatives discussed in this chapter could be a starting point. More active efforts at concentrated public education on specific issues could be a further contribution. Another central strategy might be to nurture the development of coalitions of individuals and groups dedicated to change outside established political parties and interest groups. Instead of preaching, churches would focus on organizing. Acts of public witness could be another means toward conversion. Relatedly, the empowerment of those most affected by injustice and inequity would be critical.

That the model of transformational politics discussed here is inconsistent with a continued focus on legislative advocacy reflects three sets of considerations. Although the involvement of national religious lobbies has contributed to expanding the representativeness of the American polity, it has done so at a major cost. As the analysis in the third chapter indicated, investment of staff and resources in the legislative process has tended to conform mainline denominations to the political system rather than to challenge it on a faith basis. This has made the advocacy initiatives of these churches generally reactive, captive to the secular Washington agenda and the dynamics of interest-group lobbying. Their experience also suggests that there is a trade-off between involvement in short-term incremental policy approaches and more long-term visioning of new alternatives and initiatives with a more profound potential for change. For example, distracted by their full lobbying agenda on public policy issues, mainline churches failed to use and implement their economic and peace pastorals effectively. There are many public interest actors potentially capable of addressing particular issues and needs. Mainline churches, however, by virtue of their ethical and theological frame of reference, standing, and global relationships, have a unique perspective and capacity to consider fundamental questions involving the future of humanity and the integrity of creation. Legislative advocacy therefore seems appropriate only on a very selective range of issues in conjunction with other strategies or conducted through specialized ecumenical organizations.

5. *Empowering the poor and disadvantaged:* As the United States Catholic bishops note, the option for the poor imposes a prophetic mandate to speak for those who have no one to speak for them (National Conference of Catholic Bishops 1986, par. 52). Yet beyond such representation is the more important need for empowerment of the poor. In the Jesus model, solidarity with the poor in its most fundamental sense entails active efforts to enable those disadvantaged by the current order to become full and equal members. Advocacy on behalf of the poor, no matter how well intentioned and well organized, is not equivalent to providing the poor with the means to speak for themselves. To be able to do so, such groups must be able to express their own views within the economic and political systems and to compete in relative equality with privileged economic interests. This means the establishment of countervailing power dedicated to the creation of a more just order. It also entails changing the basic rules or structures to make systems function more justly and equitably.

Much has already been said about strategies of empowerment. Consistent with the biblical model, greater inclusivity in church membership has been discussed as one of the mandates of church reformation. By intentionally and aggressively reaching out to the poor, racial and ethnic minorities, and immigrants, predominantly white, middle-class churches would be able to incorporate these groups into communities of equality and mutual support. The sharing of resources and power within the churches to compensate for their uneven distribution within the society, economy, and political system is another approach. The design of ministries of service to include recipients in the decision-making and management of programs and to enable them to minister to others is a third strategy discussed in this chapter. In undertaking research and analysis, organizing networks and coalitions, and developing alternative models, the churches would be connecting with constituencies often marginal to the political process.

Beyond these approaches, there are three others. The first is the improvement of listening skills. Mainline churches have a predilection for preaching to the world to such an extent that it inhibits their ability to listen to and learn from others. A theological and social emptying is probably a prerequisite for an openness to listening. The second is a fuller response to programs, projects, and political objectives that originate within groups outside the church. Consultation, to the extent it happens, now often appears as part of the church agenda at the church's initiative. Openness to receiving would mean cultivating channels to a more authentic partnership. And, finally, organization is critical. This does not mean that churches would undertake direct efforts at organizing. Rather, they would make resources available to groups within the various constituencies to enable them to engage in organizing. Networking with these groups would not only help establish coalitions dedicated to change, it would provide access to a greater diversity of perspectives. It would also bring members of the coalition into ongoing contact with others with similar commitments, thus enhancing the possibilities for mutual support.

REFLECTION

Does the strenuous and demanding conception of political ministries presented here have relevance and applicability for major Protestant churches? Components of the model — the focus on a faith vocation providing a distinctive identity and lifestyle, the emphasis on community bonds as the locus of faith relationships, and the intensity of the demands made and commitments expected — have affinities with some sectarian forms of religious expression. Other dimensions, particularly the balance between the faithfulness of the community and its activity to convert and transform the world, go beyond conventional sectarian typologies but are still very different from the character of American denominations in the closing years of the twentieth century. It can be argued that the church/sect typologies developed by Ernst Troeltsch (1931), which have subsequently influenced much thinking on this subject, have serious flaws, particularly when applied to American denominations. Moreover, many of the issues that divided state churches and dissenting sects during the Reformation and gave rise to the differences between them have little contemporary significance. Even so, it would take major and, perhaps, unprecedented changes for an American denomination to emulate this model, particularly because it is put forward not as a plan for a small confessing church but for the wider church as a community.

Images of a more God-centered world and church, like the kingdom vision infusing them, offer a challenge and an inspiration. At a minimum, the model of political ministry has provided a relevant way to uncover critical limitations, contradictions, and inconsistencies within the major Protestant churches. Beyond this analysis, it has pointed to potential thresholds of reformation and renewal. To show that the mainline churches are at a major turning point that will determine their character, faithfulness, and viability into the next century and beyond may enhance the prospect that they will respond appropriately. And it is hoped that by envisioning a renewed and reformed community of church communities, the study will energize and propel the mainline churches toward a more faithful future.

I believe that there are real possibilities for movement in the direction of this model. Whether or not it is clearly acknowledged, the major churches are in a period of transition and reconfiguration opening new horizons and possibilities. The "disestablishment" of the mainline denominations will continue to present challenges of identity and role. As Christianity moves into its third millennium as a global church of the poor, it is likely that denominations with international ties will continue to be drawn into the search for new forms of theological expression, enhanced modes of community spirituality, reconceptualization of church structures, and a redefinition of ministry. And the problems of a global society attempting to resolve crises and groping toward new types of relationships will continue to confront the churches. Although the model presented here may appeal initially to only a minority, their commitment could provide the inspiration and momentum for significant transformation. As the unprecedented political events of recent years have shown, significant change may occur unpredictably, more by leaps of discontinuity than by gradual evolution. Time and again, from the origins of the Jesus movement and through church history, there has been the affirmation that with God all things are possible.

References

Advisory Council on Church Society. 1985. *Toward a Just, Caring and Dynamic Political Economy*. New York: Presbyterian Church (U.S.A.).

Ahlstrom, Sydney E. 1975. *A Religious History of the American People*. 2 vols. New Haven: Yale University Press.

American Baptist Churches in the U.S.A. 1989. *American Baptist Policy Statements and Resolutions*. Valley Forge, Pa.: National Ministries.

Banks, Robert. 1980. *Paul's Idea of Community: The Early House Churches in Their Historical Setting*. Grand Rapids, Mich.: William B. Eerdmans Publishing Company.

Barreiro, Alvaro. 1982. *Basic Ecclesial Communities: The Evangelization of the Poor*. Trans. Barbara Campbell. Maryknoll, N.Y.: Orbis Books.

Bass, Dorothy C. 1989. "Reflections on the Reports of Decline in Mainstream Protestantism." *The Chicago Theological Seminary Register* 80 (Summer): 5–15.

Baum, Gregory. 1987. *Theology and Society*. New York: Paulist Press.

Bellah, Robert N. 1975. *The Broken Covenant*. New York: Seabury Press.

———. 1980. "Religion and the Legitimation of the American Republic." In Robert N. Bellah and Phillip E. Hammond. *Varieties of Civil Religion*. Cambridge: Harper & Row, Publishers.

Bellah, Robert N., et al. 1985. *Habits of the Heart*. Berkeley and Los Angeles: University of California Press.

Benson, Peter L. and Carolyn H. Eklin. 1990. *Effective Christian Education: A National Study of Protestant Congregations*. Minneapolis: Search Institute.

Berger, Peter L. 1967. *The Sacred Canopy: Elements of a Sociological Theory of Religion*. New York: Archer Books.

Biblical Witness Fellowship. 1989. *The Witness*. (February, April, May).

Birch, Bruce C., and Larry L. Rasmussen. 1978. *The Predicament of the Prosperous*. Philadelphia: The Westminster Press.

———. 1989. *Bible and Ethics in the Christian Life*. Minneapolis: Augsburg.

Blank, Rebecca and Audrey R. Chapman. 1989. "Linking Faith and Economics: The UCC Experience." *Global Advocates Bulletin* 13 (September): 1–3.

199

Board of Christian Education. n.d. *The Church's Purpose in Public Affairs.* Philadelphia: The United Presbyterian Church U.S.A.

Boff, Leonardo. 1984. *Jesus Christ Liberator: A Critical Christology for Our Time.* Trans. Patrick Hughes. Maryknoll, N.Y.: Orbis Books.

————. 1988. *Church: Charism and Power: Liberation Theology and the Institutional Church.* Trans. John W. Diercksmeier. New York: Crossroad.

Bonino, José Míguez. 1983. *Toward a Christian Political Ethics.* Philadelphia: Fortress Press.

Borg, Marcus, J. 1987. *Jesus, a New Vision: Spirit, Culture and the Life of Discipleship.* San Francisco: Harper & Row Publishers.

Brown, Raymond E. 1979. *The Community of the Beloved Disciple: The Life, Loves, and Hates of an Individual Church in New Testament Times.* New York: Paulist Press.

Brown, Robert McAfee, and Sydney Thomson Brown. 1989. *A Cry for Justice: The Churches and Synagogues Speak.* New York: Paulist Press.

Brueggemann, Walter. 1978. *The Prophetic Imagination.* Philadelphia: Fortress Press.

Burkholder, John Richard. 1988. "Mennonites in Ecumenical Dialogue on Peace and Justice," *MCC Occasional Paper* 7 (August).

Camara, Dom Helder. 1984. *Hoping Against All Hope.* Trans. Matthew J. O'Connell. Maryknoll, N.Y.: Orbis Books.

Camendisch, Paul F. 1987. "Recent Mainline Protestant Statements on Economic Issues." In Diane M. Yeager, ed. *The Annual Society of Christian Ethics 1987.* Washington, D.C.: Georgetown University Press.

Cassidy, J. Richard. 1978. *Jesus, Politics, and Society: A Study of Luke's Gospel.* Maryknoll, N.Y.: Orbis Books.

Chapman (Smock), Audrey R. 1987. *Christian Faith and Economic Life: A Study Paper Contributing to a Pronouncement for the Seventeenth General Synod of the United Church of Christ.* New York: United Church Board for World Ministries.

Chikane, Frank. 1988. *No Life of My Own: An Autobiography.* Maryknoll, N.Y.: Orbis Books.

Chopp, Rebecca S. 1989. *The Power to Speak: Feminism, Language, God.* New York: Crossroad.

Christian Church (Disciples of Christ). 1987. *Economic Systems — Their Impact on the Third World: A Beginning Christian Study.* Indianapolis: Division of Overseas Ministries.

Committee of Fifteen. 1989. *Report to the Governing Board.* New York: National Council of Churches.

Crosby, Michael H. 1988. *House of Disciples: Church, Economics, and Justice in Matthew.* Maryknoll, N.Y.: Orbis Books.

Daly, Mary. 1975 (1968). *The Church and the Second Sex.* New York: Harper Colophon Books.

Drimmelen, Rob van. 1987. "Homo Oikomenicus and Homo Economicus." *Transformation* 4 (June–December): 66–84.

Dudley, Carl S., and Earle Hilgert. 1987. *New Testament Tensions and the Contemporary Church*. Philadelphia: Fortress Press.

Dulles, Avery. 1974. *Models of the Church*. New York: Image Books.

Eagleson, John, and Philip Scharper, eds. 1979. *Puebla and Beyond: Documentation and Commentary*. Maryknoll, N.Y.: Orbis Books.

Effective Christian Education: A Report for the United Church of Christ. Minneapolis: The Search Institute.

Ellacuría, Ignacio. 1984. "The Political Nature of Jesus' Mission." In José Míguez Bonino, ed. *Faces of Jesus: Latin American Christologies*. Maryknoll, N.Y.: Orbis Books.

Episcopal House of Bishops (Urban Bishops Coalition). 1987. *Economic Justice and the Christian Conscience*. Marquette, Mich.: Unpub.

Evangelical Lutheran Church in America. 1989. *Social Statements in the Evangelical Lutheran Church in America: Principles and Procedures*. Chicago: Department for Studies, Commission in America.

Falwell, Jerry. 1987. "An Agenda for the 1980s." In Richard John Neuhaus and Michael Cromartie, eds. *Piety and Politics: Evangelicals and Fundamentalists Confront the World*. Washington, D.C.: Ethics and Public Policy Center.

Fiorenza, Elisabeth Schüssler. 1983. *In Memory of Her: A Feminist Theological Reconstruction of Christian Origins*. New York: Crossroad.

Fowler, Robert Booth. 1989. *Unconventional Partners: Religion and Liberal Culture in the United States*. Grand Rapids, Mich.: William B. Eerdmans Publishing Company.

Freire, Paulo. 1984. *Pedagogy of the Oppressed*. Trans. Myra B. Ramos. New York: Continuum Publishing Corporation.

General Assembly Presbyterian Church (U.S.A.). 1980. *Peacemaking: The Believer's Calling*. New York: Office of the General Assembly.

———. 1983. *Reformed Faith and Politics*. New York and Atlanta: The Office of the General Assembly.

———. 1988. *Christian Obedience in a Nuclear Age*. Louisville, Ky.: The Office of the General Assembly.

General Council of the Congregational Christian Churches. 1971. *Digest of Minutes of the Meetings of the General Council of the Congregational Christian Churches of the United States, 1931–1965*. New York: The Executive Committee of the General Council.

General Synod of the United Church of Christ. 1959. *Minutes of the Second General Synod*. New York: Office of the Secretary.

———. 1985. Pronouncement "Affirming the United Church of Christ as a Just Peace Church." *Minutes of the Fifteenth General Synod*. St. Louis: Church Leadership Resources.

———. 1989. Pronouncement on "Christian Faith: Economic Life and Justice." *Minutes of the Seventeenth General Synod*. St. Louis: Church Leadership Resources.

Gutiérrez, Gustavo. 1984. *We Drink from Our Own Wells: The Spiritual Journey of a People.* Trans. Matthew J. O'Connell. Maryknoll, N.Y.: Orbis Books.

Hall, Douglas John. 1986. *Imaging God: Dominion as Stewardship.* Grand Rapids, Mich.: William B. Eerdmans Publishing Company, and New York: Friendship Press.

Handy, Robert T. 1984 (1971). *A Christian America: Protestant Hopes and Historical Realities.* New York: Oxford University Press.

Hanson, Paul D. 1986. *The People Called: The Growth of Community in the Bible.* San Francisco: Harper & Row Publishers.

Hartsock, Nancy C. 1983. *Money, Sex and Power: Toward a Feminist Historical Materialism.* Boston: Northeastern University Press.

Hauerwas, Stanley. 1983. *The Peaceable Kingdom.* Notre Dame, Ind.: University of Notre Dame Press.

———. 1985. "The Gesture of a Truthful Story," *Theology Today* 42 (July): 181–189.

Hauerwas, Stanley, and William H. Willimon. 1989. *Resident Aliens.* Nashville: Abingdon Press.

Hellwig, Monika. 1983. *Jesus: The Compassion of God.* Wilmington, Del.: Michael Glazier, Inc.

Hertzke, Allen D. 1988. *Representing God in Washington: The Role of Religious Lobbies in the American Polity.* Knoxville: The University of Tennessee Press.

Hessel, Dieter T., and George M. Wilson. 1981. *Congregational Life-Style Change for the Lean Years.* New York: United Presbyterian Program Agencies.

Heyward, Carter. 1982. *The Redemption of God: A Theology of Mutual Relation.* Lanham, Md.: University Press of America.

———. 1984. *Our Passion for Justice: Images of Power, Sexuality and Liberation.* New York: Pilgrim Press.

Holland, Joseph, and Peter Henriot. 1983 (1980). *Social Analysis: Linking Faith and Justice.* Maryknoll, N.Y.: Orbis Books in collaboration with The Center of Concern.

Institute for Religion and Democracy. 1989. "Working for Church Reform." *Religion and Democracy* (February): 5.

Jeremias, Joachim. 1969. *Jerusalem in the Time of Jesus.* Philadelphia: Fortress Press.

Kairos Central America: A Challenge to the Churches of the World. 1988. New York: Circus Publications Incorporated.

Kairos Theologians. 1986. *The Kairos Document: Challenge to the Church.* New York: William B. Eerdmans Publishing Company and Theology in Global Context Association.

Kee, Howard Clark. 1983 (1977). *Community of the New Age: Studies in Mark's Gospel.* Macon, Ga.: Mercer University Press.

Kelley, Dean M. 1986 (1972). *Why Conservative Churches Are Growing*. Macon, Ga.: Mercer University Press.

Klein, Christa R., with Christian D. von Dehsen. 1989. *Politics and Policy: The Genesis of Social Statements in the Lutheran Church in America*. Minneapolis: Fortress Press.

Lebacqz, Karen. 1985. *Professional Ethics: Power and Paradox*. Nashville: Abingdon Press.

———. 1987. *Justice in an Unjust World: Foundations of a Christian Approach to Justice*. Minneapolis: Augsburg.

Lind, Millard C. 1980. *Yahweh as a Warrior: The Theology of Warfare in Ancient Israel*. Scottsdale, Pa.: Herald Press.

Mainwaring, Scott, and Alexander Wilde, eds. 1989. *The Progressive Church in Latin America*. Notre Dame, Ind.: University of Notre Dame Press.

Marty, Martin E. 1987. "Fundamentalism as a Social Phenomenon." In Richard John Neuhaus and Michael Cromartie, eds. *Piety and Politics: Evangelicals and Fundamentalists Confront the World*. Washington, D.C.: Ethics and Public Policy Center, 303–320.

McFague, Sallie. 1987. *Models of God: Theology for an Ecological, Nuclear Age*. Philadelphia: Fortress Press.

McKinney, William. 1989. "The NCC in New Times." *Christianity and Crisis* 48 (January): 465–466.

Mead, Sidney. 1975 (1963). *The Lively Experiment*. New York: Harper & Row.

Meeks, M. Douglas. 1989. *God the Economist: The Doctrine of God and Political Economy*. Minneapolis: Fortress Press.

Metz, Johann Baptist. 1980. *Faith in History and Society: Toward a Practical Fundamental Society*. New York: Seabury Press.

Miller, Donald E. 1986. "Constituencies for Liberal Protestantism: A Market Analysis." In Robert S. Michaelsen and Wade Clark Roof, eds. *Liberal Protestantism: Realities and Possibilities*. New York: Pilgrim Press.

Moltmann, Jürgen. 1967. *Theology of Hope*. New York: Harper & Row Publishers.

———. 1985. *God in Creation: A New Theology of Creation and the Spirit of God*. San Francisco: Harper & Row Publishers.

National Conference of Catholic Bishops. 1983. *The Challenge of Peace: God's Promise and Our Response*. Washington, D.C.: U.S. Catholic Conference.

———. 1986. *Economic Justice for All*. Washington, D.C.: U.S. Catholic Conference.

Neuhaus, Richard John. 1981. "The Post-Secular Task of the Churches." In Carol Friedley Griffith, ed. *Christianity and Politics*. Washington, D.C.: Ethics and Public Policy Center.

———. 1984. *The Naked Public Square: Religion and Democracy in America*. Grand Rapids, Mich.: William B. Eerdmans Publishing Company.

Neuhaus, Richard John, and Michael Cromartie, eds. 1987. *Piety and Politics: Evangelicals and Fundamentalists Confront the World*. Washington, D.C.: Ethics and Public Policy Center.

Newman, Paul W. 1987. *A Spirit Christology: Recovering the Biblical Paradigm of the Christian Faith*. Lanham, Md.: University Press of America.

Niebuhr, H. Richard. (1984) 1929. *The Social Sources of Denominationalism*. Gloucester, Mass.: Peter Smith.

————. 1943. *Radical Monotheism and Western Culture*. New York: Harper & Brothers Publishers.

————. 1951. *Christ and Culture*. New York: Harper & Brothers Publishers.

Niebuhr, H. Richard, Wilhem Pauck, and Francis Miller. 1935. *The Church Against the World*. Chicago and New York: Willett, Clark & Company.

Nolan, Albert. 1988. *God in South Africa: The Challenge of the Gospel*. Grand Rapids, Mich.: William B. Eerdmans Publishing Company.

Noll, Mark A. 1988. *One Nation Under God? Christian Faith and Political Action in America*. San Francisco: Harper & Row Publishers.

Office for Research, Planning, and Evaluation. 1990. *Faith, the Church, and the World: ELCA Members See the Connections*. Chicago: Evangelical Lutheran Church in America.

Office of the General Assembly. 1984. *Christian Faith and Economic Justice*. Atlanta: Presbyterian Church (U.S.A.).

Office of the Treasurer. 1990. *Memorandum: The 1991 Annual Allocation*. Cleveland: United Church of Christ.

Presbyterian Panel Report. 1988. *Communication of Social Justice Issues Among Presbyterians*. Louisville, Ky.: Presbyterian Church (U.S.A.).

Rasmussen, Larry. 1989. "The Power of Morality and the Morality of Power." In Charles R. Strain. *Prophetic Visions and Economic Realities*. Grand Rapids, Mich.: William B. Eerdmans Publishing Company, pp. 134–145.

Redekop, Calvin Wall, and Samuel J. Steiner, eds. 1988. *Mennonite Identity: Historical and Contemporary Perspectives*. Lanham, Md.: University Press of America.

Reichley, A. James. 1985. *Religion in American Public Life*. Washington, D.C.: Brookings Institution.

————. 1987. "The Evangelical and Fundamentalist Revolt." In Richard John Neuhaus and Michael Cromartie, eds. *Piety and Politics*. Washington, D.C.: Ethics and Public Policy Center, pp. 69–98.

The Road to Damascus: Kairos and Conversion. 1989. London: Catholic Institute for International Relations.

Roehlkepartain, Eugene C. 1990. "What Makes Faith Mature?" *The Christian Century* 107 (May): 496–499.

Roof, Wade Clark, and William McKinney. 1987. *American Mainline Religion: Its Changing Shape and Future*. New Brunswick, N.J., and London: Rutgers University Press.

Royle, Marjorie H., 1989. "A Report of the People of the UCC in the Indiana-Kentucky Conference." Unpublished paper. United Church Board for Homeland Ministries.

Royle, Marjorie H., and Richard A. Bolin. 1983. "Justice by Resolution." Paper presented at the meeting of the Religious Research Association, Knoxville, Tenn.

Ruether, Rosemary R. 1983. *Sexism and God-Talk: Toward a Feminist Anthropology*. Boston: Beacon Press.

Russell, Letty M. 1979. *The Future of Partnership*. Philadelphia: The Westminster Press.

——. 1981. *Growth in Partnership*. Philadelphia: The Westminster Press.

Schell, Jonathan. 1982. *The Fate of the Earth*. New York: Alfred A. Knopf.

Shinn, Roger. 1988. "Christian Social Ethics in North America." *The Ecumenical Review* 40 (April): 223–232.

Sider, Ronald J., ed. 1982. "Living More Simply for Evangelism and Justice." In *Lifestyle in the Eighties: An Evangelical Commitment to a Simple Lifestyle*. Philadelphia: The Westminster Press, pp. 23–41.

Smith, Adam. 1937 (1776). *The Wealth of Nations*. New York: Random House.

Sobrino, Jon. 1988. *Spirituality of Liberation: Toward Political Holiness*. Trans. Robert R. Barr. Maryknoll, N.Y.: Orbis Books.

Strain, Charles R., ed. 1989. *Prophetic Visions and Economic Realities*. Grand Rapids, Mich.: William B. Eerdmans Publishing Company.

Swomley, John M., Jr. 1984. *The Politics of Liberation*. Elgin, Ill.: Brethren Press.

Tenth Biennial Convention of the Lutheran Church in America. 1980. *Economic Justice: Stewardship of Creation in Human Community*. New York: Division for Mission in North America.

Thistlethwaite, Susan Brooks. 1983. *Metaphors for the Contemporary Church*. New York: Pilgrim Press.

Thistlethwaite, Susan Brooks, ed. 1986. *A Just Peace Church*. New York: United Church Press.

Tinder, Glen. 1989. *The Political Meaning of Christianity: An Interpretation*. Baton Rouge and London: Louisiana State University.

Troeltsch, Ernst. 1931 (1981). *The Social Teaching of the Christian Churches*. Trans. Olive Wyon. Chicago and London: The University of Chicago Press.

Tutu, Desmond. 1983. *Hope and Suffering*. Grand Rapids, Mich.: William B. Eerdmans Publishing Company.

Twelfth Biennial Convention of the Lutheran Church in America. 1984. "Peace and Politics." Reprinted in Christa R. Klein with Christian D. von Dehsen. 1989. *Politics and Policy: The Genesis and Theology of Social Statements in the Lutheran Church in America*. Minneapolis: Fortress Press.

United Church Board for Homeland Ministries. 1988. *The Churches Speak: Findings 1986–1987 UCC Soundings Project.* New York: United Church of Christ.

United Church of Christ. 1989. "Advance Materials — Section II Seventeenth General Synod." Unpublished papers. New York.

United Congregational Church of Southern Africa. 1989. *Pastoral Plan: Hearing the Bible Today.* Unpublished document. Johannesburg.

United Methodist Church. 1988. *The Book of Resolutions of the United Methodist Church.* Nashville: The United Methodist Publishing House.

United Methodist Council of Bishops. 1986. *In Defense of Creation: The Nuclear Crisis and a Just Peace.* Nashville: Graded Press.

Villa-Vicencio, Charles. 1988. *Trapped in Apartheid: A Socio-Theological History of the English-Speaking Churches.* Maryknoll, N.Y.: Orbis Books.

Weigel, George. 1989. "Still Blind on the Road to Damascus." *American Purpose* 3 (November): 65–67.

Welch, Sharon D. 1985. *Communities of Resistance and Solidarity: A Feminist Theology of Liberation.* Maryknoll, N.Y.: Orbis Books.

Wills, Gary. 1989. "Right Wing Religiosity: The Changing Face of the Church in Politics." *Sojourners* 18 (July): 24-27.

Wink, Walter. 1984. *Naming the Powers: The Language of Power in the New Testament.* Philadelphia: Fortress Press.

————. 1987. *Violence and Nonviolence in South Africa: Jesus' Third Way.* Philadelphia: New Society Publishers.

Wogaman, J. Philip. 1988. *Christian Perspectives on Politics.* Philadelphia: Fortress Press.

Wood, James R. 1981. *Leadership in Voluntary Organizations: The Controversy over Social Action in Protestant Churches.* New Brunswick, N.J.: Rutgers University Press.

World Council of Churches. 1989. "Guidelines for Sharing." In Huibert van Beek, ed. *Sharing Life: Official Report of the WCC Consultation on Koinonia: Sharing Life in a World Community.* Geneva: WCC Publications.

Wuthnow, Robert. 1988. *The Restructuring of American Religion.* Princeton, N.J.: Princeton University Press.

————. 1989. *The Struggle for America's Soul: Evangelicals, Liberals, and Secularism.* Grand Rapids, Mich.: William B. Eerdmans Publishing Company.

Yoder, John Howard. 1964. *The Christian Witness to the State.* Newton, Kans.: Faith and Life Press.

————. 1972. *The Politics of Jesus.* Grand Rapids, Mich.: William B. Eerdmans Publishing Company.

————. 1984. *The Priestly Kingdom: Social Ethics as Gospel.* Notre Dame, Ind.: University of Notre Dame Press.

Index